THE MOVING PAGEANT

The Moving Pageant presents a stunning variety of writings inspired by the street-life of London. Focusing on the period between 1700 and the First World War, when London was unique in its size, diversity and alarming rate of growth, Rick Allen presents a broad selection of contemporary writings.

Such authors as Daniel Defoe, James Boswell, Horace Walpole, Flora Tristan, Charlotte Brontë, Charles Dickens, Oscar Wilde and H.G. Wells fill this volume with explorations of London life. Through their descriptions of the city's streets and sites of popular assembly, of state pageants and processions, we see the modern urban world in the making.

The works presented here cover all spheres of London life in the period and represent genres and writing styles ranging from the novel and epic poems to street-ballads and music-hall songs, newspaper accounts and private diaries.

Each writer's entry has a full biography and commentary, and the Introduction provides a critical context for the rich diversity and historical range of texts in this unique book.

Rick Allen is Principal Lecturer in English at Anglia Polytechnic University in Cambridge.

Frontispiece: London Bridge, Looking North-West, c. 1890, *The Queen's London*.

THE MOVING PAGEANT

A Literary Sourcebook on London
Street-life, 1700–1914

Rick Allen

London and New York

First Published 1998
by Routledge
11 New Fetter Lane, London EC4P 4EE

Simultaneously published in the USA and Canada
by Routledge
29 West 35th Street, New York, NY 10001

Typeset in Garamond by
J&L Composition Ltd, Filey, North Yorkshire

Printed and bound in Great Britain by
Biddles Ltd, Guildford and King's Lynn

British Library Cataloguing in Publication Data
A catalogue record for this book is available from the British Library

Library of Congress Cataloguing in Publication Data
The moving pageant: a literary sourcebook on London street-life,
1700–1914/Rick Allen.
Includes bibliographical references and index.
1. London (England)–Literary collections.   2. London (England)–Social
life and customs–18th century–Sources.   3. London (England)–Social life
and customs–19th century–Sources.   4. London (England)–Social life and
customs–20th century–Sources.   5. English literature–England–London.
I. Allen, Rick.
PR1111.L6M68 1998
820.8′032421–dc21   97-38277

ISBN 0–415–15307–7 (hbk)
ISBN 0–415–15308–5 (pbk)

To the memory of my father,
Clifford Allen

CONTENTS

PART II
'A Mask of Maniacs'

PART III
'The Attraction of Repulsion'

PART IV
'In Darkest England and Some Ways out'

ILLUSTRATIONS

PREFACE

As the twentieth century draws to its close, in our increasingly urbanised world no aspect of eighteenth- and nineteenth-century recorded experience has greater immediacy for us than that of the city. The writers represented in this anthology – mostly eye-, ear- and nose-witnesses to the physical environment and to the social and cultural life of the streets – testify that the city then as now generated excitement and revulsion, creating both centripetal and centrifugal waves throughout those periods, as it still does. Urban studies – an academic growth area within and across several disciplines – have developed interesting approaches to such material in recent years; by returning the 'gaze' of the flaneur, for instance, they have ensured that urban spectatorship itself is subject to as much critical scrutiny as the objects of its attention.

However, a good deal of the rich abundance of documentary and imaginative writing about the city in the two hundred years or so before the First World War is now inaccessible, and this makes it difficult to judge what is representative – and distinctive – in the more celebrated works which have survived. Moreover, the interesting changes and continuities of view and experience from the early eighteenth to the early twentieth century have not often been closely examined since the stimulating work of Raymond Williams and Richard Sennett over twenty years ago. Hence this anthology, which offers synchronic juxtapositions of the familiar and the unfamiliar and of pieces in very different styles and genres (though the lack of space for drama is regrettable), and which in other ways aims to facilitate cross-periodic comparisons. Needless to say, however, it makes absolutely no claim to comprehensiveness: the proliferation of the literature of London between 1700 and 1914 is as vast and relentless as that by which this flood-tide of writing repeatedly characterises the city itself. If this book did no more than encourage an enlightened publisher to bring out a paperback edition of, say, *The Diary of Dudley Ryder*, Francis Place's *Autobiography* or Olive Malvery's *The Soul Market* , its production would have been worthwhile.

ACKNOWLEDGEMENTS

Many people have contributed to the production of this book. My largest debt of gratitude is owed to Rick Rylance, without whose encouragement and expert advice I should never have begun, and who has remained a guiding light throughout. To another colleague at Anglia Polytechnic University, Mary Abbott, I am greatly indebted for many valuable suggestions; she helped me delimit a potentially limitless subject and brought Dudley Ryder to my attention. Other Anglia colleagues I particularly wish to thank for their generous help are: Nora Crook, Simon Featherstone (especially on music-hall), Felicia Gordon, Mary Joannou (especially on suffragists), Tony Kirby, Rebecca Stott, John Tyler, Nigel Wheale and, not least, Bruce Robertson, whose photographic skills are in evidence in most of the illustrations. Elsewhere, I am grateful to James Austin, Kate Campbell, Mike Garner, Philip Grover, Philip Landon, Morag Shiach and Michael Slater for various kinds of valuable assistance, as well as to my scrupulous and patient editors at Routledge, Talia Rodgers, Diane Stafford and Sophie Powell. For her constancy as a true sounding-board I am most appreciative of the support of Jenny Bamborough.

I gratefully acknowledge permission to include the following material in copyright:

E. Baynes and E. Bateman, 'A Nice Quiet Day'. Words © 1901 Francis Day & Hunter Ltd. Reproduced by permission of International Music Publications Ltd.

A. Bennett, *A Man from the North*. Reprinted by permission of A. P. Watt Ltd on behalf of Mme V. M. Eldin.

S. Frosterus, 'London Rhapsody'. Reprinted by permission of the translator, Michael Garner.

F. H. Hueffer (Ford Madox Ford), *The Soul of London*. Reprinted by permission of David Higham Associates.

G. Le Brunn, B. Lloyd and E. Bateman, 'The Girls from Bryants & May'. Words © 1901 Francis Day & Hunter Ltd. Reproduced by permission of International Music Publications Ltd.

A. J. Munby, 'Diaries'. Reprinted by permission of Adam Matthew Publications and the Master and Fellows of Trinity College, Cambridge.

M. Thale (ed.), *The Autobiography of Francis Place*. Reprinted by permission of the editor and Cambridge University Press.

W. H. Quarrell and Margaret Mare (trans. and eds), *London in 1710: From the Travels of Z. C. von Uffenbach*. Reprinted by permission of Faber & Faber Ltd.

B. Webb, *My Apprenticeship*, Longman, Green & Co., 1926. Copyright © The Passfield Trust.

H. G. Wells, *Ann Veronica*. Reprinted by permission of A. P. Watt Ltd on behalf of the Literary Executors of the Estate of H. G. Wells.

H. G. Wells, *Tono-Bungay*. Reprinted by permission of A. P. Watt Ltd on behalf of the Literary Executors of the Estate of H. G. Wells.

I also gratefully acknowledge permission to reproduce the following numbered illustrations: **4**, **6** and **11**: by permission of the Syndics of Cambridge University Library. **5**: by permission of Guildhall Library, Corporation of London. **7**: Copyright © The British Museum. **12**: Copyright © The University of Oxford: Ashmolean Museum. **21**: by permission of The Museum of London.

In a few cases, efforts to discover the identity and/or whereabouts of copyright holders have proved unsuccessful. The editor and the publishers would welcome information to rectify any such omissions in future editions.

INTRODUCTION

'Is there any other sight in the Metropolis . . . so thoroughly Londonesque as . . . the several miles of crowd . . . flooding the leading thoroughfares of this giant city[?]'

Mayhew, 1862

I

The growth of cities is among the most salient features of modern history and quite directly associated with all other major changes – political, economic, technological, social and cultural – in the Western world over the past 300 years. Throughout the eighteenth and nineteenth centuries London was the largest city in the world, the metropolis of the first industrial nation, the commercial and political hub of a global empire. It was unique in its immensity (a favourite word among those describing it) and in its social and cultural variousness. But it was also representative of the more extensively urbanised world coming into being in Europe and America during this period: in, for example, the politico-economic divisions and polarities starkly manifested in its social geography (with the separateness of the cities of Westminster and London continuing well into the eighteenth century, and the yet sharper opposition of West End and East End a conspicuous phenomenon from early in the nineteenth); and in the equally marked tensions between tradition and innovation in cultural practice and in the very fabric of the buildings.

This selection of writing about London displays some of the city's own variousness in its range of genres, viewpoints, styles, tones and functions, and in the social and national diversity of its contributors. However, the impossible task of representing every significant facet of urban life has not been attempted. Instead, the majority of pieces in this collection deal directly or indirectly with what I take to be the most fundamental, the defining aspects of the city in both physical and social terms: the human crowd, and its prime location, the streets – where its members throng to pursue licit and illicit forms of work and pleasure, to buy and to sell, and in the most consciously collective spirit, to celebrate and to protest.

1

The political character or significance of the crowd is often explicit in these latter activities. However, this dimension is also at least implicit in the unorganised crowd, by virtue of the levelling tendencies of a heterogeneous mix of street users: 'Your only true Republic/Is a crowded city street', a poet declared in *The True Briton* in 1851 (Winter 1993: 10). A similar sentiment is comically intimated by Tom Brown as early as 1700: 'Here a sooty chimney-sweeper takes the wall of a grave alder-man, and a broom-man jostles the parson of the parish. There a fat greasy porter runs a trunk full-butt upon you, while another salutes your antlers with a basket of eggs and butter' (doc. 1). The anti-hierarchical promiscuity of the crowd, at least in the city's central thoroughfares, is a familiar feature of urban life. But it deserves emphasis given the yet more familiar facts about class segregation in residential districts and in most other occupational and recreational venues in the city.

Above all, though, the crowded streets are characterised by movement; they are emblems of the essentially kinetic quality of modern city life. This is primarily why I have borrowed Wordsworth's wonderful phrase, 'the moving pageant', for the title of this anthology. It is also pertinent that commentaries on the urban world are themselves typically kinetic: the observer himself – whether purposeful investiga-tor or idle wanderer – is constantly on the move, discovering a different scene round every corner. (For most of the period covered in this anthology, such observers did tend to be male, for reasons discussed later.)

Moreover, there is a significant sub-genre of descriptive writing on the city which might be called the 'time-and-motion' essay, since the scene-shifting is simultane-ously spatial and temporal. Such pieces give us a day in the life of the city, the commentator providing round-the-clock dispatches from a range of distinctive loca-tions. Steele's *Spectator* essay, known as 'The Hours of London' (1712, doc. 7), a prime model for the use of this format, declares: 'The hours of the day and night are taken up, in the cities of London and Westminster, by people as different from each other as those who are born in different centuries.' This particular way of con-veying the city's social diversity and restless mobility attracted many writers, includ-ing the young Dickens ('The Streets: Day' and 'The Streets: Night' in *Sketches by Boz* (1836)) and graphic artists too (e.g., Hogarth in *The Four Times of Day* (1738) and Doré in *London: A Pilgrimage* (1872)); it reached a peak of loquacious ampli-tude in Sala's *Twice Round the Clock* (1859, doc. 54).

An important variant of this sub-genre offers a blend of topographical documen-tary and comic fiction; in its most typical format, a pair of metropolitan tourists – one experienced and streetwise and the other a newcomer filled with callow won-der, constantly liable to fall victim to deception – embark on a daylong inspection of London life in all its copious variety. Brown's *Amusements* and Ned Ward's *The London Spy* (1700, doc. 2) are notable prototypes of the form, Pierce Egan's *Life in London* (1821, doc. 28) the best-known and probably most influential variant upon it. In the case of these semi-fictional tours too, 'daylong' certainly means 'round the clock', since to a visitor, especially one from the country, the most astonishing aspect of the city is its vibrant night-life. Dickens is restating a truism when he remarks – significantly in a London-by-night piece – that 'all great towns' are 'out of Nature' (doc. 38); in no respect is this more strikingly the case than in their disturbance of the natural rhythms of the diurnal cycle, their violation of Night's 'natural' properties of darkness, peace and stasis. In writing of all kinds the quintessence of London life has been found in nocturnal scenes; Flora Tristan speaks for many when she exclaims: 'But it is really at night that London must be seen!' (1980: 2). The tone of such pronouncements ranges between, and often combines, horror and exhilaration. (A distinctive variant in the late nineteenth and early twentieth centuries, represented by Arthur Symons and other self-conscious impressionists, takes pure aesthetic delight in the atmospheric power and flickering chiaroscuro of the nocturnal city.) And even when, more conventionally, the peace and stillness of night are celebrated – as, for example, in Wordsworth's *Prelude* (VII, 625–35, doc. 25) – the brevity and rarity of such an experience amid the *perpetuum mobile* of urban life are heavily emphasised.

II

Nowhere is the continuous (and sometimes rapid) process of social and cultural change more conspicuous than in the city streets: in demolition and building projects, with the flaunting of new architectural styles (a particularly marked feature of the London of both the early eighteenth and the early twentieth century, in which respectively this anthology begins and ends); in fashions of dress and behaviour; in the class and ethnic composition of groups parading or flouting these fashions; in vehicle style and technology (this collection takes us from sedan chairs and stage coaches to motor cars and underground trains); and in advertisements and shop signs. To this process, too, the image of 'the moving pageant' is applicable: one of the precise meanings of pageant is a parade or dramatic enactment of successive historical periods. This anthology, offering a chronological sequence of items grouped in period sections, is itself a sort of pageant in that sense. One historical change to which it bears witness is in the dominant identity of the street crowd itself. Scholarly studies of the crowd have tended to be about assembled gatherings, as in Le Bon's classic treatise in collective psychology (1896); George Rudé's *The Crowd in History* (1964) is also about popular assemblies, organised or spontaneous, to hold a protest meeting, to march or to run riot. The crowd in this sense was a feature of the eighteenth-century city in particular; whether gathered for violent protest or for carnivalesque pleasure (or both) it was generally perceived and referred to by those of a higher social class as 'the mob' – an abbreviation of *mobile vulgus* ('the excitable crowd') or of 'the mobility' (the facetious antithesis to 'the nobility'; see Ward, doc. 2). The crowd as mob was, then, by definition a kinetic body. But it should

3

not thereby be confused with what Mayhew, in the passage from which the epigraph to this introduction is taken, described as 'the one distinctive mark' of the London of his day; 'the vast human tide – the stupendous living torrent of thousands upon thousands of restless souls . . . for ever rushing along the great leading thoroughfares of the Metropolis' (1967: 53). The distinction between these two kinds of crowd is neatly drawn in a Horace Walpole lettrer to the Miss Berrys, 8 June 1791 (Cunningham 1857–9: IX (1859), 324), a testimony to the fact that in the late eighteenth century the crowd in Mayhew's sense was still something of a novelty: 'London is, I am certain, much fuller than ever I saw it. I have twice this spring been going to stop my coach in Piccadilly, to inquire what was the matter, thinking there was a mob – not at all; it was only passengers.'

With good reason Walpole attributed this new kind of crowd, the continuous flow of pedestrians, to a large increase in the population of the metropolis and to a consequent expansion of its built-up areas: 'There will soon be one street from London to Brentford.' He also recognised the effect of these factors on the number and kinds of private conveyances in the streets: '[T]he tides of coaches, chariots, curricles, phaetons, etc. are endless. Indeed, the town is so extended, that the breed of chairs is almost lost; for Hercules and Atlas could not carry anybody from one end of this enormous capital to the other.' There were other reasons for the onset of these endless tides of passengers and vehicles through the streets of London (and other cities), and hence for the profusion of water imagery in nineteenth-century urban writing. Related to the physical expansion of the city and the growth of residential suburbs was the creation of large-scale commuting, especially on the part of an augmented class of white-collar workers employed in the city's commercial and administrative sectors. And a crucial precondition for the tidal flow of pedestrians and traffic was the implementation of street-improvement schemes. This had clearly not happened by 1716 when John Gay published his mock-cautionary poem *Trivia: or the Art of Walking the Streets of London* (doc. 9), a detailed guide to the hazards and obstructions to be encountered in metropolitan perambulation:

> Where the low penthouse bows the walker's head,
> And the rough pavement wounds the yielding tread;
> Where not a post protects the narrow space,
> And strung in twines, combs dangle in thy face;
> Summon at once thy courage, rouze thy care,
> Stand firm, look back, be resolute, beware.
>
> (III, 19)

Gay's poem shows why the crowd as, in Wordsworth's phrase, an 'endless stream of men and moving things' (doc. 25, 158) was a physical impossibility before legislation in the 1760s provided for the surfacing and widening of roads and footpaths, and for the clearance of obstructions, especially large, overhanging trade signs. The work of Hogarth, the supreme pictorial chronicler of eighteenth-century urban life, offers evidence of a similar kind. Kinetic crowdedness is the very hallmark of his technique and vision, yet it is mobs rather than passengers who pack his street-scenes (plate 2). In nineteenth-century writing and art we still encounter mobs, but passenger-crowds are more common. London's greatest novelist, Dickens, gives us some memorable mobs, but most of them appear in historical novels about late eighteenth-century riot and revolution. A more typical crowd scene is the set-piece in Chapter 32 of *Nicholas Nickleby* (doc. 35), where imagery of tide and torrent is combined with that of dreamlike, ritualistic, promiscuous procession ('all these jumbled each with the other and flocking side by side, seemed to flit by in motley dance like the fantastic groups of the old Dutch painter') to give a paradigmatic evocation of the moving pageant.

III

And so to the *locus classicus* for this kind of description in Book VII of Wordsworth's *Prelude*, composed 1804–5. The poet recalls, from his temporary residence in 'this great city' of London in the early 1790s, sensations repeatedly experienced when going 'forwards with the crowd' through 'the overflowing streets'. The mass anonymity of the stream of strangers pouring past induces in him a powerful sense of alienation, of personal and collective identity obliterated. He enters a dreamlike state: 'the shapes before my eyes became/A second-sight procession' and he is 'lost/Amid the moving pageant' (lines 594–609). In a famous appraisal Raymond Williams identified 'these important lines' as 'the first expression of what has since become a dominant experience of the city' (1973: 186). We have noted some of the contextual factors which help to account for the timing of this 'first expression'; what is then remarkable is how rapidly such observations become commonplace – as has clearly already happened when Robert Mudie's journalistic account (1825, doc. 31) states that 'in the crowds of London, individual man is lost in the mass'. The case for the subsequent dominance of such experience of the city can find plenty of supportive evidence in this anthology, among pieces which not only testify to the experience of identity lost amid the crowd, but register a shift into phantasmagoric modes of perception. A striking instance is 'The City of Dis' in Melville's *Israel Potter* (doc. 49), the Dantean overtones of which give it a central place in a Romantic tradition of urban-apocalyptic visions. Earlier examples are Blake (doc. 23), de Quincey (doc. 33) and Shelley's 'Hell is a city much like London' (1943: 350–3) in *Peter Bell the Third* (1819), the most celebrated later one the 'Unreal City' passage (I, 60–8; Eliot 1965: 65) in *The Waste Land* (1922).

But despite the potency of the literary witness to urban alienation, it is by no means uncontested. Lamb and Hazlitt mount direct challenges to Wordsworth by insisting on the sociability as opposed to the loneliness of the crowd (docs 24 and

30), and this conflict is sustained in later writing. Often, indeed, it is found within single works, including – if we take Books VII and VIII as a whole – *The Prelude* itself. Hazlitt's essay, 'On Londoners and Country People', disputes Wordsworth's later, more extreme image of urban man as a dehumanised atom. Yet Hazlitt himself presents a thoroughly equivocal view of the Londoner's personality and outlook, and thence of the nature of urban society (see Section IV below). There is, then, a representativeness about Dickens' ambivalence towards the city, expressively summed up in the phrase 'the attraction of repulsion'. Dickens has usually been credited with inventing this memorable term, the best-known usage of which is actually in his friend John Forster's biography (1872–4), citing the novelist's memory of his boyhood fascination with 'the real town' (i.e., inner-city slums): 'But, most of all, he had a profound attraction of repulsion to St. Giles's' (Forster 1969: I, 14). Dickens himself introduces the phrase into 'The City of the Absent' (*The Uncommercial Traveller*), an essay not on slums but on City churchyards, first published in the early 1860s. Two decades before that, however, the phrase is used with regard to the ambiguous appeal of the metropolis at large by an older contemporary of Dickens, John Fisher Murray, in a pertinent passage on solitude and society: 'the attraction of London is the attraction of repulsion' (doc. 39). This equivocal view is especially typical of the early and middle years of the nineteenth century; it remains in evidence, for example in Gissing (docs 65 and 68) and in James' confession of attachment to 'the dreadful, delightful city' (doc. 67), even when moralism has started to give way to an aesthetic-impressionist appreciation of the urban scene.

IV

The word 'pageant' has general connotations of spectacle and this, as I have already suggested, is certainly appropriate to many pieces throughout this collection, if only because their writers have experienced London as spectators. Some of the characteristics of what has been called 'the tourist gaze' (Urry 1990) can often be recognised here, not least those of daydreaming and fantasy. The latter tendencies are also associated with the role of *flâneur*, the loafing observer of the nineteenth-century city, most notably celebrated and enacted by the Parisian poet, Charles Baudelaire, and most brilliantly interpreted in the 1930s by the cultural theorist and critic, Walter Benjamin. It has been argued that the *flâneur* was a sociological phenomenon peculiar to the urban geography of Paris and that he was 'virtually unknown in London . . .; "loiter" [sic] which Harrap's gives as a translation of "flâneur", has a distinctly sinister meaning in English' (Bedarida and Sutcliffe 1980: 390). This view might seem to be supported by Benjamin's treatment of the *flâneur* as a type specific to the arcades of Paris, but it is unduly exclusive. 'The loafer' and 'the lounger' frequently figure in nineteenth-century accounts of London street-life; Angus Reach's vignette (1849, doc. 43) identifies different breeds of lounger in topographic and social terms, but characterises them all as observers of the crowds of people more busily occupied than themselves. In this respect they are synonymous with *flâneurs*. It is not surprising, therefore, that 'flaneur' is a term much used recently by cultural historians concerned with male voyeurism. In cases where the urban observer is no idle loafer this can seem distortive, as when the earnest sociologist Charles Booth is labelled a flaneur by Walkowitz (1992: 33). Elizabeth Wilson (1992) follows Benjamin (1983: 170–1) in pointing out that the flaneur was a socially or economically marginal figure and, in Baudelaire's classic account, 'The Painter of Modern Life' (1863), his identity is certainly ambiguous (see Tester 1994: 6, 16–17). A dandy who nevertheless 'loves being incognito', he strolls in apparent idleness amidst the bustling crowd, but this pose is redeemed by the artistic results of creative observation in which 'the weird pageant has been distilled from nature' (1972: 395, 402). The particular hero of Baudelaire's essay, Constantin Guys, was a Dutchman occasionally resident in Paris who wrote and drew for *The Illustrated London News*. His cosmopolitanism made him the ideal flaneur: '[t]o be away from home and yet to feel at home anywhere . . .' (pp. 399–400). But Baudelaire, a native Parisian, was also writing about himself; though adoption of an alien's or cosmopolitan's eye is a much-favoured strategy to achieve freshness or penetration of vision, visitors are obviously not the only discerning spectators of the urban pageant – consider the title and explicit functions of the most famous eighteenth-century London periodical. Addison and Steele (docs 6 and 7), under the persona of 'Mr Spectator', prefigure certain aspects of *flânerie*, delighting in their absorption within the purposeful crowd without really being involved in its business. However, Mr Spectator is a gregarious street-conversationalist whereas, according to one influential modern view (Sennett 1977: 27, 196), his nineteenth-century successors observe in silence (not always: see, for example, docs 37, 50 and 56). The idea of the gazer as a detached outsider is interestingly reversed in the early nineteenth century by Hazlitt, who sees the indigenous crowd itself as a bunch of *un*discerning gapers – *badauds* rather than *flâneurs* (Benjamin 1983: 69). His 'true Cockney' is a perennial spectator of the moving pageant ('an endless phantasmagoria') whose gaze has thereby become a daze: 'He sees everything near, superficial, little, in hasty succession. The world turns round, and his head with it, like a roundabout at a fair, till he becomes stunned and giddy with the motion' (doc. 30).

Hazlitt's simile here is an apt one given the longstanding prominence of fairs as centres of popular culture and consumerism in and near the London streets: Bartholomew, Southwark, Greenwich and May Fairs were the biggest and best known of such annual events, where pageant and theatre in the literal sense figured significantly in the range of entertainments. It is even more appropriate that Wordsworth's description of Bartholomew Fair should constitute the disturbing climax to Book VII of *The Prelude*, since the greater part of what precedes it in this recollection of 'Residence in London' consists of a documentary survey (more equivocal in tone than the finale) of the capital's rich variety of popular shows and exhibitions. But the poet's summative claim that Bartholomew Fair, 'This Parliament of Monsters,' is 'a type not false/Of what the mighty City is itself' has been given further artistic validation by the treatment of proceedings in law court and church as exercises in histrionic display on the part of the principal actors. Wordsworth was registering a deep-seated distrust of what he regarded as the fundamental artifice, the unnatural exhibitionism, of urban life, a hostility which was rooted in puritan as well as rural values. This was perceived by Charles Lamb, who accompanied him on a visit to Bartholomew Fair in 1802 and whose first 'Londoner' essay of the same year (doc. 24) constitutes an implicit rejoinder: 'The very deformities of London, which give distaste to others . . . excite in me no puritanical aversion.' But wherever one's sympathies lie in this interesting debate, there is no doubt that public life itself in this ancient and imperial capital has long been strongly characterised by pageantry and theatrical ritual, much of it performed in and through the streets. As Hogarth ironically demonstrated in *Industry and Idleness* by juxtaposing images of the Lord Mayor's Procession and that of the condemned criminal to Tyburn (see plates 1 and 2), these nominally contrasting pieces of street theatre licensed the same (ritualised) unruliness in the assembled crowds, in the eighteenth century at least. Yet these and most other officially sponsored rituals are clearly symbolic forms of social and political control. On the ideologically ambiguous effects of metropolitan spectacle Hazlitt is again a compelling witness: he characterises the typical Londoner as a proud egalitarian through vicarious identity with glamorous display:

> He meets the Lord Mayor's coach, and without ceremony treats himself to an imaginary ride in it. He notices the people going to court or to a city-feast, and is quite satisfied with the show. He takes the wall of a Lord, and fancies himself as good as he . . . *Your true Cockney is your only true leveller.*
>
> (emphasis in original)

Although Hazlitt echoes Tom Brown on the brash republicanism of the city street and its denizens, he treats it as largely hollow, an assertion of egalitarianism which actually betokens its opposite: a deferential loyalism.

This latter emphasis may at first sight seem questionable, or at any rate unrepresentative, given that in 1823 Hazlitt could look back on a golden half-century of popular radicalism centred on London. Accounts of mass gatherings, from the 'Wilkes and Liberty' riots of the late 1760s and early 1770s to the pro-Reform and pro-Caroline demonstrations of the post-Napoleonic era (docs 19, 21, 27), suggest a London populace with strongly anti-Establishment leanings. But aside from the question of whether the participants in such assemblies were typical of the populace at large, much of this radical activism did in fact take forms which confirm rather than refute Hazlitt's image of the Londoner as 'a great man by proxy, . . . dazzled with noise, show and appearances'. There is first the obvious point that a 'great' man (or woman) – Wilkes, Gordon, Hunt, Queen Caroline – was often the instigator or the heroic occasion of mass action; in the case of Wilkes, violent demonstrations supported not only his campaigns to become an MP but also those to become Lord Mayor. This corroborates the second and more significant point: that in a tradition going back at least as far as the Civil War, the City of London as a social and political entity tended to stand in opposition to the Court and often to the government of the day. In the eighteenth century it did so, moreover, on a 'patriotic' platform, this being one of the factors accounting for the element of collusion on occasions between the City authorities and violently xenophobic rioters. Third, radical demonstrations against the state often conducted elaborate parodies of its pageants and rituals. For example, according to Rudé, popular protests against the imprisonment of the Lord Mayor in the Tower in 1771 included mock executions of all the most prominent 'enemies of the people' (1971: 218). And, as Roger Sales (1983) has shown, the procession escorting Queen Caroline through huge crowds of supporters to her trial at the House of Lords in 1820 was a carnivalesque parody of state pageantry.

This context of popular radicalism helps explain why Hazlitt ends his essay with an affirmative view of the London populace as 'a visible body-politic' wherein 'we learn to venerate ourselves as men, and to respect the rights of human nature'. Except on rare occasions, such as the Hyde Park pro-Reform demonstrations of 1866–7 (see doc. 59 and plate 14), mid-Victorian popular assemblies took place in a rather less highly charged atmosphere, politically speaking. Observers thus tended to echo the converse emphasis in Hazlitt upon the bedazzled gazer. According to Fisher Murray, 'Processions, parades, and reviews form one of the principal sources of innocent recreation to the Londoner. He is a perfect child in his admiration of spectacle' (1843: II, 41). This anticipates the famous Bagehot (1867) thesis regarding a deferential people:

> They defer to what we may call the theatrical show of society . . . . The higher world, as it looks from without, is a stage on which actors walk their parts much better than the spectators can . . . . As a rustic on coming to London finds himself in the presence of a great show and vast exhibition of inconceivable mechanical things, so by the structure of society, he finds himself face to face with a great exhibition of political things which he could not have imagined, which he could not make – to which he feels in himself scarcely anything analogous.
>
> (Bagehot 1993: 249)

Although there are some obvious continuities with Hazlitt here regarding spectators of the great metropolitan show, more striking is the complete reversal of Hazlitt's image of the Londoner as 'a great man by proxy'. Bagehot posits a theatre of alienation in which, however, the very unBrechtian effect of distance is deferential awe rather than cerebral criticism. The analogy he draws between a provincial at the Great Exhibition and 'the common man . . . face to face with a great exhibition of political things' is a significant one; the orderly behaviour, good humour and patriotic enthusiasm of the vast crowds visiting the Crystal Palace in 1851 were hailed by many as evidence that class conflict and the threat of revolution now belonged to this country's past.

However, this signal event in the history of London tourism and London crowds, though actively patronised by the Royal Family, especially the Prince Regent, stressed modernity rather than tradition and occurred well before 'the heyday of "invented tradition", . . . when old ceremonials were staged with an expertise and appeal which had been lacking before' (Cannadine 1983: 108). According to David Cannadine the presentation of the British monarchy in this way began only with the bestowal upon Victoria of the title of Empress of India in 1877: 'the most important point about Bagehot's . . . picture of the power and pomp of the monarchy was that it was not so much description as prescriptive' (1983: 107 n. 18). Cannadine's case regarding the belatedness of effective stage-management of royal pageantry is partly borne out by accounts of the arrival in London of Princess Alexandra of Denmark to marry the Prince of Wales in 1863. Two diarists of the day, Arthur Munby and William Hardman, give vivid descriptions of the enormous crush of people blocking the route of the procession and in physical touch with the chief celebrities when their carriages were brought to a halt: none of Bagehot's desired distance here! 'The arrangements of the City were execrable,' complains Hardman. Yet his record of the event opens on an entirely different note of portentous affirmation: 'London has been convulsed by the Prince of Wales's wedding. The air has been filled with the sounds of joy-bells, and the streets by shouting millions. This generation has never seen such sights, nor indeed has the world before' (Ellis 1923: 268, 265). This mass enthusiasm for a royal occasion is arguably of greater significance than poor organisation; indeed, its significance is heightened thereby, given the degree of popular indifference if not outright hostility to the monarchy and its public ceremonials during the previous 150 years.

Crowds computed in millions are obviously heterogeneous in composition, but can anything further be said about the social profile of these loyalist masses in the London streets? This is Munby's useful record: 'Men of all classes, and women of the lower and lower middle, made up the crowd; and more women than men; but the ladies – luckless beings – were rooted in omnibus & carriage.' But the relative precision of this view is sharpened when, a year later, he describes another great popular assembly in London for the visit of Garibaldi, with this royal occasion still in mind:

It was a crowd composed mainly of the lowest classes; a very shabby and foul smelling crowd . . . . [T]hey surged & struggled round the carriage, they shouted with a mighty shout of enthusiasm that took one's breath away to hear it . . . . There was an ardour and a sort of deep pathetic force about this sound that distinguished it plainly from the shouts of simple welcome which I heard given last year to the Princess Alexandra . . .

(doc. 56)

From our perspective Munby's moving and discriminating account is likewise invaluable for its demonstration of distinctive social and political identities among mass gatherings in the centre of Victorian London, and of the fact that not every category of Londoner then (or, surely, at any other time?) was 'a perfect child in his admiration of spectacle'. The suffragist processions of half a century later provide an interesting comparison to those viewed by Hardman and Munby: meticulously organised, colourful and iconographically complex pageants, their participants predominantly but not exclusively female, mainly but by no means entirely middle class, these events also attracted enormous crowds from all social classes whose respectful if not enthusiastic admiration (see doc. 90) belied the media propaganda characterising the general public as contemptuously hostile to 'the shrieking sisterhood'.

V

We have seen that on the historic occasion of Garibaldi's visit, the spectacle Munby most admires is the crowd itself. Like most of the other writers represented in this anthology he is an equally keen observer of quotidian urban life and, although obsessional case-studies of working women are a peculiarity of this private diarist, an acute class-consciousness is not. However, the tone in which the class divisions of urban society are represented varies considerably. For much of the eighteenth century, writers mostly treated 'low life' (an elastic term covering anything disreputable as well as of humble status) with a mixture of amusement and contempt; low burlesque, as in Ward (doc. 2) or Pope (doc. 3), is rather more characteristic than the moralistic pathos of Whitehead's 'The Sweepers' (doc. 16). However, by the era of the French Revolution (Part II of this anthology), the tone of writing about the poor has typically become more serious: thereafter, their condition variously invokes pity, indignation, apprehension, but, above all, a sense of responsibility on the part of the writer to leave the reader better informed about it. Admittedly, Egan's *Life in London* (1821, doc. 28) treats active enquiry into this subject as a kind of aristocratic field-sport; yet even this predominantly light-hearted exploration of metropolitan polarities has an educative function in presenting the city as 'a complete CYCLOPEDIA', in which 'even the *poorest* cellar contains some trait or other, in union with the manners and feelings of this great city, that may be put down in the note-book' (p. 24). In Henry Trumbull's *Life and Remarkable Adventures of Israel R. Potter* (1824), the source for Melville's novel thirty years later, the narrator remarks 'That one half the world knows not how the other half lives, is a common and just observation' (Hayford *et al.* 1982: 361). It was indeed proverbial by then, as we can see from its use as the subtitle of the anonymous round-the-clock satire of 1752, *Low-Life* (doc. 15). But whereas the latter offers a promiscuous, often humorous sequence of snapshots of unedifying urban customs and behaviour performed by members of various social groups, Trumbull's Israel Potter purports to offer eye-witness accounts 'of the extreme poverty and distress of the wretched poor of London' (p. 75). And by the Victorian period the cliché has been modified to read: 'One half of the world lives without knowing how the other half dies' (Collins 1971: 81).

Low-life comedy is still allowed, as Dickens most obviously demonstrates. But Sam Weller, the working-class Cockney wag in *The Pickwick Papers* (1837), is someone we laugh with rather than at; his humour, moreover, is often specifically informative of how the other half lives . . . and dies:

> I had unfurnished lodgin's for a fortnight . . . – the dry arches of Waterloo bridge. Fine sleeping place – within ten minutes' walk of all the public offices – only if there is any objection to it, it is that the sitivation's rayther too airy. I see some queer sights there . . . . Sights, sir, . . . as 'ud penetrate your benevolent heart and come out on the other side. You don't see the reg'lar wagrants there; trust 'em, they knows better than that. Young beggars, male and female, as hasn't made a rise in their profession, takes up their quarters there sometimes; but it's generally the worn-out, starving, houseless creeturs as rolls themselves in the dark corners o' them lonesome places . . .
>
> (Dickens 1874: 106, Ch. 16)

When Dickens presents such 'creeturs' directly, unmediated by Wellerian patter, for example in 'A Nightly Scene in London' (1856, doc. 50), their plight is, of course, no laughing matter. In this sombre essay he describes an encounter, on a dark, wet evening, with a group of homeless women shut out from the Casual Ward of Whitechapel Workhouse. The repetition of such phrases as 'five bundles of rags', 'five great beehives', 'five dead bodies taken out of graves' and 'five ragged mounds' emphasises their liminal status on the very edge not only of society but of humanity. The next phrase in this sequence requires the reader to consider the perilous implications for us all of such exclusion: 'Five awful Sphinxes by the wayside, crying to every passer-by, "Stop and guess! What is to be the end of a state of society that leaves us here!"' In this case the answer to Dickens' rhetorical question seems to be collective moral insensibility rather than the revolutionary turmoil he was also wont to predict in the mid-1850s. When the narrator does stop to speak to these figures and offer them money, their 'dull and languid' response confirms an advanced stage of desensitisation. Limited communication with them is still possible, but expressions of anger as much as of gratitude are beyond them. The horror of the scene is augmented by the implication of the title of the piece that, far from being unusual, such situations are a nightly occurrence which might be witnessed in many parts of London.

Yet Dickens does not – cannot – leave such bleakness unmitigated: 'let me close this terrible account with a redeeming and beautiful trait of the poorest of the poor.' The main incident in this essay closely resembles Munby's encounter with down-and-out females in St James' Park eight years later (doc. 56), where there is no redemptive outcome ('it was Dante and Virgil gazing on the damned'). But Dickens' coda is reminiscent instead of the way in which Wordsworth's dark vision of a monstrous urban 'Swarm, . . . melted and reduced/To one identity' in Book VII of *The Prelude* is somewhat lightened in Book VIII:

> And is not, too, that vast Abiding-place
> Of human Creatures, turn where'er we may,
> Profusely sown with individual sights
> Of courage, and integrity, and truth,
> And tenderness, which, here set off by foil,
> Appears more touching.
>
> (lines 836–41)

The example the poet then gives is the 'tender scene' of a man cradling 'a sickly babe . . . with unutterable love'. Underlying the foil image in the lines above is the idea that such scenes dramatise resistance to the dehumanising forces of an urban environment.

The extent to which faith in such resistance can be retained is a question looming large over nineteenth-century urban writing. The Dante revival in English Romantic and post-Romantic culture no doubt encouraged the use of Inferno imagery to represent the urban environment and those trapped within it. However, very few writers on London from Wordsworth's generation to Dickens' subscribed to the idea of absolute perdition for its poorer inhabitants which that imagery implies. Only in the later nineteenth century do these depths of pessimism begin to be plumbed, in such imaginative works as Thomson's 'The City of Dreadful Night' (1874) and Gissing's *The Nether World* (1889, doc. 68), followed in the early twentieth century by some of the documentary writing in which the inferno image has been replaced by, or merged with, that of the abyss.

Fin-de-siècle gloom on the condition of the London poor might seem surprising given that over the previous half-century in the capital there had been extensive slum clearance, an enlarged provision of public parks, and improvements in sanitation, public transport, education, cultural amenities, policing and (mainly voluntary-sector) welfare services. The first point to make here is that there is actually a rich variety of moods and attitudes as well as modes displayed in late nineteenth- and early twentieth-century writing on the city. Socialists (Morris, Shaw, Jack London), salvationists (William Booth) and the Garden City Association (Ebenezer Howard) saw The Way Out of Darkest London, and there were many others (for example, Octavia Hill, 'Mark Rutherford', Beatrice Potter, Charles Booth, C. F. G. Masterman and Olive Malvery) strenuously involved in different ways, through the Charity Organisation Society, the settlement movement and the first systematic sociological surveys of poverty, in efforts to lighten the darkness. Nevertheless, there are three major historical factors sufficient to account for the deeper pessimism of some observers. One is the relentless growth of the city, especially eastwards to create vast working-class or under-class ghettoes. The fear this generated is clearly spelt out by Masterman in *From the Abyss* (1902):

> We had thought that a city of four millions of people was merely a collection of one hundred cities of forty thousand. We find it differing not only in degree, but in kind, producing a mammoth of gigantic and unknown possibility . . . . How long before, in a fit of ill-temper, it suddenly realizes its tremendous unconquerable might?

> (doc. 80)

The other two factors, which perhaps make Masterman's apprehensions better founded than Dickens' anxieties about revolution in the 1850s, were the steady economic decline of industrial London between 1870 and 1914 and the consequent rise of the 'New Unionism' and socialist organisation in the 1880s, manifested in unemployment marches into central London and in a series of strikes, most notably the Great Dock Strike of 1889.

According to a leading authority on 'Outcast London',

> By the 1880s, the inner industrial perimeter . . . was fast becoming an industrial vacuum . . . . [It] developed into an area of chronic male under-employment, female sweated labour, and low paid, irregular artisan work in declining trades; an area associated with small dealing, petty criminality and social desolation . . . . London workers of the 1830s and 1840s . . . lived within walking distance of their work within the tight confines of the central area . . . . Despite a large growth of population, the industrial structure of London, and the geographical distribution of its inhabitants were little different from that of the eighteenth century.

> By the early years of the twentieth century the whole physiognomy of central London had been transformed beyond recognition. Large and packed residential areas had given way to acres of warehouses, workshops, railway yards, and offices.

> (Stedman Jones 1971: 154, 159)

This summary of industrial and demographic changes in London through our period provides a useful context for the tradition of urban writing known as 'social exploration', writing which, as we have seen, deplores the fact that 'one half the world knows not how the other half lives' and aims to make this truism less true. A number of the essays in Dickens' first book, *Sketches by Boz* (1835–6), are composed on this principle, but in none of these does he need to venture beyond the two-mile radius of Temple Bar within which a large proportion of low-class London lived as well as worked at that time. In 'Gin Shops', for instance, we are taken 'through the narrow streets and dirty courts which divide [Drury Lane] from Oxford Street': 'The filthy and miserable appearance of this part of London can hardly be imagined by those (and there are many such) who have not witnessed it' (Dickens 1877b: 86). Only five years later, a foreign (and socialist) visitor, Flora Tristan, saw a clear tripartite geographical division in 'the monster city' – the West End, the City and the suburbs – corresponding to a tripartite social class structure. However, she confirmed that these residential suburbs were within walking distance of workplaces in central London, if only to claim that this daily trek helped to account for the workers being 'forever broken with fatigue' (1980: 3). Dickens was a formidable walker (and noctambulist in particular), and this is reflected in the geographical range of his post-*Sketches* writing on the London poor, fictional and non-fictional. But the strategy of ironic contrast between wealth and poverty at the heart of his urban vision continued to be founded on a sense of the proximity if not contiguity of these extremes. His exact contemporary, Henry Mayhew, viewed London in much the same way – as 'a strange incongruous chaos of wealth and want' (Mayhew and Binny 1968: 28). And when, in the Preface to his best-known work, Mayhew described himself as a 'traveller in the undiscovered country of the poor' about whom 'the public had less knowledge than of the most distant tribes of the earth' (1967: I, xv), he was again making an ironic distinction between geographical and social distance.

But later in the nineteenth century the construction of tram and underground rail systems made it possible for London's burgeoning workforce to reside much further from the centre, 'in the unknown lands beyond' as Masterman put it (doc. 80), and thus become an even more alien race. Moreover, the social and economic decline of the areas in between, on the fringes of the inner industrial perimeter, made them seem more inhospitable than before to the casual middle-class explorer. No doubt mid-Victorian London had its 'no-go' areas for such as he: one thinks of Dickens enjoying the privilege of entering some of them under Inspector Field's protection. On the other hand, he begins 'A Nightly Scene in London' by saying he 'accidentally strayed' into Whitechapel with an unofficial companion. And the whole point of the episode's conclusion – the 'redeeming and beautiful trait of the poorest of the poor' – is that when a crowd gathers round these two gentlemen with money in their hands as well as in their pockets, no one begs from them, nor do they feel in the least threatened. Oliveira Martins' account (doc. 75) of a visit to the same area in 1892, with the Ripper murders still fresh in mind, has an utterly different atmosphere. The broad-shouldered detective who acts as guide and bodyguard tells him: '"It would be rash to come alone to these places even by day. By night, even inhabitants of London do not venture – much less strangers! This is no longer London. London ends with the City. This is the East End."'

One feels that Martins heard and saw mostly what conformed to his expectations (rare is the travel writer who does not!). Arthur Morrison was not a mere traveller in that undiscovered country of the poor, being himself a product of the East-End working class. He begins 'A Street' (1891, doc. 70) by challenging stereotyped images of the East End as a region of colourful violence, disorder and squalor: 'Many and misty are the people's notions of the East End; and each is commonly but the distorted shadow of a minor feature.' Aided by the unadorned prose of naturalism, Morrison proceeds to correct these distorted notions of 'spectacular' slums, want and misery by showing them as facets of an inescapably dull and monotonous existence. The main effect, then, is not to refute the pessimists but to join them: 'every day is hopelessly the same . . . . Nobody laughs here – life is too serious a thing; nobody sings . . .'.

The ghettoisation of London working-class life is strongly evident in Morrison's work. He himself had escaped from the confinement he describes, but it was not until well after the terminal date of our survey that the liberating effects of universal education, the welfare state and urban-industrial regeneration started to be more generally experienced. In many ways, of course, the lot of the London poor, including educational provision, had been even worse in earlier parts of our period, and this, obviously enough, explains why there are so few accounts of it from an inside perspective, and why, indeed, genuinely working-class views of the wider London scene are equally rare. The copious writings of Francis Place, a substantial proportion of them still unpublished, are all the more noteworthy on both counts (see doc. 34). On the other hand, their very exceptionality, and that of Place's career as social and political reformer, raise difficult questions about how representative, in class terms, we might take his viewpoint to be.

Probably the best available evidence in print of working-class attitudes and tastes in nineteenth-century London is the street-literature of the time: ballads, broadsheets and the like produced, most famously, or notoriously, by the Catnach Press in Seven Dials and sold and sung by patterers and chaunters in the surrounding streets. Mayhew's *London Labour and the London Poor* (1851–2), a richly detailed source of information about this major aspect of urban popular culture, includes samples of the various kinds of material and interviews with a writer as well as several salesmen of it (1967: I, 213–323). These confirm Mayhew's own statement regarding the narrow tyrannies of the market imposed upon the composers of street literature: 'It must be borne in mind that the street author is closely restricted in the quality of his effusion. It must be such as the patterers approve, as the chaunters can chaunt, the ballad-singers sing, and – above all – such as street-buyers will buy' (1967: I, 220). A poet in very poor circumstances and health tells him: 'Writing poetry is no comfort to me in my sickness. It might if I could write just what I please. The printers like hanging subjects best, and I don't. But when any of them sends to order a copy of verses for a "Sorrowful Lamentation" of course I must supply them' (1967: I, 280). Existing collections of street ballads and modern research confirm that crime and especially murder was by far the most popular subject in street literature. However, what were known as Ballads on a Subject and Ballads Local, focusing respectively on topical events and on local topographical features and issues, do provide interesting vignettes and views of London life from a popular perspective. Some, such as 'The Opening of the New Viaduct' and 'The New Streets Act' (doc. 59), comment on changes to the streets themselves from the point of view of those who work in them. In the first of these two examples, Holborn Viaduct is welcomed primarily because it will spare horses which have hitherto had to struggle with their loads up Holborn Hill. 'The New Streets Act', on the other hand, reflects the viewpoint of humbler street-workers than carriers (or their employers); it is an ironic satire on the restrictive provisions, especially as regards street vending and entertainment, of the 1867 Metropolitan Streets Act. This latter example corroborates the argument of James Winter's splendid book, *London's Teeming Streets* (1993), that street 'improvements' in the Victorian period aimed to facilitate vehicular freedom of passage at the expense of more traditional freedoms to use the streets for other purposes.

VI

As well as the poor, another major category heavily under-represented in the ranks of reporters of London street life before the First World War is that of women. Their minority status here seems more marked than in other kinds of writing, but this is scarcely surprising. At a time when female novelists felt impelled to adopt male personae (as did, for example, two nineteenth-century women whose fiction contains notable evocations of the urban scene, Charlotte Brontë and Margaret Harkness), the genre of street exploration must have seemed even less open to women writers. We are speculating here, but I suspect that such conventional gender restrictions on an 'unfeminine' mode of writing may have operated more tightly than those on physical experience of the city streets. Eliza Haywood's best-known novel (1751, doc. 14) suggests a more permissive situation in the eighteenth century, but less decisively if one takes account of the censure her work received. It is no doubt true that for much of our period only females euphemistically designated as street-walkers would have felt completely free (though that is hardly the right word for the situation of most of them) to do just that – to walk the streets unaccompanied. (Not surprisingly, very few prostitutes wrote about the experience; the letter from 'Another Unfortunate' to *The Times* in 1858 (doc. 53) is a remarkable exception.) Indeed, it is obviously the case that in certain areas of London and at certain times of day no solitary walkers of *either* sex would have felt entirely safe. Nevertheless, the current debate about the 'flaneuse' has shown the proposition that in the nineteenth century 'women could not stroll alone in the city' (Wolff 1990: 41) to be an exaggeration (see, for example, Nord 1995: 11–12). Judith Walkowitz's detailed contextual study of 'narratives of sexual danger in late-Victorian London' concludes that streets of both the East and the West End had by then become areas of 'contested terrain' on the part of respectable women engaged in charitable and shopping expeditions respectively (1992: 41–80). And well before the period to which this refers, Charlotte Brontë, through her narrator in *Villette*, described – in authentic-sounding terms – a sense of 'freedom and enjoyment' in walking 'utterly alone' in London (doc. 47). However, a non-fictional work of acknowledged female authorship and largely devoted to such solitary saunterings would certainly have been extraordinary before the twentieth century. Indeed, the new century's first notable presentation of flaneuse experience, in H. G. Wells's *Ann Veronica* (doc. 88), is actually an account – with an eerily *late*-twentieth-century ring – of its freedoms being violated by a stalker's harassment; but, just as significantly, the author is a man. On the other hand, it might be argued that the importance of the great suffragist processions of the same Edwardian period (see doc. 90) partly lay in the fact that they enabled women in lawful and respectable collectivity to claim possession of the streets still often denied them individually. In any case, singleness is not an essential component of the authentic urban experience; we have seen that a favourite device in narrated tours of London was a pairing of male wanderer-observers, and the value of women's eye-witness accounts of nineteenth-century street-life is not diminished as a result of the observers having usually been accompanied.

However, the point remains that such accounts are very scarce. Here, briefly, are four cases from which we might infer the various reasons why there aren't a lot more.

Celia Fiennes was a remarkably courageous and enterprising explorer at the very beginning of our period: in the 1690s and early 1700s she took several journeys on horseback around Britain in the company only of two or three servants. A substantial portion of her travel journal (Morris 1947) is devoted to London, but in contrast to her often lively personal accounts of small provincial communities this section offers only impersonal description of public ceremonies, institutions and buildings. The streets and their inhabitants are ignored . . . or avoided.

An upper-class German, Sophie von la Roche, who visited London nearly a century later in 1786 (doc. 22), mildly chafed at the constraints of gender and class which prevented her from getting closer to the people en route from Harwich to the capital: 'I should have loved to travel by cheap stage-coach like a common woman, and with some wise friend by my side, to get to know everybody and gain some knowledge of popular character, habits and speech, and thus I should have returned with a far richer harvest' (Roche 1933: 83–4). Arrived in London, Sophie lightheartedly conforms to further constraints imposed upon her as a woman: '[Mr Hurter's] pleasant eldest daughter is getting me a cap and hat, as women here may not go out without a hat. So the land with the greatest freedom of thought, creed and custom is yet in some measure fettered by convention' (p. 88). Needless to say, she requires the hat not to visit the slums but the major sites of tourism and consumerist culture. When, however, she emerges from the theatre on a rainy evening to find there is no cab or chair to be had, 'I decided to hurry along, keeping to the houses, as the streets are so well lit – for it was quite impossible for me to loiter outside the theatre with the crowd of light women' (p. 122). Sophie is much more at ease strolling with companions in the most fashionable shopping ares, the Strand and Oxford Street, and best of all she seems to like being inside these splendid emporia. She welcomes in principle the fact that they are open to all, but when she benignly looks out of Boydell's printshop window at the crowd looking in the comfortable distance seems symbolic. Nevertheless, her liberal-humanist sensibilities are not deadened by the glamour of the new commodity culture: eulogies to its elegance and luxury are more than once tempered by sympathetic thoughts about the producers, especially 'our black, yellow and brown brothers' (p. 172) exploited in colonial gold- and silver-mines.

In such comments Sophie almost begins to sound like Flora Tristan, whose *London Journal* of 1840 (doc. 36) continuously represents the city as a monstrous embodiment of capitalist greed and exploitation. The reinforcements of this pre-conceived view come from a tourist agenda totally different from Sophie's, and from that of most other female (and indeed, male) visitors at any time. She goes to see the prostitutes in and off Waterloo Road, 'accompanied by two men armed with canes . . . . It would be extremely dangerous to walk there alone in the evening'. She also visits the Irish quarter in St Giles, accompanied by a Frenchman after failing to find an Englishman who would even acknowledge its existence: 'The visitor cannot venture into Bainbridge Street, that dark and narrow alley, without a feeling of trepidation . . . . When I reached the end of the street . . . I felt my resolve beginning to abandon me . . . . I was about to give up . . . when suddenly I remembered that these were human beings, my fellow men, all about me . . .'.

More than sixty years later Olive Malvery (doc. 83) confronted scenes just as nauseating and heartrending. Motivated for sure by Christian compassion and an indignant sense of injustice, but probably also by adventurist and histrionic impulses, this remarkable young Indian woman pursued the role of social explorer much further, not merely visiting the poorest of the poor but temporarily joining their ranks. A few men (e.g., James Greenwood and Jack London) had already adopted this practice of slumming in disguise in order to write more authoritatively about how the other half lived; in Malvery's case, though, it involved a great deal more than sleeping rough in the Casual Ward for a night (though she did do that). She enlisted for a succession of gruelling, low-paid jobs, such as busking musician, coster girl, street pedlar and fried-fish-shop assistant; as fraternities with distinctive skills and customs, these called forth all her resources of performative dexterity as well as of courage and resilience. And steadily she pushed lower and lower, to the point of trying 'the Simple Life of London' – i.e., living on no more than sixpence a day. Malvery proved highly adept at disguising her real identity, but she could not do it alone: a similar virtuosity was required of her ever-present 'minder', Mr C. (probably Stuart Cunningham, managing editor of *Pearson's Magazine* in which many of her accounts were first published):

> It is in no wise easy to 'slip' into a new life. Among the 'people', as we term the labouring and poor classes, an outsider is very quickly recognised. I found, however, that my foreign appearance really helped me, for as I dealt mostly with women and girls, they made their own stories about me. By maintaining a discreet silence, I managed to get through. Being small and young-looking too helped me. I get tired very quickly and show it, and poor Mr C., who was nearly always with me, got the rough side of several 'gentle' tongues for ill-treating me. It helped me wonderfully to have a man so big and burly, and such a splendid Cockney actor, to assume command of me. Together we were able to do what one alone could never have accomplished.
>
> (1906: 135)

When Malvery decided to sample life in 'the worst street in London', a different kind of disguise was called for. She went to stay with Captain Molly, a Salvation Army Officer and even more devoted Slum Sister, who actually lived among the criminal fraternity in one of the 'dirty, dark, insanitory hovels'. 'My uniform's a protection,' says Molly, to which Olive replies: 'I shall wear a uniform also, if you will let me' (p. 238). Despite evincing an almost childlike delight in dressing up, Malvery assumed false identities for essentially serious purposes, not least that of realising for herself and her readers the classic maxim, *Nihil humanum a me alienum pute* (I regard nothing human as alien to me). However, she discovered that new waves of literally alien groups were pouring into parts of the East End, so that 'there are some localities in London which are almost entirely foreign' (p. 217; compare Sims in doc. 84). She began to campaign vigorously against permissive immigration policies allowing 'hordes of foreigners of the lowest class . . . to flood this country, to the unspeakable detriment of our poorer working classes' (1908: 90). A familiar argument, but Malvery's later description of herself as 'the worst Little Englander that ever lived' (1912: 231) is sadly anomalous given the admission that her own foreign appearance greatly helped her 'gain a practical insight into the lives of the submerged tenth' (1908: 4). Thus, even as she strives, through empathetic role-play, to break down long-established class barriers, Malvery heralds the multicultural city of the later twentieth century, in which ethnic divisions will prove an equally difficult nut to crack.

VII

Three of the four women just discussed were foreigners in London; in each of these cases, and in that of most of the multitude of other visitors from overseas who wrote about the experience during our period, the response to Britain's capital is significantly shaped by the writer's alien identity and perspective. This might seem too predictable a fact to remark on, except for two others which often make the distinctiveness of the foreign viewpoint less obvious. First, and just as predictably, this viewpoint, no less than its British counterpart, tends also to be representative of its time and its social class. The preponderance of middle- and upper-class views is naturally greater among foreigners than among natives. And foreign attitudes to London's poor show a similar general shift from early eighteenth-century disdain to nineteenth-century solicitude. Second, there is a real sense in which most native British writers on London, especially from about 1780, likewise view this vast, densely-packed 'city of strangers' as aliens. Even those permanently resident in the capital are likely not to have been born there; this is true of the London population as a whole through most of our period, the primary reason for continuous growth even when death rates were higher than birth rates. For many writers in this category, as for those in more temporary residence (as we saw in the case of Wordsworth) or for those just visiting, their first encounter with the city leaves an indelible impression of overwhelming size, noise and chaotic movement, and of the individual in the crowd as an insignificant and isolated atom. There are cases of this being recalled many years after the event: by de Quincey (doc. 33) and James (doc. 67), for example, and in David Masson's memoir looking back half a century to this paradigmatic experience soon after his arrival in London as a semi-foreigner from Aberdeen in 1843:

> Certainly to a stranger in London, beginning his chances of fortune there, or looking forward to that likelihood, I can conceive nothing more saddening than a solitary reverie on one of those seats in the Green Park, with that roar of Piccadilly as continuous in his ear as if a sea-shell were held close to it, and telling of the pitiless immensity of life and motion amid which he, one poor atom more, means to find a home.
>
> (1908: 23)

The powerfully symbolic role accorded the unremitting roar of street traffic here is reminiscent (partly because of the sea-shell image) of that performed by the 'melancholy, long, withdrawing roar' of the tide in the most famous Victorian poem of alienation, 'Dover Beach', by Masson's exact contemporary Matthew Arnold (1890: 226). But in Masson 'the pitiless immensity of life and motion' is London itself. Yet he did find a home there for several decades. Foreign writers on London who are not looking for one often testify to similarly intense feelings of alienation, exacerbated by the language barrier. For Heine (doc. 32) and Dostoyevsky (doc. 55), for example, the sights and sounds of a city apparently given over entirely to frenzied commercialism and consumerism were made all the more bewildering thereby.

It is striking, indeed, how many foreign commentators, while duly impressed by the bright lights and bustling energy in the streets, and by all the luxury and finery on display among the prosperous classes, nevertheless find London to be pervaded by a spirit of melancholy. This impression is attributable to a variety of features which seem to distinguish this city, absolutely or by degree, from foreign ones with which the visitor might already be familiar: the damp and dreary climate compounded with a continuous pall of smoke, soot and smog (already the dominant physical characteristic in von Uffenbach's account of 1710 and the basis of Grosley's analysis of the national temperament and culture in the 1760s); the air of confinement in a vast network of narrow streets monotonously lined with unstately buildings (a 'stone forest' in Heine's expressive phrase); and the manifestations of English puritanism, especially in the Sabbatarian prohibitions making the only day of rest even gloomier than the other six. Observations on climate, architecture and ideology illustrate two related aspects of the foreign perspective on London which often distinguish it from that of native observers. There is first the assumption that the capital exemplifies English life and character in general, whereas British writers tend to stress the contrasts between London and the rest of the country. For example, the bumptious arrogance of the common Cockney is, as we have seen, presented by Hazlitt as a trait distinguishing Londoners from country people; foreign commentators, especially eighteenth-century Frenchmen such as de Saussure (doc. 11) and Grosley (doc. 18), can cite personal abuse in regarding it as regrettably typical of a national xenophobia. Second and conversely, foreign writers on London are naturally drawn into comparative observation and appraisal in relation to foreign cities and countries, especially their own. It is not surprising, given the contempt for foreigners repeatedly experienced in London, that in some cases this procedure is coloured by nostalgia or wounded patriotism. In others such as Taine (doc. 60), however, sustained and systematic reflection along these lines results in an impressive level of balanced critical insight.

VIII

The street-stroller's engulfment in the flowing crowd was not the only source of changing urban visions at the beginning of the nineteenth century; another was the panoramic bird's-eye view. Indeed, a new predilection for the latter was probably in part a reaction to the former experience, a search for extended vistas over a city now too large and overcrowded to permit anything other than close-up snapshots at ground level. Trends in documentary and imaginative writing should not be considered in isolation here; there are significant parallels not only in the visual arts but in popular culture and entertainment. In particular, the phenomenon which became known as 'panoramania' (Hyde 1988), a veritable craze for public shows of large-scale 360-degree or moving panoramic scenes, raged through precisely the period (the first half of the nineteenth century) when literary visions of the city often adopted this perspective.

In talking about vision one has more than merely physical perspectives in mind, of course. For many nineteenth-century writers, including Mudie, Dickens and Mayhew (docs 31, 38, 44), panoramic views were a means of retaining philosophic purchase on the city as a human construct and organism, a way of rediscovering the 'mighty heart' (Wordsworth 1950: 214) in the Babylonian Monster. Now we might interpret the appeal of this angle of vision less benignly in the light of Michel Foucault's influential discussion, in *Discipline and Punish* (1975), of Bentham's panopticon design. In this late-eighteenth-century architectural blueprint for institutional buildings such as prisons, factories and workhouses, with a centrally located overview of every single inmate, Foucault identified a paradigm of power relations in industrial-capitalist society. According to this view the 'indefinitely generalizable mechanism of "panopticism"' (Rabinow 1986: 206) was a means by which those in authority (or allied to it) sought to retain control when the urban mass was reaching unmanageable proportions. However, the technological aspect – by which the controllers themselves are controlled - is crucial to Foucault's interpretation of panopticism and it would be simplistic to extend this reading to every other kind of elevated surveillance. The mass panoramania referred to above makes an ideological equation of literary panoramas with panopticism seem unlikely. On the other hand, panopticism itself does receive favourable literary treatment in Egan's immensely popular *Life in London*, significantly written in the Benthamite era and with particular reference to prison security: 'On ascending to the top of Newgate, the TRIO expressed themselves much pleased, on looking down into the different yards, and witnessing the excellent mode of discipline . . .' (1822: 343). Might we find more oblique or unconscious collusion in such practice in some later descriptions of the London poor from a physically elevated standpoint? The evidence seems to me inconclusive on the basis of instances in this collection – see, for example, Masterman (doc. 80) and Wells (doc. 87) – or indeed of most other Victorian or Edwardian examples with which I am familiar.

The *locus classicus* for metropolitan panoramas was the dome of St Paul's, for this was London's highest building, constructed on high ground in the very heart of the city. The cathedral had become a standard feature of the tourist itinerary long before the finish – notoriously protracted – of Wren's grand design; the earliest account of the prospect from the dome that I know of is von Uffenbach's, describing a visit in the very year of structural completion, 1710. The account, though, is brief and, in translation at least, rather garbled; Uffenbach is far more interested in the elevated view of the interior of the cathedral. There is a similar effect in Dudley Ryder's record of a visit six years later, when Thornhill was still at work on the mural painting of the dome's interior. The detailed account of Ryder's unofficial encounter with the artist is fascinating, whereas the fulfilment of the purpose of going to St Paul's, 'to view the City from the top of it', is dealt with in a mere five words: 'It was a fine sight . . .'. Although numerous later eighteenth-century commentaries include this scene, they offer little more than elaboration of Ryder's judgement.

Nineteenth-century London panoramas, for which St Paul's remains the prime vantage-point, tend to be functionally and qualitatively different, infused with a blend of Romantic aesthetics and social or moral philosophy. In Southey's *Letters from England* (1807) we can see the shift taking place; some physical features of the view are itemised, but the real significance does not lie in such aggregation of empirical detail: 'few objects . . . are so sublime, if by sublimity we understand that which completely fills the imagination to the utmost measure of its powers . . . . It was a sight which awed me and made me melancholy.' And Southey thus modulates from a Romantic evocation of the sublime to proto-Victorian moralism: 'I was looking down upon . . . the single spot whereon were crowded together more wealth, more splendour, more ingenuity, more worldly wisdom, and, alas! more worldly blindness, poverty, depravity, dishonesty and wretchedness, than upon any other spot in the whole habitable earth' (1951: 153–4).

There are echoes of Southey's conclusion, but in a less melancholic key, in a nocturnal meditation of 1840 by Dickens (doc. 38, already mentioned in section I above). Although the location is again the dome of St Paul's, there is no attempt here at literal visualisation of the prospect. Instead, in an exercise of the moral imagination, the commentator strives to hear or feel that 'mighty heart' of the urban organism beating; to this end, the great cathedral clock is itself designated and addressed as 'Heart of London'. The moralistic conclusion firmly relates this temporary visionary retreat to the quotidian challenge 'as I elbow my way among the crowd . . . to turn away with scorn and pride from none that bear the human shape': *nihil humanum a me alienum pute* again.

Henry Mayhew might claim to be the leading literary panoramist of the Victorian metropolis, even if in this regard he was less of an innovator than in his close-up studies of London labour and street-life. His panoramas include a 'bird's eye view' from the Golden Gallery of St Paul's in the midday smog (Mayhew and Binny 1968: 24–7), a remarkable piece of phantasmagoric impressionism, a survey of the port of London, and the 'silent highway' running through it, from the roof of the Custom

House (1968: 21–3), a balloon view of London 'dwindled into a mere rubbish-heap' (1968: 7–9) and a contemplation of 'the great city . . . by night, afar off from an eminence' (doc. 44). Most of these tend to be elaborations of the Southey formula, combining aesthetic sensations of Romantic sublimity with philosophic observations on the 'city of antithesis' (1968: 28). However, we should keep in mind that all except the balloon view were originally published in the *Morning Chronicle* as introductory passages to Mayhew's survey of 'Labour and the Poor' (1849–50); in the context of his empirical social investigations there and in *London Labour and the London Poor* (1851–2), their significance is not merely that of rhetorically conventional set-pieces. Anne Humpherys (1977: 37–8) observes that, as an aspirant social 'scientist', Mayhew tried – with limited success – to combine deductive procedures with the inductive ones, the microscopic techniques, wherein his achievment really lay. I would argue, though, that his panoramas of the 'monster city' serve a deductive function in the 'moving . . . story of essentially isolated individuals' (Humpherys 1977: 63) which is mainly told through inductive methods. In the balloon passage he writes of the thrill of being able 'to grasp [London] . . . in all its incongruous integrity, at one single glance' (1968: 9), an experience by this time unattainable at any lower altitude. The sheer scale of the city's growth, and the sense of atomisation within it, make it harder and harder to retain a grasp, even imaginatively, of the integrity of this human agglomeration. That is what Mayhew and Dickens are still striving for as panoramists; later generations simply give up the struggle, in this form at least. When F. M. Hueffer goes in search of 'the Soul of London' in 1905 (doc. 83), he begins by discounting the possibility of such an overview, now that London is 'illimitable'. The only valid bird's-eye view now is that of a bird pecking seeds on the ground: 'it will be some minute detail of the whole' that we must rely on for a sense of what London is. Thus Hueffer's method is to build up clusters of impressionistic vignettes; it is the subjective literary-artistic contemporary counterpart, perhaps, to the more objective inductive sociology collectively undertaken by Booth and his team (doc. 72). While each of these procedures is effective in a way characteristic of its time, they tend to suggest that by the early twentieth century the age of the grand panoramic vision in urban writing has passed.

IX

Large periodic generalisations are bound to be more or less crude. The one I have just made might be challenged by citing, say, the collected works of H. G. Wells, perhaps especially *Tono-Bungay* (1909, doc. 87), in which 'the tumourous growth-process' of London is surveyed as evidence of the pathological Condition of England; or Masterman's large-scale diagnoses, *The Heart of Empire* (1901) and *The Condition of England* (1909), itself strongly influenced by *Tono-Bungay*, as Lodge

(1984: 217) has shown. The period divisions in this anthology and the titles given to each part invite challenge in the same way. The arrangement of individual documents as far as possible in chronological order of composition encourages a testing of historical generalisations, and will certainly show period tendencies to be offset both by contemporaneous diversities and by more perennial perceptions and responses over more than two centuries of London crowd-watching.

Part I covers the first seven decades of the eighteenth century during which the dominant mode employed in urban literature is burlesque, even when the more disturbing aspects of city life are being documented. A corresponding tone of levity tends to be adopted in treating 'low life', the casual but controlled encounter with which is one of the recreations which the London streets offer to men of leisure. Despite such major exceptions as Johnson's *Life of Savage* (doc. 13), Tom Brown's title *Amusements Serious and Comical* may be taken as representative of this period's attitude to street-life and its literary documentation. By the later 1760s, however, the physical and socio-political character of London was changing markedly in ways already substantially registered in *Humphry Clinker* (1771, doc. 20), the opening piece of Part II, which I have entitled 'A Mask of Maniacs'. De Quincey's phrase (doc. 33) suggests the grim frenzy which, in the eyes of fresh beholders in the London streets of the late eighteenth and early nineteenth centuries, seemed to possess the continuous tide of purposeful pedestrians. It also conveys the phantasmagoric quality of such impressions, the nightmarish sense of estrangement and infernal repetition often encountered in such descriptions, and combines this, through the word 'mask', with the ideas of role-playing and theatrical performance which pervade early nineteenth-century evocations of the urban scene. As proposed earlier, the phrase supplying the title of Part III, 'The Attraction of Repulsion', encapsulates the ambiguous attitude to the city shared by a much larger number of writers than the two (Murray and Dickens) who actually use it. Though not confined to the mid-nineteenth century this attitude often takes on a distinctively Victorian colouring of conscientious or guilty fascination with wretched squalor, a state of mind exemplified or perhaps exploited in, for example, Reynolds (doc. 41), Mayhew (doc. 44) and Munby (doc. 56). It is of course still prevalent in the later nineteenth century and, in such cases as Stead's (doc. 63), even more highly coloured. But exploration of the increasingly remote *terra incognita* of Outcast London, now necessarily more systematic, starts to be accompanied by a millenial spirit of reclamation and renewal, whether tentatively pragmatic or boldly utopian, a spirit manifested in a different way in rapturous discoveries of the urban landscape's aesthetic appeal by, for example, Henley (doc. 73), Frosterus (doc. 81), Symons (doc. 82) and Markino (doc. 89). Although I have not found room in this selection for the Salvationist William Booth's *In Darkest London and The Way Out*, its representativeness in this respect is acknowledged in the title to Part IV. The very last item (doc. 90) appropriately describes a ceremonial procession which is both a funereal protest against these unreconstructed times and a colourful expression of collective faith in a more enlightened future – in yet another sense a moving pageant.

The texts used in this anthology have, where necessary, been modernised in respect of punctuation, spelling and typography, except when, as in the cases of Smollett (doc. 20) and Egan (doc. 28), the original version of one or more of these elements remains rhetorically significant.

PART I
'AMUSEMENTS SERIOUS AND COMICAL'
The Early and Mid-Eighteenth Century

1 TOM BROWN, FROM *AMUSEMENTS SERIOUS AND COMICAL, CALCULATED FOR THE MERIDIAN OF LONDON* (1700)

Brown (1663–1704) had a rather dubious reputation as a satirist – at least once imprisoned for libel – and as a connoisseur of the London scene, including its low life: '[his] life was as licentious as his writings', according to the *Dictionary of National Biography*. Remarkably, these excerpts display a prototypical way of seeing and describing the city in at least five respects: London as a 'world'; use of the foreign, innocent eye; the republican street atmosphere; the physiological image of 'circulation'; and the blindly frenetic anti-sociability of the crowd. 'Meridian' in the title means 'distinctive local character'.

London is a world by itself; we daily discover in it more new countries and surprising singularities than in all the universe besides. There are among the Londoners so many nations differing in manners, customs, and religions, that the inhabitants themselves don't know a quarter of 'em. Imagine, then, what an Indian would think of such a motley herd of people, and what a diverting amusement it would be to him to examine with a traveller's eye all the remarkable things of this mighty city. A whimsy takes me in the head to carry this stranger all over the town with me; no doubt but his odd and fantastical ideas will furnish me with variety, and perhaps with diversion.

Thus I am resolved to take upon me the genius of an Indian who has had the curiosity to travel hither among us, and who has never seen anything like what he sees in London. We shall see how he will be amazed at certain things which the prejudice of custom makes to seem reasonable and natural to us. . . .

I will therefore suppose this Indian of mine dropped perpendicularly from the clouds, to find himself all on a sudden in the midst of this prodigious and noisy city, where repose and silence dare scarce shew their heads in the darkest night. At first dash the confused clamours near Temple Bar stun him, fright him, and make him giddy.

He sees an infinite number of different machines, all in violent motion, with some riding on the top, some within, others behind, and Jehu on the coach-box, whirling towards the devil some dignified villain who has got an estate by cheating the public. He lolls at full stretch within, with half a dozen brawny, bulk-begotten footmen behind.

In that dark shop there, several mysteries of iniquity have seen light; and it's a sign that our Saviour's example is little regarded, since the money-changers are suffered to live so near the Temple. T'other side of the way directs you to a house of a more sweet-smiling savour than its owner's conscience; and you can no sooner prepare yourself to make water near his back window, but you shall have an obliging female look through her fingers to take the dimensions of the pipe that emits it. . . .

Some carry, others are carried. 'Make way there,' says a gouty-legged chairman, that is carrying a punk of quality to a morning's exercise; or a Bartholomew baby-beau, newly launched out of a chocolate-house, with his pockets as empty as his brains. 'Make room there,' says another fellow, driving a wheelbarrow of nuts, that spoil the lungs of the city 'prentices and make them wheeze over their mistresses as bad as the phlegmatic cuckolds, their masters, do when called to family duty. One draws, another drives. 'Stand up there, you blind dog,' says a carman, 'will you have the cart squeeze your guts out?' One tinker knocks, another bawls. 'Have you brass-pot, iron-pot, kettle, skillet or a frying-pan to mend?' Another son of a whore yelps louder than Homer's stentor, 'Two a groat, and four for sixpence, mackerel.' One draws his mouth up to his ears and howls out, 'Buy my flounders,' and is followed by an old burly drab that screams out the sale of her 'maids' and her 'soul' at the same instant.

Here a sooty chimney-sweeper takes the wall of a grave alderman, and a broom-man jostles the parson of the parish. There a fat greasy porter runs a trunk full-butt upon you, while another salutes your antlers with a basket of eggs and butter. 'Turn out there, you country putt,' says a bully with a sword two yards long jarring at his heels, and throws him into the kennel. By and by comes a christening, with the reader screwing up his mouth to deliver the service *à la mode de Paris*, and afterwards talks immoderately nice and dull with the gossips, the midwife strutting in the front with young original sin as fine as fippence; followed with the vocal music of 'Kitchen-stuff ha' you maids,' and a damned trumpeter calling in the rabble to see a calf with six legs and a top-knot. There goes a funeral with the men of rosemary after it, licking their lips after three hits of white sack and claret at the house of mourning, and the sexton walking before, as big and bluff as a beefeater at a coronation. Here a poet scampers for't as fast as his legs will carry him, and at his heels a brace of bandog bailiffs, with open mouths ready to devour him and all the nine muses; and there an informer ready to spew up his false oaths at the sight of the common executioner. . . .

'While I behold this town of London,' said our contemplative traveller, 'I fancy I behold a prodigious animal. The streets are so many veins, wherein the people circulate. With what hurry and swiftness is the circulation of London performed?' 'You behold,' cried I to him, 'the circulation that is made in the heart of London, but it moves more briskly in the blood of the citizens; they are always in motion and activity. Their actions succeed one another with so much rapidity that they begin a thousand things before they have finished one, and finish a thousand others before they may properly be said to have begun them.'

They are equally incapable both of attention and patience, and though nothing is more quick than the effects of hearing and seeing, yet they don't allow themselves time either to hear or see; but, like moles, work in the dark and undermine one another.

(Brown 1927: 10–12, 20–1)

2 EDWARD WARD, FROM *THE LONDON SPY* (1700), PTS 12, 13

Ned Ward (1667–1731), a London inn-keeper, wrote prolifically about the city in both prose and verse, his distinctive vein being low burlesque and related forms of vulgar comedy (unexpurgated editions since the eighteenth century are rare). He was twice pilloried as the author of *Hudibras Redivivus* (1705), a political and religious verse satire; his rough treatment by the crowd on those occasions ironically verified the character of the 'mobility' light-heartedly sketched in this passage. Saussure (doc. 11) and Hogarth (plates 1 and 2) provide further corroboration.

Having now wasted our time till about nine at night, we thought it a reasonable hour to take leave of the coffee-house and repair to our own lodgings, where my business engaged me to continue close till the triumphs of the City called me to make one of the innumerable multitude of the gaping spectators. When the morning came that my Lord Mayor and his attendants were to take their amphibious journey to Westminster Hall, where his Lordship, according to the custom of his ancestors, was by a kiss of calves' leather, to make a fair promise to Her Majesty, I equipped my carcase in order to bear with little damage the hustles and affronts of the unmannerly mobility, of whose wild pastimes and unlucky attacks I had no little apprehension. And when my friend and I had thus carefully sheltered ourselves under our ancient drabdeberries against their dirty assaults, we ventured to move towards Cheapside, where I thought the triumphs would be most visible and the rabble most rude, looking upon the mad frolics and whimsies of the latter to be altogether as diverting (provided a man takes care of the danger) as the solemn grandeur and gravity of the former.

When I came to the end of Blow-Bladder Street, I saw such a crowd before my eyes that I could scarce forbear thinking the very stones of the street, by the harmony of their drums and trumpets, were metamorphosed into men, women and children. The balconies were hung with old tapestry and Turkey-work tablecloths, for the cleanly leaning of ladies with whom they were chiefly filled, which the mob had soon pelted into so dirty a condition with their kennel[1] ammunition that some of them looked as nasty as the cover cloth of a . . . horse that had travelled from St Margaret's[2] to London in the midst of winter. The ladies at every volley quitt[ed] their post and retreat[ed] into dining-rooms, as safer garrisons to defend them from the assaults of their mischievous enemies; some fretting at their daubed scarves like a godly old woman that had dropped her Bible in the dirt . . . , others wiping their new commodes which they had bought on purpose to honour his Lordship, each expressing as much anger in their looks as a disappointed bride. . . . The windows of each house, from the top to the bottom, [were] stuffed with heads piled one upon another like skulls in a charnel-house, all gazing at the lob-cocks in their coney-skin pontificalibusses[3] with as much intention as if an Indian prophetess had been riding through the City upon the back of a tiger.

Whilst my friend and I were thus staring at the spectators much more than the show, the pageants were advanced within our view, upon which such a tide of mob overflowed the place we stood in that the women cried out for room, the children for breath, and every man, whether citizen or foreigner, strove very hard for his freedom. For my own part I thought my entrails would have come out of my mouth . . .; I was so closely imprisoned between the bums and bellies of the multitude that I was almost squeezed as flat as a napkin in a press, [or] I heartily would have joined with the rabble to have cried 'Liberty! Liberty!' In this pageant was a fellow riding a-cock-horse upon a lion, but without either boots or spurs, as if intended by the projector to show how the citizens ride to Epsom on a Saturday night to bear their wives company till Monday morning.

> Or else to let the hen-pecked cuckolds know
> A lion's tamed more easier than a shrew.

At the base of the pedestal were seated four figures representing, according to my most rational conjecture, the four principal vices of the city, viz., Fraud, Usury, Seeming Sanctity and Hypocrisy. As soon as this was past, the industrious rabble, who hate idleness, had procured a dead cat, whose reeking puddings hung dangling from her torn belly, covered all over with dirt, blood and nastiness, in which pickle she was handed about by the babes of grace as an innocent diversion, every now and then being tossed into the face of some gaping booby or other . . . .

In every interval between pageant and pageant the mob had still a new project to put on foot. By this time they had got a piece of cloth of a yard or more square; this they dipped in the kennel till they made it fit for their purpose, then tossed it about. It, expanding itself in air and falling on the heads of two or three at once, made 'em like so many bearers under a pall, everyone lugging a several way to get it off his head, oftentimes falling together by the ears about plucking off their cover-slut. By th[e] time forty or fifty of the heedless spectators were made as dirty as so many scavengers, the fourth pageant was come up, which was a most stately, rich and noble chariot made of slit-deal and paste-board, and in it sitting a woman representing (as I fancy) the Whore of Babylon, drawn by two goats, signifying her lust, and upon the backs of them two figures representing Jealousy and Revenge; her attendance importing the miseries that follow her. . . .

The rabble having changed their sport to a new scene of unluckiness, had got a bullock's horn, which they filled with kennel water and poured it down people's necks and into their pockets, that it run down their legs into their shoes. The ignorant sufferers not readily discovering from whence the wet came, were apt to think they had bepissed themselves. . . .

The triumphs of the City being now passed by, they drew after them the mobility, to our safe deliverance, my friend and I clinging as fast to a post as a bear to a ragged staff, to avoid being carried away by the resistless torrent of the rabble; which, if we had quitted our hold, would have inevitably happened to the farther bruising of our ribs and the great penance of our toes. But on the contrary, finding ourselves safe, we began to consider in what new adventure we should spend the remainder of the day.

(Ward 1924: 297–303)

Notes

1 *kennel*: gutter.
2 *St Margaret's*: St Margaret's Hill, site of Southwark Fair.
3 *lob-cocks . . . pontificalibusses*: clowns in their rabbit-furred gowns.

3 ALEXANDER POPE, 'SPENSER: THE ALLEY' (WRITTEN BY 1709, PUB. 1727)

In this youthful imitation Pope (1688–1744) employs the *Faerie Queene* stanzaic form for a piece of low realism remote from Spenserian romance, a disdainful view of riverside working-class communities at the opposite end of London to his own Twickenham retreat and to other places with pastoral (and Spenserian) associations mentioned in the last two lines.

In ev'ry town where Thamis rolls his tide,
A narrow pass there is, with houses low,
Where ever and anon the stream is eyed,
And many a boat soft sliding to and fro,
There oft are heard the notes of infant woe,
The short thick sob, loud scream, and shriller squall:
How can ye, mothers, vex your children so?
Some play, some eat, some cack[1] against the wall,
And as they crouchen low for bread and butter call.

And on the broken pavement, here and there,   10
Doth many a stinking sprat and herring lie;
A brandy and tobacco shop is near,
And hens, and dogs, and hogs are feeding by;
And here a sailor's jacket hangs to dry.
At ev'ry door are sunburnt matrons seen
Mending old nets to catch the scaly fry;
Now singing shrill, and scolding eft between,
Scolds answer foul-mouthing scolds; bad neighbourhood I ween.

The snappish cur (the passenger's annoy)
Close at my heel with yelping treble flies;   20
The whimp'ring girl, and hoarser screaming boy,
Join to the yelping treble shrilling cries;
The scolding quean to louder notes doth rise,
And her full pipes those shrilling cries confound:
To her full pipes the grunting hog replies;
The grunting hogs alarm the neighbours round,
And curs, girls, boys and scolds in the deep bass are drowned.

Hard by a sty, beneath a roof of thatch,
Dwelt Obloquy, who in her early days
Baskets of fish at Billingsgate did watch,   30
Cod, whiting, oyster, mackrel, sprat, or plaice:
There learned she speech from tongues that never cease.
Slander beside her like a magpie chatters,
With Envy (spitting cat), dread foe to peace;
Like a cursed cur, Malice before her clatters,
And, vexing ev'ry wight, tears clothes and all to tatters.

Her dugs were marked by ev'ry collier's hand,
Her mouth was black as bulldog's at the stall:
She scratchèd, bit, spared ne lace ne band,

And 'bitch' and 'rogue' her answer was to all;   40
Nay, e'en the parts of shame by name would call:
Yea, when she passèd by or lane or nook,
Would greet the man who turned him to the wall,
And by his hand obscene the porter took,
Nor ever did askance like modest virgin look.

Such place hath Deptford, navy-building town,
Woolwich and Wapping, smelling strong of pitch;
Such Lambeth, envy of each band and gown,
And Twick'nham such, which fairer scenes enrich,
Grots,^{2} statues, urns, and Jo – – n's dog and bitch:^{3} 50
Ne village is without, on either side,
All up the silver Thames, or all adown;
Ne Richmond's self, from whose tall front are eyed
Vales, spires, meand'ring streams, and Windsor's tow'ry pride.

(Ward 1870: 177–9)

Notes

1 *cack*: defecate.
2 *grots*: Pope's own garden famously contained a grotto.
3 *Jo–n's . . . bitch*: James Johnston, Pope's neighbour, displayed a pair of leaden dogs on his garden wall.

4 JONATHAN SWIFT, 'A DESCRIPTION OF A CITY SHOWER' (1710)

First published in *The Tatler*, no. 238, 17 October 1710, this poem notably exemplifies the mock-pastoral/heroic vein in which the contemporary city was characteristically treated by Augustan writers (see also docs 3 and 9) – to equivocal tonal effect.
Swift (1667–1745) parodies in structure and sometimes in diction the account of a
portentously violent storm in the countryside in Virgil's *Georgics I* (and more particularly, Dryden's 1697 translation thereof), wittily exposing the artificiality of modern
urban civilization, and in the final paragraph (especially the resonantly climactic alexan-
drine triplet) erasing its veneer of refinement with a sordid mass of organic garbage
pouring (with topographical precision) through the London streets.

Careful observers may foretell the hour
(By sure prognostics) when to dread a show'r:
While rain depends,^{1} the pensive cat gives o'er
Her frolics, and pursues her tail no more.
Returning home at night, you'll find the sink^2
Strike your offended sense with double stink.

If you be wise, then go not far to dine,
You spend in coach-hire more than save in wine.
A coming show'r your shooting corns presage,
Old aches throb, your hollow tooth will rage.   10
Saunt'ring in coffee-house is Dulman seen;
He damns the climate, and complains of spleen.
    Meanwhile the South, rising with dabbled wings,
A sable cloud athwart the welkin flings,
That swilled more liquor than it could contain,
And like a drunkard gives it up again.
Brisk Susan whips her linen from the rope,
While the first drizzling show'r is borne aslope;
Such is that sprinkling which some careless quean
Flirts on you from her mop, but not so clean.   20
You fly, invoke the gods; then turning, stop
To rail; she singing, still whirls on her mop.
Not yet the dust had shunned th' unequal strife,
But aided by the wind, fought still for life;
And wafted with its foe by violent gust,
'Twas doubtful which was rain, and which was dust.
Ah! where must needy poet seek for aid,
When dust and rain at once his coat invade?
Sole coat, where dust cemented by the rain
Erects the nap, and leaves a cloudy stain.   30
    Now in contiguous drops the flood comes down,
Threat'ning with deluge this devoted[3] town.
To shops in crowds the daggled[4] females fly,
Pretend to cheapen[5] goods, but nothing buy.
The Templar spruce, while ev'ry spout's a-broach,[6]
Stays till 'tis fair, yet seems to call a coach.
The tucked-up sempstress walks with hasty strides,
While streams run down her oiled umbrella's sides.
Here various kinds, by various fortunes led,
Commence acquaintance underneath a shed.   40
Triumphant Tories and desponding Whigs[7]
Forget their feuds, and join to save their wigs.
Boxed in a chair the beau impatient sits,
While spouts ran clatt'ring o'er the roof by fits;
And ever and anon with frightful din
The leather sounds, he trembles from within.

So when Troy chair-men bore the wooden steed,
Pregnant with Greeks impatient to be freed
(Those bully[8] Greeks, who, as the moderns do,
Instead of paying chair-men, run them through),   50
Laocoön struck the outside with his spear,
And each imprisoned hero quaked for fear.
    Now from all parts the swelling kennels flow,
And bear their trophies with them as they go:
Filth of all hues and odours seem to tell
What streets they sailed from, by the sight and smell.
They, as each torrent drives, with rapid force
From Smithfield or St. Pulchre's[9] shape their course,
And in huge confluent join at Snow Hill ridge,
Fall from the Conduit prone to Holborn Bridge.   60
Sweepings from butchers' stalls, dung, guts, and blood,
Drowned puppies, stinking sprats, all drenched in mud,
Dead cats and turnip-tops come tumbling down the flood.

(Browning 1910: I, 78–80)

Notes

1 *depends*: impends.
2 *sink*: sewer.
3 *devoted*: doomed.
4 *daggled*: bespattered.
5 *cheapen*: bargain for.
6 *a-broach*: flush.
7 *Triumphant . . . Whigs*: the Tories had very recently won a General Election.
8 *bully*: hired ruffian.
9 *St Pulchre's*: St Sepulchre's Church, Holborn.

5   Z. C. VON UFFENBACH, FROM *CURIOUS TRAVELS IN BELGIUM, HOLLAND AND ENGLAND* (WRITTEN 1710–11, PUB. 1753)

Uffenbach (1683–1734) was a German bibliophile whose collection of books numbered 12,000 by 1711. This indicates one of the main purposes of his visit to London in 1710, the detailed record of which remained unpublished in his lifetime and untranslated until the twentieth century. However, his account of a predictable round of metropolitan high culture – libraries, galleries, cathedrals, opera – is interspersed with remarkably vivid and relatively dispassionate descriptions of often barbaric popular entertainments – cock-fighting, bull- and bear-baiting, as well as this sword-and-buckler fight. Hockley in the Hole, an insalubrious locality in Clerkenwell, was the main London venue for such 'sports' in the early eighteenth century.

In the afternoon we drove to the Bear Garden at Hockley in the Hole to watch the fights that take place there, a truly English amusement. First a properly printed challenge was carried round and dealt out. Not only were all the conditions of the fight there set forth, but also the weapons to be used. The combatants were an Englishman and a Moor. The Englishman was a short, thick-set man but the Moor was as tall, well-made and pretty a fellow as I had ever seen. The former was called Thomas Wood and the latter George Turner. The Moor is by profession a fencing master; there are, in fact, such a quantity of Moors of both sexes in England that I have never seen so many before. . . .

The females wear European dress and there is nothing more diverting than to see them in mobs or caps of white stuff and with their black bosoms uncovered, as we often saw them. The place where the fight took place was fairly large. In the middle was a platform as tall as a man of middling height; it had no rail and was open all round, so that neither of the fighters could retreat. All round the upper part of the open space were wretched galleries with raised seats, like those on which the spectators sit at the play. But the common people, who do not pay much, are below on the ground. They tried with violence to clamber up on to the galleries and scaffolding, and when some would have hindered them, they cast up such monstrous showers of stones, sticks and filth, and this with no respect of persons, that we were not a little anxious; as we, however, were sitting on the best side, they did not come near us. They behaved like madmen and things looked very ugly.

After we had sat there a little while, four fellows got up on the platform and laid about them prodigiously with sticks, to the end of which muzzles were fastened. This is a sport peculiar to the English, and one can see it any day practised by children in Morefield or any other wide open space in London. It is diverting to watch how skilfully they can parry each other's blows with their sticks and how those lacking practice get fearful knocks, especially on the head and shins. The fellows gained nothing by it but the shillings thrown them by the spectators. When they had finally stopped, half a crown came flying down to them; thereupon they were at it again violently to decide which of them should have the half-crown.

Then the master and the fighter I mentioned above appeared themselves. They had taken off their coats and tied only a handkerchief round their heads. First they bowed in every direction, and then showed their swords all round. These were very broad and long and uncommonly sharp. Each of the combatants had his second by him with a large stick in his hand; they were not there to parry blows, but only to see that there was fair play on all sides. They began the fight with broadswords. The Moor got the first wound, above the breast, which bled not a little. Then the onlookers began to cheer and call for Wood; they threw down vast quantities of shillings and crowns, which were picked up by his second. This seemed to me quite the wrong way round, as one should have compassion on the fellow that is hit, especially since the winner receives two-thirds of the money that is taken at the gate. In the second round the Englishman, Wood, took a blow above the loins of such force that, not only did his shirt hang in tatters, but his sword was knocked out of his hand and all the buttons on one side of the open breeches he wore were cut away.

Then they went for each other with sword and dagger and the Moor got a nasty wound in his hand, which bled freely. It was probably due to this that, when they had attacked each other twice with 'sword and buckler', that is to say with broadsword and shield, the good Moor received such a dreadful blow that he could not fight any longer. He was slashed from the left eye right down his cheek to his chin and jaw with such force that one could hear the sword grating against his teeth. Straightway not only the whole of his shirt front but the platform too was covered with blood. The wound gaped open as wide as a thumb, and I cannot tell you how ghastly it looked on the black face. A barber-surgeon immediately sprang towards him and sewed up the wound, while the Moor stood there without flinching. When this had been done and a cloth bound round his head, the Moor would have liked to continue the fight, but, since he had bled so profusely, neither the surgeon nor the seconds, who act as umpires, would allow this. So the combatants shook hands (as they did after each round) and prepared to get down.

Then there arose a prodigious cheering, and one could hear nothing but shouts of Wood! Wood! while yet more money was thrown down to him. An Englishman sitting behind us, who had probably drunk a considerable amount, was making a vast uproar and throwing down whole handfuls of shillings. His wife, who was sitting with him, was also rather vociferous; she assured us herself that two years ago she had fought another female in this place without stays and in nothing but a shift. They had both fought stoutly and drawn blood, which was apparently no new sight in England. When I asked whether it had ever happened that people had been killed or died subsequently of their wounds, I was answered in the affirmative; they told me that four years ago the brother of this identical Moor, Turner, had lost his life. Nothing was done to the perpetrator, unless it could be proved that he had transgressed the rules of fighting and wounded his adversary with malicious intent. The most diverting thing of all was that, when the fighters had got down, so many little boys climbed up on to the platform that it would scarce hold them, and called out asking the spectators for money to scramble for. It was amazing to see them swoop down on it in groups of ten or a dozen; sometimes a couple of them would roll down together, but, straightway picking themselves up, plunge afresh into the fray, which lasted for at least an hour. We left while it was still going on, since we had a long way to go. . . .

(Uffenbach 1934: 88–91)

6   RICHARD STEELE, FROM 'A DISCOURSE UPON WENCHES', *THE SPECTATOR*, NO. 266 (4 JANUARY 1712)

After running *The Tatler* (see doc. 4) in 1709–11, Steele (1672–1729), soldier, journalist, playwright, established *The Spectator* in partnership with Joseph Addison, and wrote nearly half of the first series comprising 555 issues between March 1711 and December 1712. Not least among the factors contributing to the periodical's enormous influence was its metropolitanism, its evocation of and commentary upon the physical and cultural character of contemporary London. This essay also typifies *The Spectator*'s promotion of a humanitarian ethos, which on this particular subject proved controversial among its 'tea-table' audience, and which might be seen to conflict with the equally characteristic claim to spectatorial disinterestedness in the second paragraph.

No vice or wickedness, which people fall into from indulgence to desires which are natural to all, ought to place them below the compassion of the virtuous part of the world; which indeed often makes me a little apt to suspect the sincerity of their virtue, who are too warmly provoked at other people's personal sins. The unlawful commerce of the sexes is of all other the hardest to avoid; and yet there is no one which you shall hear the rigider part of womankind speak of with so little mercy. . . .

The other evening passing along near Covent Garden I was jogged on the elbow as I turned into the Piazza, on the right hand coming out of James Street, by a slim young girl of about seventeen, who with a pert air asked me if I was for a pint of wine. I do not know but I should have indulged my curiosity in having some chat with her, but that I am informed the man of the Bumper[1] knows me; and it would have made a story for him not very agreeable to some part of my writings, though I have in others so frequently said that I am wholly unconcerned in any scene I am in, but merely as a spectator. This impediment being in my way, we stood under one of the arches by twilight; and there I could observe as exact features as I had ever seen, the most agreeable shape, the finest neck and bosom, in a word the whole person of a woman exquisitely beautiful. She affected to allure me with a forced wantonness in her look and air, but I saw it checked with hunger and cold; her eyes were wan and eager, her dress thin and tawdry, her mien genteel and childish. This strange figure gave me much anguish of heart, and to avoid being seen with her I went away, but could not forbear giving her a crown. The poor thing sighed, curtsied, and with a blessing expressed with the utmost vehemence, turned from me. This creature is what they call 'newly come upon the town',[2] but who, I suppose, falling into cruel hands, was left

40

in the first month from her dishonour and exposed to pass through the hands and discipline of one of those hags of hell whom we call bawds. . . .

It must not be thought a digression from my intended speculation to talk of bawds in a discourse upon wenches, for a woman of the town is not thoroughly and properly such without having gone through the education of one of these houses. But the compassionate case of very many is that they are taken into such hands without any the least suspicion, previous temptation or admonition to what place they are going. The last week I went to an inn in the city to enquire for some provisions which were sent by a waggon out of the country; and as I waited in one of the boxes till the chamberlain had looked over his parcels, I heard an old and a young voice repeating the questions and responses of the Church-Catechism. I thought it no breach of good manners to peep at a crevice and look in at people so well employed, but who should I see there but the most artful procuress in the town examining a most beautiful country-girl, who had come up in the same waggon with my things. Whether she was well educated, could forbear playing the wanton with servants and idle fellows, 'of which this town', says she, 'is too full'. At the same time, whether she knew enough of breeding as that if a squire or a gentleman or one that was her betters should give her a civil salute, she could curtsy and be humble nevertheless. Her innocent 'forsooth's, 'yes'es, and ''t please you's, and 'she would do her endeavour', moved the good old lady to take her out of the hands of a country bumpkin her brother, and hire her for her own maid. I stayed till I saw them all marched out to take coach; the brother loaded with a great cheese he prevailed upon her to take for her civilities to sister. This poor creature's fate is not far off that of hers whom I spoke of above, and it is not to be doubted but after she has been long enough a prey to lust she will be delivered over to famine.

(Smith 1897–8: IV, 57–60)

Notes

1   *Bumper.* The Bumper Tavern in St James's Street, Covent Garden.
2   *newly . . . town:* recently taken into prostitution; but as the final paragraph and, for example, Hogarth's *The Harlot's Progress* show, this sense of the phrase and the literal one were all too often synonymous.

7   RICHARD STEELE, FROM 'THE HOURS OF LONDON', *THE SPECTATOR*, NO. 455 (11 AUGUST 1712)

See Introduction, pp. 2 and 7 and headnote to doc. 6.

It is an inexpressible pleasure to know a little of the world, and be of no character or significancy in it. To be ever unconcerned, and ever looking on new objects with an endless curiosity, is a delight known only to those who are turned for speculation: nay, they who enjoy it must value things only as they are the objects of speculation, without drawing any worldly advantage to themselves from them, but just as they are what contribute to their amusement, or the improvement of the mind. I lay one night last week at Richmond; and being restless, not out of dissatisfaction, but a certain busy inclination one sometimes has, I arose at four in the morning, and took boat for London, with a resolution to rove by boat and coach for the next four and twenty hours, till the many different objects I must needs meet with should tire my imagination, and give me an inclination to a repose more profound than I was at that time capable of. I beg people's pardon for an odd humour I am guilty of, and was often that day, which is saluting any person whom I like, whether I know him or not. This is a particularity would be tolerated in me, if they considered that the greatest pleasure I know I receive at my eyes, and that I am obliged to an agreeable person for coming abroad into my view, as another is for the visit of conversation at their own houses.

The hours of the day and night are taken up, in the cities of London and Westminster, by people as different from each other as those who are born in different centuries. Men of six o'clock give way to those of nine, they of nine to the generation of twelve; and they of twelve disappear, and make room for the fashionable world, who have made two o'clock the noon of the day.

When we first put off from shore, we soon fell in with a fleet of gardeners bound for the several market-ports of London; and it was the most pleasing scene imaginable to see the cheerfulness with which those industrious people plied their way to a certain sale of their goods. The banks on each side are as well peopled, and beautified with as agreeable plantations, as any spot on the earth; but the Thames itself, loaded with the product of each shore, added very much to the landscape. It was very easy to observe by their sailing, and the countenances of the ruddy virgins who were supercargoes, the parts of the town to which they were bound. There was an air in the purveyors for Covent Garden, who frequently converse with morning rakes, very unlikely the seemly sobriety of those bound for Stocks Market.[1]

Nothing remarkable happened in our voyage; but I landed with ten sail of apricot boats at Strand Bridge, after having put in at Nine Elms, and taken in melons, consigned by Mr. Cuffe of that place, to Sarah Sewell and company, at their stall in Covent Garden. We arrived at Strand Bridge at six of the clock, and were unloading; when the hackney-coachmen of the foregoing night took their leave of each other at the Dark House, to go to bed before the day was too far spent. Chimney-sweepers passed by us as we made up to the market, and some raillery happened between one of the fruit-wenches and those black men, about the devil and Eve, with allusion to their several professions. I could not believe any place more entertaining than Covent Garden, where I strolled from one fruit-shop to another, with crowds of agreeable young women around me, who were purchasing fruit for their respective families. . . .

The day of people of fashion began now to break, and carts and hacks were mingled with equipages of show and vanity; when I resolved to walk it out of cheapness; but my unhappy curiosity is such that I find it always my interest to take coach, for some odd adventure among beggars, ballad-singers, or the like, detains and throws me into expense. It happened so immediately; for at the corner of Warwick Street, as I was listening to a new ballad, a ragged rascal, a beggar who knew me, came up to me, and began to turn the eyes of the good company upon me by telling me he was extreme poor, and should die in the streets for want of drink, except I immediately would have the charity to give him sixpence to go into the next alehouse and save his life. He urged, with a melancholy face, that all his family had died of thirst. All the mob have humour, and two or three began to take the jest; by which Mr. Sturdy carried his point, and let me sneak off to a coach. As I drove along, it was a pleasing reflection to see the world so prettily chequered since I left Richmond, and the scene still filling with children of a new hour. This satisfaction increased as I moved towards the City; and gay signs, well-disposed streets, magnificent public structures, and wealthy shops, adorned with contented faces, made the joy still rising till we came into the centre of the City, and centre of the world of trade, the Exchange of London. As other men in the crowds about me were pleased with their hopes and bargains, I found my account in observing them in attention to their several interests. I, indeed, looked upon myself as the richest man that walked the Exchange that day; for my benevolence made me share the gains of every bargain that was made. It was not the least of the satisfactions in my survey to go upstairs, and pass the shops of agreeable females; to observe so many pretty hands busy in the foldings of ribands, and the utmost eagerness of agreeable faces in the sale of patches, pins, and wires, on each side the counters, was an amusement in which I should longer have indulged myself, had not the dear creatures called to me to ask what I wanted, when I could not answer only 'To look at you.' I went to one of the windows which opened to the area below, where all the several voices lost their distinction, and rose up in a confused humming; which created in me a reflection that could not come into the mind of any but of one a little too studious; for I said to myself, with a kind of pun in thought, 'What nonsense is all the hurry of this world to those who are above it?' In these or not much wiser thoughts I had like to have lost my place at the chop-house; where every man, according to the natural bashfulness or sullenness of our nation, eats in a public room a mess of broth, or chop of meat, in dumb silence, as if they had no pretence to speak to each other on the foot of being men, except they were of each other's acquaintance.

I went afterwards to Robin's,[2] and saw people who had dined with me at the fivepenny ordinary just before, give bills for the value of large estates; and could not but behold with great pleasure, property lodged in and transferred in a moment from such as would never be masters of half as much as is seemingly in them, and given from them every day they live. But before five in the afternoon I left the City, came to my common scene of Covent Garden, and passed the evening at Will's in attending the discourses of several sets of people, who relieved each other within my hearing on the subjects of cards, dice, love, learning, and politics. The last subject kept me till I heard the streets in the possession of the bellman, who had now the world to himself, and cried, 'Past two of clock'. This roused me from my seat, and I went to my lodging, led by a light, whom I put into the discourse of his private economy, and made him give me an account of the charge, hazard, profit, and loss of a family that depended upon a link, with a design to end my trivial day with the generosity of sixpence, instead of a third part of that sum. When I came to my chamber I writ down these minutes; but was at a loss what instruction I should propose to my reader from the enumeration of so many insignificant matters and occurrences; and I thought it of great use, if they could learn with me to keep their minds open to gratification, and ready to receive it from anything it meets with. This one circumstance will make every face you see give you the satisfaction you now take in beholding that of a friend; will make every object a pleasing one; will make all the good which arrives to any man, an increase of happiness to yourself.

(Smith 1897–8: VI, 208–13)

Notes

1 *Stocks Market*: a market for meat and fish in the City; stocks for the punishment of lawbreakers once stood there.
2 *Robin's*: a coffeehouse in Exchange Alley.

8 DUDLEY RYDER, FROM *DIARY* (1715–16)

Ryder (1691–1756), who was to prosecute leaders of the second Jacobite Rebellion in 1745 and to become Lord Chief Justice in 1754, kept this diary as a law student. Unpublished until the twentieth century, it provides vivid testimony to the fervid atmosphere of political conflict and uncertainty in London shortly after the accession of George I and the 1715 Rebellion. Ryder's Dissenting background is reflected in the meditation on sudden death occasioned by the execution of the rebel leaders, while in his mainly sympathetic account of the loyalist Mug-houses (so-called because the drinking mugs bore portraits of the king and his ministers) there is underlying anxiety about their provoking civil war on the streets.

Thursday, October 20 [1715].

Went to brother's at 4. There were several ladies to see the procession of figures of the Pope, the Devil and the Pretender which were expected to be burnt. There was a great mob about the streets and much holloing for King George. It pleased me exceedingly well. The streets rang with huzzas for the King, but I could not but feel a great displeasure when I heard once a hiss mixed with the shoutings. The society of young men at the Roebuck had prepared the effigies of the Pope, Devil and Pretender and some others to be carried in procession, but the Tories had spread about a malicious report that they intended to burn the Queen. It was therefore thought advisable not to prosecute that design, but they made a vast large bonfire over against Bow Church and burnt some images there with a prodigious crowd of people that were continually crying 'God bless King George' and drank his and all the royal family's health. The streets were very well illuminated.

Friday, February 24 [1716].

The whole hill was full of people that I never saw so large a collection of people in my life, and a vast circle was made by the horse guards round about the scaffolds and a great many foot guards in the middle. At length Lord Derwentwater and Kenmure came in two hackney coaches from the Tower to the transport office over against the scaffolds. I saw them both. Lord Derwentwater looked with a melancholy aspect, but Lord Kenmure looked very bold and unconcerned.

Lord Derwentwater was executed first. After he was brought upon the stage and was saluted by several officers and others that were there, he prayed and spoke to them and told them, as I am informed, that since he was to die he was sorry he pleaded guilty, for he was an innocent man, for he knew no king but King James III. He was a papist and therefore had no priest along with him. He seemed to behave himself very well and make his exit decently enough, though with but a melancholy and pious aspect. . . . The executioner struck off his head at one blow and then held it in his hand and showed it to the people and said, 'Here is the head of the traitor. God bless King George!' His head and body were wrapped in a black cloth and put into the coach in which he came and carried back to the Tower. . . . There was no disturbance made at all, while the mob were as quiet as lambs, nor did there seem to be any face of sorrow among the multitude.

It is very moving and affecting to see a man that was but this moment in perfect health and strength sent the next into another world. Few that die in their bed have so easy an end of life. But then what must be the thoughts of a man in that condition, that could count every moment before his death and reflect to the very last, it is impossible to conceive, because one cannot put one-self into that form and temper of mind which these circumstances will necessarily put a man into. The pain of dying is nothing. It is but like a flash of lightning, begun and ended in the compass of a thought. Life itself is attended in every one with much more grievous pains. Why then are we afraid to die? Is it the loss of the pleasures of life, of all the agreeable things in which we delighted? That cannot be all. No, the strange uncertain dark prospect that is before us terrifies us and makes afraid to be we know not what and go we know not where.

I was very well pleased to see that the King had resolution enough to execute these lords. I think he has given in this a greater proof than ever of his fitness to govern this nation, and I am persuaded it will have a good effect both at home to make the Tories partly despair and partly come over to the King, and abroad to raise his character in foreign nations, and convince them that it is not the clamour and noise of rebels or the mob that shall interrupt the course of justice or shake his resolute mind. . . .

Friday, July 20

. . . Went to the coffee-house and at the Gill House met with some company that asked me to go with them to the Mug-House in Salisbury Court and I went with them to see the manner of it. I like the design of this institution very well. It is to encourage the friends to King George and keep up the spirit of loyalty and the public spirit among them. They have a president who proposes the healths. Between every health some of the company sing a song that is composed against the Tories and Jacobites. There is something in their manner of singing, which is generally attended with a chorus at the end of each stanza of the song, which has an effect upon those that hear it, something like the drums and trumpets in an army, to raise the courage and spirits of the soldiers. Methought it put me into a very brisk intrepid state to hear them huzza and clap hands and sing together. . . . I am persuaded these mug-houses are of service to the Government to keep up the public spirit and animate its friends, and I believe in time it will gain over the populace and make King George become popular.

There was a mob gathered about the door and we heard that there were some of the Bridewell boys come to attack us. This came to the ears of the society at the Roebuck and they sent some of their members to inquire into our circumstances and offer their assistance if we needed it and others came from the Tavistock Mug-House, so that our room was quite full. But we were not attacked and I came off very peaceably. The worst of it is I find some of the members of these societies are apt to be too flushed with their strength and attack persons whom they suspect before they are insulted themselves. However, I believe they do service to the Government in keeping its friends in countenance and dispiriting its enemies. There were several gentlemen among them but many as I guess only prentices and ordinary tradesmen. However, we are all upon a level there and those that can entertain the company with the most songs is the most taken notice of, his health being always drunk after he has sung a song. But between every song the public state health is drunk, which the President composes, who is elected new every night. . . .

Monday, July 23. . . .
Came home at 11 o'clock. There was a mob got about the Mug-House in Salisbury Court. There had been some fighting there before to defend it and they dispersed the mob, but then one of the Mug-House men was taken into custody by the constable and his friends were resolved to rescue him and broke the windows of the house where he was and made a great deal of noise and a vast mob was gathered about. However, they dispersed soon after. . . .

Tuesday, July 24. . . .
When I went out to dinner I saw a mob gathered together about the Mug-House. The Tory mob were resolved to be revenged for what the Whigs did to them last night and therefore to-day assembled against the Mug-House and broke all the lower part of the inside of it in pieces, quite destroying all the furniture and goods in it and beat and wounded some that defended it, but those few that were in the house defended themselves and killed one man of the mob and wounded several others. At length the soldiers came and dispersed the mob. . . .

(Matthews 1939: 121, 187–8, 279–80, 283)

9 JOHN GAY, FROM *TRIVIA, OR THE ART OF WALKING THE STREETS OF LONDON* (1716)

Trivia (Latin for 'streets') is a mock-georgic poem which transfers classical georgic's instructive treatment of the labours and rhythms of rural life to the more hazardous, disorderly and man-made environment of the modern city. Gay (1685–1732) amplifies his friend Swift's strategy (see doc. 4) of fusing formal burlesque (including epic similes and allusions) with social and topographical realism; the result is a work of far from trivial significance in urban literature (see Rogers 1974: 219–20 and Corfield 1990: 136–7).

BOOK II

'Of Walking the Streets by Day'

... If drawn by business to a street unknown,   *Of whom*
Let the sworn porter point thee through the town;   *to enquire*
Be sure observe the signs, for signs remain,   *the way.*
Like faithful landmarks to the walking train.
Seek not from 'prentices to learn the way,
Those fabling boys will turn thy steps astray;   70
Ask the grave tradesman to direct thee right,
He ne'er deceives, but when he profits by't.

Where famed Saint Giles's ancient limits spread,
An inrailed column[1] rears its lofty head,
Here to sev'n streets, sev'n Dials count the day,
And from each other catch the circling ray.
Here oft the peasant, with enquiring face,
Bewildered, trudges on from place to place;
He dwells on ev'ry sign, with stupid gaze,
Enters the narrow alley's doubtful maze,   80
Tries ev'ry winding court and street in vain,
And doubles o'er his weary steps again.
Thus hardy Theseus, with intrepid feet,
Traversed the dang'rous labyrinth of Crete;
But still the wand'ring passes forced his stay,
Till Ariadne's clue unwinds the way.
But do not thou, like that bold chief, confide
Thy vent'rous footsteps to a female guide;
She'll lead thee, with delusive smiles along,
Dive in thy fob, and drop thee in the throng.   90

. . .

Successive cries the seasons' change declare,   *Remarks*
And mark the monthly progress of the year.   *on the Cries*
Hark, how the streets with treble voices ring,   *of the Town.*
To sell the bounteous product of the spring!
Sweet-smelling flow'rs, and elder's early bud,
With nettle's tender shoots, to cleanse the blood;   430
And when June's thunder cools the sultry skies,
Ev'n Sundays are profaned by mack'rel cries.

Walnuts the fruit'rers hand, in autumn, stain,
Blue plums and juicy pears augment his gain;
Next, oranges the longing boys entice
To trust their copper fortunes to the dice.

When rosemary and bays, the poet's crown, *Of*
Are bawled in frequent cries through all the town, *Christmas.*
Then judge the festival of Christmas near,
Christmas, the joyous period of the year. 440
Now, with bright holly all your temples strow,
With laurel green and sacred mistletoe.
Now, heav'n-born Charity, thy blessings shed;
Bid meagre Want uprear her sickly head:
Bid shiv'ring limbs be warm; let plenty's bowl
In humble roofs make glad the needy soul . . . .

BOOK III

'Of Walking the Streets by Night'

. . . When Night first bids the twinkling stars appear, *The*
Or with her cloudy vest inwraps the air, 10 *Evening.*
Then swarms the busy street; with caution tread,
Where the shop-windows falling threat thy head;
Now lab'rers home return, and join their strength
To bear the tott'ring plank, or ladder's length;
Still fix thy eyes intent upon the throng,
And as the passes open, wind along.

Where the fair columns of Saint Clement stand, *Of the*
Whose straitened bounds encroach upon the Strand; *Pass of*
Where the low penthouse bows the walker's head, *St. Clement's.*
And the rough pavement wounds the yielding tread; 20
Where not a post protects the narrow space,
And strung in twines, combs dangle in thy face;
Summon at once thy courage, rouse thy care,
Stand firm, look back, be resolute, beware.
Forth issuing from steep lanes, the collier's steeds
Drag the black load; another cart succeeds,
Team follows team, crowds heaped on crowds appear,
And wait impatient, till the road grow clear.
Now all the pavement sounds with trampling feet,
And the mixed hurry barricades the street. 30

Entangled here, the waggon's lengthened team
Cracks the tough harness; here a pond'rous beam
Lies overturned athwart; for slaughter fed,
Here lowing bullocks raise their hornèd head.
Now oaths grow loud, with coaches coaches jar,
And the smart blow provokes the sturdy war;
From the high box they whirl the thong around,
And with the twining lash their shins resound:
Their rage ferments, more dang'rous wounds they try,
And the blood gushes down their painful eye.   40
And now on foot the frowning warriors light,
And with their pond'rous fists renew the fight;
Blow answers blow, their cheeks are smeared with blood,
Till down they fall, and grappling roll in mud . . . .

. . .

O! may thy virtue guard thee through the roads   *An*
Of Drury's mazy courts and dark abodes,   260 *Admonition*
The harlots' guileful paths, who nightly stand   *to Virtue.*
Where Catherine Street descends into the Strand.
Say, vagrant Muse! their wiles and subtle arts,
To lure the strangers' unsuspecting hearts;
So shall our youth on healthful sinews tread,
And city cheeks grow warm with rural red.

                                                    How to
'Tis she who nightly strolls with saunt'ring pace,   *know a*
No stubborn stays her yielding shape embrace;   *whore.*
Beneath the lamp her tawdry ribbons glare,   270
The new-scored mantua and the slattern air;
High-draggled petticoats her travels show,
And hollow cheeks with artful blushes glow;
With flatt'ring sounds she soothes the cred'lous ear,
My noble captain! charmer! love! my dear!
In ridinghood near tavern-doors she plies,
Or muffled pinners[2] hide her livid eyes;
With empty bandbox she delights to range,
And feigns a distant errand from the 'Change;
Nay, she will oft the Quaker's hood profane,   280
And trudge demure the rounds of Drury Lane:
She darts from sarcenet ambush wily leers;
Twitches thy sleeve, or with familiar airs

Her fan will pat thy cheek: these snares disdain,
Nor gaze behind thee when she turns again . . . .

(Gay 1720: I, 135–203)

Notes

1 *column*: a Doric pillar which bore the eponymous seven dials (though some
accounts say there were only six), each facing one of the streets converging at this
spot; the column was removed in 1774.
2 *pinners*: long flaps pinned to the cap.

10 DANIEL DEFOE, FROM *THE FORTUNES AND MISFORTUNES OF THE FAMOUS MOLL FLANDERS* (1722)

Defoe (1660?–1731) was a lifelong Londoner with an abiding interest in the problems and dynamics of the urban environment, including the layout of streets and the
relationship of poverty and crime. *Moll Flanders*, the first-ever novel with a predominantly urban setting, is also notable for the number of street-scenes integral to the
main action. Born in Newgate prison, Moll enjoys a colourful career of sexual adventure until in middle age 'mere necessity', so she claims, forces her into crime. This
account of her second robbery displays Defoe's characteristic accumulation of
authenticating detail, for example in the precise routing of Moll's flight from dark alley
to crowded thoroughfare, and in the more subtle psychological realism of her self-
exculpatory fancies regarding her victim's circumstances.

I went out now by daylight, and wandered about I knew not whither, and
in search of I knew not what, when the devil put a snare in my way of a
dreadful nature indeed, and such a one as I have never had before or since.
Going through Aldersgate Street, there was a pretty little child who had
been at a dancing-school, and was going home, all alone; and my prompter,
like a true devil, set me upon this innocent creature. I talked to it, and it
prattled to me again, and I took it by the hand and led it along till I came
to a paved alley that goes into Bartholomew Close, and I led it in there. The
child said that was not its way home. I said, 'Yes, my dear, it is; I'll show you
the way home.' The child had a little necklace on of gold beads, and I had
my eye upon that, and in the dark of the alley I stooped, pretending to
mend the child's clog that was loose, and took off her necklace, and the
child never felt it, and so led the child on again. Here, I say, the devil put
me upon killing the child in the dark alley, that it might not cry, but the very
thought frighted me so that I was ready to drop down; but I turned the
child about and bade it go back again, for that was not its way home. The
child said, so she would, and I went through into Bartholomew Close, and
then turned round to another passage that goes into Long Lane, so away
into Charterhouse Yard and out into St. John Street; then, crossing into

Smithfield, went down Chick Lane and into Field Lane to Holborn Bridge, when, mixing with the crowd of people usually passing there, it was not possible to have been found out; and thus I enterprised my second sally into the world.

The thought of this booty put out all the thoughts of the first, and the reflections I had made wore quickly off; poverty, as I have said, hardened my heart, and my own necessities made me regardless of anything. The last affair left no great concern upon me, for as I did the poor child no harm, I only said to myself, I had given the parents a just reproof for their negligence in leaving the poor little lamb to come home by itself, and it would teach them to take more care of it another time.

This string of beads was worth about twelve or fourteen pounds. I suppose it might have been formerly the mother's, for it was too big for the child's wear, but that perhaps the vanity of the mother, to have her child look fine at the dancing-school, had made her let the child wear it; and no doubt the child had a maid sent to take care of it, but she, careless jade, was taken up perhaps with some fellow that had met her by the way, and so the poor baby wandered till it fell into my hands.

However, I did the child no harm; I did not so much as fright it, for I had a great many tender thoughts about me yet, and did nothing but what, as I may say, mere necessity drove me to.

(Defoe 1923: 236–7)

11   CÉSAR DE SAUSSURE, FROM *A FOREIGN VIEW OF ENGLAND IN THE REIGNS OF GEORGE I AND GEORGE II* (WRITTEN 1725–30)

Saussure (1705–83), a Swiss traveller and writer, recorded his impressions of a five-year stay in England (mostly spent in London) in the form of long family letters. They distil the salient views among early eighteenth-century foreign visitors of, for example, the 'unpleasant' physical condition of London's roads, the aggressively declared prejudices of 'the vulgar populace', and the glamorous appeal of the principal shopping streets (showing that 'window-shopping' long predates the nineteenth century when it is sometimes said to have begun). However, Saussure's enthusiasm about a merely domestic street-lighting system exemplifies the historical relativism of views on such matters, and the same might be said for his description of particularly unsavoury aspects of a Tyburn execution as 'most amusing'.

Most of the streets are wonderfully well lighted, for in front of each house hangs a lantern or a large globe of glass, inside of which is placed a lamp which burns all night. Large houses have two of these lamps suspended outside their doors by iron supports, and some have even four. The streets of London are unpleasantly full either of dust or of mud. This arises from the

Plate 1 'The Idle 'Prentice Executed at Tyburn', W. Hogarth, 1747.

quantity of houses that are continually being built, and also from the large number of coaches and chariots rolling in the streets day and night . . . .

Another of the unpleasantnesses of the streets is that the pavement is so bad and rough that when you drive in a coach you are most cruelly shaken, whereas if you go on foot you have a nice smooth path paved with wide flat stones, and elevated above the road . . . .

The four streets – the Strand, Fleet Street, Cheapside, and Cornhill – are, I imagine, the finest in Europe. What help to make them interesting and attractive are the shops and the signs. Every house, or rather every shop, has a sign of copper, pewter, or wood painted and gilt. Some of these signs are really magnificent, and have cost as much as one hundred pounds sterling. . . . Every house possesses one or two shops where the choicest merchandise from the four quarters of the globe is exposed to the sight of the passers-by. A stranger might spend whole days, without ever feeling bored, examining these wonderful goods . . . .

The Lord Mayor's Day is a great holiday in the City. The populace on that day is particularly insolent and rowdy, turning into lawless freedom the great liberty it enjoys. At these times it is almost dangerous for an honest man, and more particularly for a foreigner, if at all well dressed, to walk in the streets, for he runs a great risk of being insulted by the vulgar populace,

53

Plate 2 'The Industrious 'Prentice Lord Mayor of London', W. Hogarth, 1747.

which is the most cursed brood in existence. He is sure of not only being jeered at and being bespattered with mud, but as likely as not dead dogs and cats will be thrown at him, for the mob makes a provision beforehand of these playthings, so that they may amuse themselves with them on the great day. ... When the people see a well-dressed person in the streets, especially if he is wearing a braided coat, a plume in his hat, or his hair tied in a bow, he will, without doubt, be called 'French dog' twenty times perhaps before he reaches his destination. This name is the most common, and evidently, according to popular idea, the greatest and most forcible insult that can be given to any man, and it is applied indifferently to all foreigners, French or otherwise. ...

On the day of execution the condemned prisoners, wearing a sort of white linen shirt over their clothes and a cap on their heads, are tied two together and placed on carts with their backs to the horses' tails. These carts are guarded and surrounded by constables and other police officers on horse-back, each armed with a sort of pike. In this way part of the town is crossed, and Tyburn, which is a good half-mile from the last suburb, is reached, and here stands the gibbet. ... When all the prisoners arrive at their destination they are made to mount on a very wide cart made expressly for the purpose, a cord is passed round their necks and the end fastened to the gibbet, which is not very high. The chaplain who accompanies the condemned men is also on the cart; he makes them pray and sing a few verses of the Psalms. The relatives are permitted to mount the cart and take farewell. When the time is up – that is to say about a quarter of an hour – the chaplain and relations get off the cart, the executioner covers the eyes and faces of the prisoners with their caps, lashes the horses that draw the cart, which slips from under the condemned men's feet, and in this way they remain all hanging together. You often see friends and relatives tugging at the hanging men's feet so that they should die quicker and not suffer. The bodies and clothes of the dead belong to the executioner; relatives must, if they wish for them, buy them from him, and unclaimed bodies are sold to surgeons to be dissected. You see most amusing scenes between the people who do not like the bodies to be cut up and the messengers the surgeons have sent for the bodies; blows are given and returned before they can be got away, and sometimes in the turmoil the bodies are quickly removed and buried. Again, the populace often come to blows as to who will carry the bought corpses to the parents who are waiting in coaches and cabs to receive them, for the carriers are well paid for their trouble. All these scenes are most diverting, the noise and confusion is unbelievable, and can be witnessed from a sort of amphitheatre erected for spectators near the gibbet.

(Saussure 1902: 67–8, 80–1, 111–2, 124–6)

12   HORACE WALPOLE, FROM LETTER TO SIR HORACE MANN (JULY 1742)

Walpole (1717–97), the fourth son of the long-serving Prime Minister Sir Robert Walpole, was a miscellaneous writer, art connoisseur and reluctant politician. His vast correspondence (more than 4,000 published letters, over 400 of them to Mann, British envoy at Florence, with whom he corresponded for almost half a century) offers a highly informative and engaging commentary upon a changing world. Walpole here sharply criticises the primitive and corrupt policing system which operated in London until the late eighteenth century. On the practice of compelling citizens, especially publicans, to serve as unpaid constables, George (1966: 47, 292, 389–90) is, as ever, illuminating.

There has lately been the most shocking scene of murder imaginable; a parcel of *drunken* constables took it into their heads to put the laws in execution against *disorderly* persons, and so took up every woman they met, till they had collected five or six-and-twenty, all of whom they thrust into St. Martin's round-house, where they kept them all night, with doors and windows closed. The poor creatures, who could not stir or breathe, screamed as long as they had any breath left, begging at least for water: one poor wretch said she was worth eighteen-pence, and would gladly give it for a draught of water, but in vain! So well did they keep them there, that in the morning four were found stifled to death, two died soon after, and a dozen more are in a shocking way. In short, it is horrid to think what the poor creatures suffered: several of them were beggars, who, from having no lodging, were necessarily found in the street, and others honest labouring women. One of the dead was a poor washerwoman, big with child, who was returning home late from washing. One of the constables is taken, and others absconded; but I question if any of them will suffer death,[1] though the greatest criminals in this town are the officers of justice; there is no tyranny they do not exercise, no villainy of which they do not partake. These same men, the same night, broke into a bagnio in Covent Garden, and took up Jack Spencer,[2] Mr. Stewart, and Lord George Graham, and would have thrust them into the round-house with the poor women, if they had not been worth more than eighteen-pence!

(Cunningham 1857–9: I (1857), 191–2)

Notes

1 *I . . . death*: according to Walpole's own note, the keeper of the round-house was tried for murder but acquitted.
2 *Spencer*: grandson of the Duke of Marlborough, the famous general.

13   SAMUEL JOHNSON, FROM *LIFE OF SAVAGE* (1744, 1781)

Though later memorialised by Boswell as an embodiment of metropolitan cultural authority, Johnson (1709–84) endured years of poverty and obscurity in Grub Street after arriving in London at the age of 27. His biography of the poet Richard Savage was first published anonymously only a year after its subject's sensational life ended in a debtor's prison. Savage always claimed to be the illegitimate son of Lady Macclesfield and Earl Rivers; Johnson not only accepts this doubtful claim (as did many others) but makes the mother's 'cruel' refusal to acknowledge it the leitmotif of a story of social exclusion and thwarted genius. This situation is vividly materialised in the account of Savage's nocturnal street-wanderings, creating, in the words of Holmes's brilliant study, 'a legend . . . of the Outcast Poet moving through an infernal cityscape, the "City of Dreadful Night"' (1993: 45). This effect is heightened by the figure's apparent solitariness, yet the night-walks were in fact a shared experience in Johnson's brief but intense friendship with Savage. The tone of indignant apologia partly reflects the fact that he is also writing about himself, and personally testifying, as he did in the juvenalian satire *London* (1738), to the 'mournful truth . . . ,/Slow rises worth, by poverty depressed' (Smith and McAdam 1941: 18).

Savage was . . . so touched with the discovery of his real mother, that it was his frequent practice to walk in the dark evenings for several hours before her door, in hopes of seeing her as she might come by accident to the window, or cross her apartment with a candle in her hand.

But all his assiduity and tenderness were without effect, for he could nei-ther soften her heart, nor open her hand, and was reduced to the utmost mis-eries of want, while he was endeavouring to awaken the affection of a mother. He was therefore obliged to seek some other means of support; and, having no profession, became by necessity an author.

But having been unsuccessful in comedy, though rather for want of oppor-tunities than genius, he resolved now to try whether he should not be more fortunate in exhibiting a tragedy. . . .

During a considerable part of the time in which he was employed upon this performance, he was without lodging, and often without meat; nor had he any other conveniences for study than the fields or the street allowed him; there he used to walk and form his speeches, and afterwards step into a shop, beg for a few moments the use of the pen and ink, and write down what he had composed, upon paper which he had picked up by accident.

If the performance of a writer thus distressed is not perfect, its faults ought surely to be imputed to a cause very different from want of genius, and much rather excite pity than provoke censure. . . .

He lodged as much by accident as he dined, and passed the night some-times in mean houses, which are set open at night to any casual wanderers, sometimes in cellars, among the riot and filth of the meanest and most prof-ligate of the rabble; and sometimes, when he had not money to support even the expences of these receptacles, walked about the streets till he was weary, and lay down in the summer upon a bulk,[1] or in the winter, with his associ-ates in poverty, among the ashes of a glass-house.[2]

In this manner were passed those days and those nights which nature had enabled him to have employed in elevated speculations, useful studies, or pleasing conversation. On a bulk, in a cellar, or in a glass-house among thieves and beggars, was to be found the Author of *The Wanderer*, the man of exalted sentiments, extensive views, and curious observations; the man whose remarks on life might have assisted the statesman, whose ideas of virtue might have enlightened the moralist, whose eloquence might have influenced senates, and whose delicacy might have polished courts. . . .

Thus he spent his time in mean expedients and tormenting suspense, liv-ing for the greatest part in fear of prosecutions from his creditors, and con-sequently skulking in obscure parts of the town, of which he was no stranger to the remotest corners. . . .

He had seldom any home, or even a lodging in which he could be private; and therefore was driven into public-houses for the common conveniences of life and supports of nature. He was always ready to comply with every invitation, having no employment to withhold him, and often no money to provide for himself; and by dining with one company, he never failed of obtaining an introduction into another.

Thus dissipated was his life, and thus casual his subsistence; yet did not the distraction of his views hinder him from reflection, nor the uncertainty of his condition depress his gaiety. When he had wandered about without any fortunate adventure by which he was led into a tavern, he sometimes retired into the fields, and was able to employ his mind in study, or amuse it with pleasing imaginations. . . .

(Johnson 1905: II, 329, 338–9, 405)

Notes

1 *bulk*: protruding stall in front of a shop.
2 *glass-house*: small factory with ovens for producing glassware.

14   ELIZA HAYWOOD, FROM *THE HISTORY OF MISS BETSY THOUGHTLESS* (1751), VOL. 2, CH. 10

Haywood (1690?–1756), daughter of a London shopkeeper, wrote plays, fiction and journalism (notably *The Female Spectator*, 1744–6). Her initial notoriety as a professional actress disowned by her clerical husband was reinforced by publication of scandalous allegories on contemporary politics and court-life. *Betsy Thoughtless* represents a shift towards moral conventionality, but the naive heroine's urban misadventures, exemplifying young women's vulnerability in a world of sexual double standards, also arise from her own independent spirit and freedom of movement about the city, which Haywood is reluctant to deplore. The following scene occurs after a visit to the theatre with an old school-friend who Miss Betsy does not yet realise is now a prostitute; the two gallants who escort them back have been invited in to Miss Forward's lodgings.

The conversation was extremely lively and, though sprinkled with some double entendres, could not be said to have anything indecent, or that could raise a blush in the faces of women who were accustomed to much company. Miss Betsy had her share in all the innocent part of what was said, and laughed at that which was less so. But not to dwell on trifles, she forgot all the cautions given her by Mr Trueworth, considered not that she was in company with two strange gentlemen, and of a woman whose character was suspected; nor, though she had a watch by her side, regarded not how the hours passed on, till she heard the nightly monitor of time cry, 'Past twelve o'clock, and a cloudy morning!'

After this she would not be prevailed upon to stay, and desired Miss Forward to send somebody for a chair. 'A chair, Madam!' cried that gentleman who, of the two, had been most particular in his addresses to her, 'you cannot sure imagine we should suffer you to go home alone at this late hour.' – 'I apprehend no great danger,' said she, 'though I confess it is a thing I have not been accustomed to.' He replied that in his company she should not begin the experiment: on this a coach was ordered. Miss Betsy made some few scruples at committing herself to the conduct of a person so little known to her. 'All acquaintance must have a beginning,' said he, 'the most intimate friends were perfect strangers at first. You may depend on it I am a man of honour and cannot be capable of an ungenerous action.'

Little more was said on the occasion, and being told a coach was at the door, they took leave of Miss Forward and the other gentleman, and went down stairs. On stepping into the coach, Miss Betsy directed the man where to drive; but the gentleman, unheard by her, ordered him to go to the bagnio in Orange Street. They were no sooner seated, and the windows drawn up to keep out the cold, than Miss Betsy was alarmed with a treatment which her want of consideration made her little expect: since the gentleman-commoner, no man had ever attempted to take the liberties which her present companion now did. She struggled – she repelled with all her might the insolent pressures of his lips and hands. 'Is this,' cried she, 'the honour I was to depend upon? Is it thus you prove yourself incapable of an ungenerous action?' – 'Accuse me not,' said he, 'till you have reason. I have been bit once, and have made a vow never to settle upon any woman while I live again. But you shall fare never the worse for that: I will make you a handsome present before we part, and if you can be constant, will allow you six guineas a week.'

She was so confounded at the first mention of this impudent proposal that she had not the power of interrupting him; but recovering herself as well as she was able, 'Heavens!' cried she, 'what means all this? What do you take me for?' – 'Take you for!' answered he, laughing, 'pr'ythee, dear girl, no more of these airs: I take you for a pretty, kind, obliging creature, and such I hope to find you, as soon as we come into a proper place. In the meantime,' continued he, stopping her mouth with kisses, 'none of this affected coyness.'

The fright she was in, aided by disdain and rage, now inspired her with an unusual strength: she broke from him, thrust down the window, and with one breath called him 'Monster! Villain!', with the next screamed out to the coachman to stop; and finding he regarded not her cries, would have thrown herself out, if not forcibly withheld by the gentleman, who began now to be a little startled at her resolute behaviour. 'What is all this for?' said he, 'would you break your neck, or venture being crushed to pieces by the wheels?' – 'Anything,' cried she, bursting into tears, 'I will venture, suffer anything, rather than be subjected to insults, such as you have dared to treat me with.'

Though the person by whom Miss Betsy was thus dangerously attacked was a libertine, or according to the more genteel and modish phrase, a man of pleasure, yet he wanted neither honour nor good sense: he had looked on

Miss Betsy as a woman of the town, by seeing her with one who was so, and her too great freedom in conversation gave him no cause to alter his opinion; but the manner in which she had endeavoured to rebuff his more near approaches greatly staggered him. He knew not what to think, but remained in silent cogitation for some minutes, and though he held her fast clasped round the waist, it was only to prevent her from attempting the violence she had threatened, not to offer any towards her. 'Is it possible,' said he, after this pause, 'that you are virtuous?' . . .

He then took the liberty of reminding her that a young lady more endangered her reputation by an acquaintance of one woman of ill fame than by receiving the visits of twenty men, though professed libertines. To which she replied that for the future she would be very careful what company she kept, of both sexes. . . .

(Haywood 1751: II, 115–19, 122)

15   ANON., FROM *LOW LIFE: OR ONE HALF THE WORLD KNOWS NOT HOW THE OTHER HALF LIVE* (1752)

See Introduction (pp. 2–3) on the 'Hours of London' genre. This example is dedicated to 'the ingenious and ingenuous Mr Hogarth', acknowledging the particular influence of *The Four Times of Day* (see plate 3). The popularity of the genre is suggested by the fact that this anonymous and undistinguished satire went into a third edition twelve years after its first appearance. The subtitle is an early (though doubtless not original) usage of what was to remain a leading catchphrase regarding urban society for at least a century. However, its main connotation here is not, as it usually would be in the nineteenth century, the woeful indifference of the prosperous to the privations of the poor, but rather the ignorance of law-abiding innocents regarding the plenitude of illicit and immoral practices in the dark metropolis.

Hour III: from two till three o'clock on Sunday morning

Young country esquires, whose whores have picked their pockets, are beaten by the bullies and sent to the watch-house for further security, during which time the villains and whores make off together with their booty. The turnkeys of gaols receiving money from prisoners to favour them in their escapes, that they may avoid condign punishment. Gaming-houses full of fools, bullies, thieves, usurers, broken gamesters and oaths. Constables going round their parishes and precincts to the several bawdy-houses to receive sufferance-money and partake of their best liquors. Pawnbrokers, after their servants are in bed, busy in altering the dates of clothes under tribulation, to defraud the poor that left them out of more money than is their due. Most private shops in and about London (as there are too many) where geneva is publicly sold in defiance of the Act of Parliament,[1] filled with whores, thieves

Plate 3 'Night', W. Hogarth, 1738.

and beggars, who have got drunk and are talking of scripture. Young fellows who have been out all night on the ran-dan,[2] stealing staves and lanterns from such watchmen as they find sleeping at their stands, which are carried to the watch-house and delivered up to the constable for the pleasure of drinking with them the remainder of the night.

The whole company of finders (a sort of people who get their bread by the hurry and negligence of sleepy tradesman) are marching towards all the markets in London, Westminster and Southwark, to make a seizure of all the butchers, poulterers, green-grocers and other market-people left behind them at their stalls and shambles when they went away. Sextons of parish-churches privately digging up and sending to the houses of surgeons the bodies of such people who were buried the preceding night, that died young and after a short illness, to be anatomised; at which time they take the opportunity of ripping the velvet and cloth off large coffins, pulling out the brass nails and tearing away the plates and handles, to sell for geneva, snuff and tobacco.

Hackney-coachmen searching the seats and boots of their coaches, in hopes of finding things of value accidentally left there in the hurry of the night.

Noblemen and gentlemen going home from bawdy-houses and gaming-tables with heavy hearts and empty pockets. Poor unfortunate whores, who have had no business the night past, creating quarrels in the streets that they may raise a mob and pick pockets for the ensuing day's sustenance. Sailors on board inward-bound merchant ships in the river, bring out their rum and brandy and contriving how to make the custom-house officers on board drunk, that they may get on shore such goods as they have neither money or inclination to pay custom for. Night-cellars about Covent Garden and Charing Cross filled with mechanics, some sleeping, others playing at cards, with dead beer before them, and link-boys giving their attendance . . . . Hostlers and stable-sweepers in general, at the principal inns in Whitechapel, Grub Street, Bishopgate Street, Goswell Street, Holborn, Piccadilly and the borough of Southwark, beginning to feed and dress the cattle which are to be rode (almost to death) the ensuing day, by new-married men, hair-brained citizens, fools just come of age, and mad sailors lately arrived from sea. . . .

(Low Life 1764: 15–17)

Notes

1 *geneva . . . Parliament*: the Gin Act of 1751 (for which Hogarth was campaigning in *Gin Lane*) banned the sale of spirits by chandlers and grocers (George 1966: 49).
2 *ran-dan*: spree, rampage.

16 WILLIAM WHITEHEAD, 'THE SWEEPERS' (1754)

Whitehead (1715–85), the son of a Cambridge baker, began to publish poetry while a Fellow at Clare College, which he had entered as a mature student. Thereafter he wrote for the London theatre as well as in a wide variety of verse forms, becoming (controversially) Poet Laureate in 1757. Whitehead's own humble origins may be a factor in what, for the eighteenth century, is an unusually sympathetic treatment of vagrant street-workers, despite its conventional 'proper-sphere' view of class divisions. The incongruity between stylistic elevation and realistic low-life subject-matter is somewhat reminiscent of Gay's *Trivia* (doc. 9), but the poem moves beyond burlesque towards a proto-Victorian sensibility.

> I sing of sweepers, frequent in thy streets,
> Augusta,[1] as the flowers which grace the spring,
> Or branches withering in autumnal shades
> To form the brooms they wield. Preserved by them
> From dirt, from coach-hire, and th' oppressive rheums
> Which clog the springs of life, to them I sing,
> And ask no inspiration but their smiles.

Hail, unowned youths, and virgins unendowed!
Whether on bulk begot, while rattled loud
The passing coaches, or th' officious hand 10
Of sportive link-boy wide around him dashed
The pitchy-flame, obstructive of the joy.
Or more propitious, to the dark retreat
Of round-house owe your birth, where Nature's reign
Revives, and prompted by untaught desire
The mingling sexes share promiscuous love.
And scarce the pregnant female knows to whom
She owes the precious burthen, scarce the sire
Can claim, confused, the many-featured child.

Nor blush that hence your origin we trace: 20
'Twas thus immortal heroes sprung of old
Strong from the stol'n embrace; by such as you,
Unhoused, unclothed, unlettered and unfed,
Were kingdoms modelled, cities taught to rise,
Firm laws enacted, Freedom's rights maintained,
The gods and patriots of an infant world!

Let others meanly chaunt in tuneful song
The blackshoe race, whose mercenary tribes
Allured by halfpence take their morning stand
Where streets divide, and to their proffered stools 30
Solicit wand'ring feet; vain pensioners,
And placemen of the crowd! Not so you pour
Your blessings on mankind; nor traffic vile
Be your employment deemed, ye last remains
Of public spirit, whose laborious hands,
Uncertain of reward, bid kennels know
Their wonted bounds, remove the bord'ring filth,
And give th'obstructed ordure where to glide.

What though the pitying passenger bestows
His unextorted boon, must they refuse 40
The well-earned bounty, scorn th' obtruded ore?
Proud were the thought and vain. And shall not we
Repay their kindly labours, men like them,
With gratitude unsought? I too have oft
Seen in our streets the withered hands of age
Toil in th' industrious task; and can we there
Be thrifty niggards? haply they have known
Far better days, and scattered liberal round

The scanty pittance we afford them now.
Soon from this office grant them their discharge,   50
Ye kind church-wardens! take their meagre limbs
Shiv'ring with cold and age, and wrap them warm
In those blest mansions Charity has raised.
    But you of younger years, while vigour knits
Your lab'ring sinews, urge the generous task.
Nor lose in fruitless brawls the precious hours
Assigned to toil. Be your contentions who
First in the dark'ning streets, when Autumn sheds
Her earliest showers, shall clear th'obstructed pass;
Or last shall quit the field when Spring distils   60
Her moist'ning dews, prolific there in vain.
So may each lusty scavenger, ye fair,
Fly ardent to your arms; and every maid,
Ye gentle youths, be to your wishes kind.
Whether Ostrea's fishy fumes allure
As Venus' tresses fragrant, or the sweets
More mild and rural from her stall who toils
To feast the sages of the Samian school.[2]
    Nor ever may your hearts elate with pride
Desert this sphere of love; for should ye, youths,   70
When blood boils high, and some more lucky chance
Has swelled your stores, pursue the tawdry band
That romp from lamp to lamp, for health expect
Disease, for fleeting pleasure foul remorse,
And daily, nightly, agonising pains.
In vain you call for Aesculapius' aid
From White-cross alley, or the azure posts
Which beam through Haydon-yard;[3] the god demands
More ample offerings, and rejects your prayer.
    And you, ye fair, O let me warn your breasts   80
To shun deluding men: for some there are,
Great lords of countries, mighty men of war,
And well-dressed courtiers, who with leering eye
Can in the face begrimed with dirt discern
Strange charms, and pant for Cynthia in a cloud.
    But let Lardella's fate avert your own.
Lardella once was fair, the early boast
Of proud St. Giles's, from its ample pound

To where the column points the seven-fold day.[4]
Happy, thrice happy, had she never known   90
A street more spacious! but ambition led
Her youthful footsteps, artless, unassured,
To Whitehall's fatal pavement. There she plied
Like you the active broom. At sight of her
The coachman dropped his lash, the porter oft
Forgot his burthen, and with wild amaze
The tall well-booted sentry, armed in vain,
Leaned from his horse to gaze upon her charms.
　　But Fate reserved her for more dreadful ills:
A lord beheld her, and with powerful gold   100
Seduced her to his arms. What can not gold
Effect, when aided by the matron's tongue,
Long tried and practised in the trade of vice,
Against th' unwary innocent! A while
Dazzled with splendour, giddy with the height
Of unexperienced greatness, she looks down
With thoughtless pride, nor sees the gulf beneath.
But soon, too soon, the high-wrought transport sinks
In cold indifference, and a newer face
Alarms her restless lover's fickle heart.   110
Distressed, abandoned, whither shall she fly?
How urge her former task, and brave the winds
And piercing rains with limbs whose daintier sense
Shrinks from the evening breeze? nor has she now,
Sweet Innocence, thy calmer heart-felt aid
To solace or support the pangs she feels.
　　Why should the weeping Muse pursue her steps
Through the dull round of infamy, through haunts
Of public lust, and every painful stage
Of ill-feigned transport, and uneasy joy?
Too sure she tried them all, till her sunk eye
Lost its languish, and the bloom of health,
Which revelled once on beauty's virgin cheek,
Was pale disease, and meagre penury.
Then loathed, deserted, to her life's last pang
In bitterness of soul she cursed in vain
Her proud betrayer, cursed her fatal charms,
And perished in the streets from whence she sprung.

　　　　　　　　　　　　(Whitehead 1754: 147–52)

Notes

1 *Augusta*: London.
2 *sages . . . school*: followers of Pythagoras, vegetarians.
3 *In vain . . . Haydon-yard*: mere potions obtainable in these two locations (the first a haunt of prostitutes; the second, more respectable, perhaps occupied by apothecaries) will be insufficient to cure venereal disease. Brightly coloured door-posts, and predominantly blue ones in London, identified houses prior to the numbering of streets in the 1760s (Lillywhite 1972: 64).
4 *the column . . . day*: Seven Dials (see doc. 9, n. 1).

17 JAMES BOSWELL, FROM *LONDON JOURNAL* (1763)

This self-revealing and self-regarding work was among extensive caches of the writer's work discovered only in the first half of this century. Boswell (1740–95) was the half-rebellious son of a Scottish laird and judge dismissive of the young man's literary ambitions. Temporarily released from paternal shackles into the heady freedoms of the English metropolis, Boswell pursued – and recorded – illicit sexual encounters as energetically as he did meetings with social and cultural celebrities. While his self-chastisements became more severe under the moral influence of Dr Johnson (whom he first met a fortnight before the episode recounted below), they remained devoid of sympathetic interest in the lower-class women with whom he trafficked. In contrast to much later cases of genuine social exploration in disguise (for example doc. 84), Boswell's role-playing in this scene is characteristic of eighteenth-century rakishness in being designed to reinforce his class identity.

Saturday 4 June

It was the King's birthnight, and I resolved to be a blackguard and to see all that was to be seen. I dressed myself in my second-mourning suit, in which I had been powdered many months, dirty buckskin breeches and black stockings, a shirt of Lord Eglinton's which I had worn two days, and little round hat with tarnished silver lace belonging to a disbanded officer of the Royal Volunteers. I had in my hand an old oaken stick battered against the pavement. And was not I a complete blackguard? I went to the Park, picked up a low brimstone, called myself a barber and agreed with her for sixpence, went to the bottom of the Park arm in arm, and dipped my machine in the Canal and performed most manfully. I then went as far as St. Paul's Church-yard, roaring along, and then came to Ashley's Punch-house and drank three three-penny bowls. In the Strand I picked up a little profligate wretch and gave her sixpence. She allowed me entrance. But the miscreant refused me performance. I was much stronger than her, and *volens nolens*[1] pushed her up against the wall. She however gave a sudden spring from me; and screaming out, a parcel of more whores and soldiers came to her relief. 'Brother soldiers,' said I, 'should not a half-pay officer r–g–r for sixpence? And here has she used me so and so.' I got them on my side, and I abused her in blackguard style, and then left them. At Whitehall I picked up another girl to whom I called myself a highwayman and told her I had no money and begged she would trust me. But she would not. My vanity was somewhat gratified tonight that, notwithstanding of my dress, I was always taken for a gentleman in disguise. I came home about two o'clock, much fatigued.

(Boswell 1950: 272–3)

Note

1   *volens nolens*: willy-nilly.

18   PIERRE JEAN GROSLEY, FROM *A TOUR TO LONDON* (WRITTEN 1766–7)

Grosley (1718–85) was a judge in his native Troyes in northern France, as well as a historian, biographer and travel-writer. Although the translator of this work commends his 'impartial eye' (p. viii), meaning a readiness to acknowledge the superiority of England to France in certain respects, Grosley's account is frequently enlivened by critical piquancy, as the following extracts illustrate. They also display the attention to physical detail which informs his general observations on, for example, the weather, popular street ceremonies and the melancholic disposition of the English. A similarly graphic passage earlier on the deplorable quality of street paving and drainage provokes patriotic rebuttal in a translator's footnote trumpeting the improvements which have occurred since Grosley's 1765 visit (though Nugent is silent about air-pollution!). The book does indeed offer a sharp and summative view of eighteenth-century London just prior to a phase of more rapid physical and cultural change.

If we add to the inconveniency of the dirt, the smoke which, being mixed with a constant fog, covers London and wraps it up entirely, we shall find in this city all those particulars which offended Horace most in that of Rome . . . . This smoke, being loaded with terrestrial particles and rolling in a thick, heavy atmosphere, forms a cloud . . . which the sun pervades but rarely; a cloud which, recoiling back upon itself, suffers the sun to break out only now and then, which casual appearance procures the Londoners a few of what they call 'glorious days'. The great love of the English for walking defies the badness of other days. On the 26th of April, St James's Park incessantly covered with fogs, smoke and rain that scarce left a possibility of distinguishing objects at the distance of four steps, was filled with walkers who were an object of musing and admiration to me during that whole day. When the spring was completely opened, all this park, trees, alleys, benches, grass-plots, were still impregnated with a sort of black stuff formed by the successive deposits which had been left by the smoke of winter. . . .

Amongst the people of London we should properly distinguish the porters, sailors, chairmen, and the day-labourers who work in the streets, not only from persons of condition . . . but even from the lowest class of shop-keepers. The former are as insolent a rabble as can be met with in countries without law or police. The French, whom their rudeness is chiefly levelled at, would be in the wrong to complain, since even the better sort of Londoners are not exempt from it. Inquire of them your way to a street: if it be upon the right, they direct you to the left, or they send you from one of their vulgar comrades to another. The most shocking abuse and ill language make a part of their pleasantry upon these occasions. . . .

Happening to go one evening from the part of the town where I lived to the Museum, I passed by the Seven Dials. The place was crowded with people waiting to see a poor wretch stand in the pillory, whose punishment was deferred to another day. The mob, provoked at this disappointment, vented their rage upon all that passed that way, whether a-foot or in coaches, and threw at them dirt, rotten eggs, dead dogs, and all sorts of trash and ordure, which they had provided to pelt the unhappy wretch according to custom. Their fury fell chiefly upon the hackney-coaches, the drivers of which they forced to salute them with their whips and their hats, and to cry 'huzza': which word is the signal for rallying in all public frays. The disturbance upon this occasion was so much the greater, as the person who was to have acted the principal part in the scene which, by being postponed, had put the rabble into such an ill humour, belonged to the nation which that rabble thinks it has most right to insult. . . .

Setting aside a few exceptions . . . melancholy prevails in London in every family, in circles, in assemblies, at public and private entertainments, so that the English nation, which sees verified in itself the *populum late regem*[1] of Virgil, offers to the eyes of strangers only *populum late tristem.*[2] The merry meetings even of the lower sort of people are dashed with this gloom. On the 26th of April the butchers' boys celebrated the anniversary of the Duke of Cumberland's birthday. Being about fifty in number, they, in uniforms, that is to say, in caps and white aprons, paraded the streets of London by break of day, having each a great marrow-bone in his hand, with which they beat time upon a large cleaver: this produced a sort of music as sharp as dissonant. The air of those who played in this manner, being as savage as their music, made them appear like a company of hangmen marching in ceremony to some great execution.

The First of May is a general holiday for milk-women and chimney-sweepers. The former, attended by a person wrapped up in a great pannier, consisting of several rows of flowers and potherbs, ramble about the streets and go amongst their customers, dancing and asking the presents generally made upon this occasion. The pannier of the milk-women is covered with pieces of plate ranged in rows as in a buffet, and these moving machines hide every part but the feet of those who carry them. The chimney-sweepers are disguised in a more ridiculous manner; their faces are whitened with meal, their heads covered with high periwigs powdered as white as snow, and their clothes bedaubed with paper-lace. And yet though dressed in this droll manner, their air is nearly as serious as that of undertakers at a funeral.

(Grosley 1772: I, 43–5, 84, 88, 183–4)

Notes

1 *populum . . . regem*: people extensively in command (*Aeneid* I, 21).
2 *populum . . . tristem*: a people generally miserable.

19   HORACE WALPOLE, FROM LETTER TO SIR HORACE MANN (1 APRIL 1768)

See headnote to document 12 on Walpole and Mann, and Introduction, pp. 8–9 on London radicalism in this period. The long-term political significance of the colourful, paradoxical career of John Wilkes (1727–97) remains a matter of debate among historians. Most, though, would agree that his first Middlesex triumph was 'perhaps the most famous single election result in the history of British parliaments' (Langford 1989: 377), and that the strong support for Wilkes on the part of lower-middle-class and artisan voters in the ballot and of the unenfranchised 'mob' in the most select streets of London presented an ominous challenge to the old oligarchical order. As usual Walpole is admirable in documenting history-in-the-making with factual precision and a touch of vivid personal testimony. But in the first and last sentences he implies that this dissolute demagogue should not be taken too seriously.

The ghost is laid for a time in a red sea of port and claret. The spectre is the famous Wilkes. He appeared the moment the Parliament was dissolved. The Ministry despise him. He stood for the City of London, and was the last on the poll of seven candidates, none but the mob, and most of them without votes, favouring him. He then offered himself to the county of Middlesex. The election came on last Monday. By five in the morning a very large body of Weavers, &c., took possession of Piccadilly, and the roads and turnpikes leading to Brentford, and would suffer nobody to pass without blue cockades, and papers inscribed '*No. 45, Wilkes and Liberty*.'[1] They tore to pieces the coaches of Sir W. Beauchamp Proctor, and Mr. Cooke, the other candidates, though the latter was not there, but in bed with the gout, and it was with difficulty that Sir William and Mr. Cooke's cousin got to Brentford. There, however, lest it should be declared a void election, Wilkes had the sense to keep everything quiet. But, about five, Wilkes, being considerably ahead of the other two, his mob returned to town and behaved outrageously. They stopped every carriage, scratched and spoilt several with writing all over them 'No. 45,' pelted, threw dirt and stones, and forced everybody to huzza for Wilkes. I did but cross Piccadilly at eight, in my coach with a French Monsieur d'Angeul, whom I was carrying to Lady Hertford's; they stopped us, and bid us huzza. I desired him to let down the glass on his side, but, as he was not alert, they broke it to shatters. At night they insisted, in several streets, on houses being illuminated, and several Scotch refusing,[2] had their windows broken. Another mob rose in the City, and Harley, the present Mayor, being another Sir William Walworth,[3] and having acted formerly and now with great spirit against Wilkes, and the Mansion House not being illuminated, and he out of town, they broke every window, and tried to force their way into the House. The Trained Bands were sent for, but did not suffice. At last a party of guards, from the Tower, and some lights erected, dispersed the tumult. At one in the morning a riot began before Lord Bute's house, in Audley Street, though illuminated. They flung two large flints into Lady Bute's chamber, who was in bed, and broke every window in the house. Next morning, Wilkes and Cooke were returned members. The day was very quiet, but at night they rose again, and obliged almost every house in town to be lighted up, even the Duke of Cumberland's and Princess Amelia's. About one o'clock they marched to the Duchess of Hamilton's in Argyle Buildings (Lord Lorn being in Scotland). She was obstinate, and would not illuminate, though with child, and, as they hope, of an heir to the family, and with the Duke, her son, and the rest of her children in the house. There is a small court and parapet wall before the house; they brought iron crows, tore down the gates, pulled up the pavement, and battered the house for three hours. They could not find the key of the back door, nor send for any assistance. The night before, they had obliged the Duke and Duchess of Northumberland to give them beer, and appear at the windows, and drink 'Wilkes's health.' They stopped and opened the coach of Count Seilern, the Austrian ambassador, who has made a formal complaint, on which the Council met on Wednesday night, and were going to issue a Proclamation, but, hearing that all was quiet, and that only a few houses were illuminated in Leicester Fields from the terror of the inhabitants, a few constables were sent with orders to extinguish the lights, and not the smallest disorder has happened since. In short, it has ended like other election riots, and with not a quarter of the mischief that has been done in some other towns.

(Cunningham 1857–9: V (1857), 91–3)

Notes

1 *No ... Liberty*: In *The North Briton* no. 45 (23 April 1763) Wilkes attacked the king's speech as untruthful regarding peace negotiations at the end of the Seven Years' War; following the issue of a 'general warrant' and Wilkes' imprisonment in the Tower, 'No. 45' was taken as a symbol of free expression and other old English liberties now tyrannously curbed.

2 *Scotch refusing*: anti-Scottish prejudice was a factor in the unpopularity of Lord Bute's current administration.

3 *Sir ... Walworth*: a wittily apt reference to the Lord Mayor who in 1381 killed Wat Tyler, the leader of the Peasants' Revolt.

PART II
'A MASK OF MANIACS'
The Late Eighteenth and Early Nineteenth Centuries

20   TOBIAS SMOLLETT, FROM *THE EXPEDITION OF HUMPHRY CLINKER* (1771)

Smollett (1721–71) was dying in Italy when he wrote his last novel. This helps to account for the vision of tumorous urban growth and a physically and morally diseased society in the commentary of the hypochondriacal main character, Matthew Bramble, and also perhaps, by virtue of his greater detachment, for the comic ironies of plural perspective in this fictional epistolary travelogue. The overall effect is to render the tensions and interplay of old and new, traditional and modern, in a world of accelerating social and physical change. This is illustrated here in the tonally conflicting impressions of London registered in successive letters by Bramble and his niece shortly after their arrival. In documentary terms Bramble's account quite accurately reflects the fresh building boom, especially in West London, in the 1760s and 1770s, together with improvements effected by the Westminster Paving Acts from 1762 onwards. In Lydia's description of the incessant 'human tide' in the streets Smollett is likewise testifying to a virtually new phenomenon. Of the two leading London pleasure-grounds described, Vauxhall, as Brambles implies, invited a more mixed clientele, with a lower entrance charge than Ranelagh's.

DEAR DOCTOR,

London is literally new to me; new in its streets, houses, and even in its situation; as the Irishman said, 'London is now gone out of town.' What I left open fields, producing hay and corn, I now find covered with streets, and squares, and palaces, and churches. I am credibly informed, that in the space of seven years, eleven thousand new houses have been built in one quarter of Westminster, exclusive of what is daily added to other parts of this unwieldy metropolis. Pimlico and Knightsbridge are now almost joined to Chelsea and Kensington; and if this infatuation continues for half a century, I suppose the whole county of Middlesex will be covered with brick.

It must be allowed, indeed, for the credit of the present age, that London and Westminster are much better paved and lighted than they were formerly. The new streets are spacious, regular, and airy; and the houses generally convenient. The bridge at Blackfriars is a noble monument of taste and public spirit – I wonder how they stumbled upon a work of such magnificence and utility. But, notwithstanding these improvements, the capital is become an overgrown monster; which, like a dropsical head, will in time leave the body and extremities without nourishment and support. . . .

The tide of luxury has swept all the inhabitants from the open country –
... The gayest places of public entertainment are filled with fashionable figures; which, upon inquiry, will be found to be journeymen taylors, serving-
men, and abigails, disguised like their betters.

In short, there is no distinction or subordination left – The different
departments of life are jumbled together – The hod-carrier, the low
mechanic, the tapster, the publican, the shop-keeper, the pettifogger, the citizen, and courtier, 'all tread upon the kibes of one another': actuated by the
demons of profligacy and licentiousness, they are seen every where, rambling, riding, rolling, rushing, justling, mixing, bouncing, cracking, and crashing in one vile ferment of stupidity and corruption – All is tumult and hurry;
one would imagine they were impelled by some disorder of the brain, that
will not suffer them to be at rest. The foot-passengers run along as if they
were pursued by bailiffs. The porters and chairmen trot with their burthens.
People, who keep their own equipages, drive through the streets at full speed.
Even citizens, physicians, and apothecaries, glide in their chariots like lightning. The hackney-coachmen make their horses smoke, and the pavement
shakes under them; and I have actually seen a waggon pass through Piccadilly
at the hand-gallop. In a word, the whole nation seems to be running out of
their wits.

The diversions of the times are not ill suited to the genius of this incongruous monster, called 'the public'. Give it noise, confusion, glare, and glitter; it has no idea of elegance and propriety – What are the amusements at
Ranelagh? One half of the company are following one another's tails, in an
eternal circle; like so many blind asses in an olive-mill, where they can neither
discourse, distinguish, nor be distinguished; while the other half are drinking
hot water, under the denomination of tea, till nine or ten o'clock at night, to
keep them awake for the rest of the evening. As for the orchestra, the vocal
music especially, it is well for the performers that they cannot be heard distinctly. Vauxhall is a composition of baubles, overcharged with paltry ornaments, ill conceived, and poorly executed, without any unity of design or
propriety of disposition. It is an unnatural assembly of objects, fantastically
illuminated in broken masses; seemingly contrived to dazzle the eyes and
divert the imagination of the vulgar. ...

The walks, which nature seems to have intended for solitude, shade, and
silence, are filled with crowds of noisy people, sucking up the nocturnal
rheums of an aguish climate; and through these gay scenes, a few lamps glim-
mer like so many farthing candles.

Yours always,
MATT. BRAMBLE.
London, May 29.

MY DEAR LETTY.

The cities of London and Westminster are spread out to an incredible extent. The streets, squares, rows, lanes, and alleys, are innumerable. Palaces, public buildings, and churches, rise in every quarter; and, among these last, St Paul's appears with the most astonishing preeminence. . . .

But even these superb objects are not so striking as the crowds of people that swarm in the streets. I at first imagined, that some great assembly was just dismissed, and wanted to stand aside till the multitude should pass; but this human tide continues to flow, without interruption or abatement, from morn till night. Then there is such an infinity of gay equipages, coaches, chariots, chaises, and other carriages, continually rolling and shifting before your eyes, that one's head grows giddy looking at them; and the imagination is quite confounded with splendour and variety. . . .

At nine o'clock, in a charming moonlight evening, we embarked at Ranelagh for Vauxhall, . . . which I no sooner entered than I was dazzled and confounded with the variety of beauties that rushed all at once upon my eye. Image to yourself, my dear Letty, a spacious garden, part laid out in delightful walks, bounded with high hedges and trees, and paved with gravel; part exhibiting a wonderful assemblage of the most picturesque and striking objects, pavilions, lodges, groves, grottos, lawns, temples, and cascades; porticoes, colonades, and rotundos; adorned with pillars, statues, and painting; the whole illuminated with an infinite number of lamps, disposed in different figures of suns, stars, and constellations; the place crowded with the gayest company, ranging through those blissful shades, or supping in different lodges on cold collations, enlivened with mirth, freedom, and good-humour, and animated by an excellent band of music. . . .

In about half an hour after we arrived we were joined by my uncle, who did not seem to relish the place. People of experience and infirmity, my dear Letty, see with very different eyes from those that such as you and I make use of. . . .

Ever affectionate,
LYDIA MELFORD.
London, May 31.

(Smollett 1831: 97–100, 103–5)

21   GEORGE CRABBE, FROM 'THE POET'S JOURNAL' (1780)

Crabbe (1754–1832) kept 'The Poet's Journal' during the first few months of poverty and failure after his arrival in London from his native Suffolk to try to launch a literary career; extracts were first published in his son's biography of 1834. This one provides an eye-witness account of the most dramatic event – the firing of Newgate – in the biggest London riots of the eighteenth century. The week-long orgy of destruction (2–9 June 1780) arose out of the campaign, spearheaded by Lord George Gordon's Protestant Association, for repeal of the Catholic Relief Act of 1778. The City authorities, sympathetic to the slogan of 'No Popery', failed to curb the rioters as long as their attacks were mainly confined to Catholic properties; Crabbe describes the consequent escalation into anarchic rebellion. His climactic image of a Miltonic inferno prefigures Dickens' highly charged narration of this episode in Chapters 64 and 65 of *Barnaby Rudge* (1841).

June 8. – Yesterday, my own business being decided, I was at Westminster at about three o'clock in the afternoon, and saw the members go to the House. The mob stopped many persons, but let all whom I saw pass, excepting Lord Sandwich, whom they treated roughly, broke his coach windows, cut his face, and turned him back. A guard of horse and foot were immediately sent for, who did no particular service, the mob increasing and defeating them.

I left Westminster when all the members, that were permitted, had entered the House and came home. In my way I met a resolute band of vile-looking fellows, ragged, dirty, and insolent, armed with clubs, going to join their companions. I since learned that there were eight or ten of these bodies in different parts of the City.

About seven o'clock in the evening I went out again. At Westminster the mob were few, and those quiet, and decent in appearance. I crossed St. George's Fields, which were empty, and came home again by Blackfriars Bridge; and in going from thence to the Exchange, you pass the Old Bailey; and here it was that I saw the first scene of terror and riot ever presented to me. The new prison was a very large, strong, and beautiful building, having two wings, of which you can suppose the extent, when you consider their use; besides these, were the keeper's (Mr Akerman's) house, a strong intermediate work, and likewise other parts, of which I can give you no description. Akerman had in his custody four prisoners, taken in the riot; these the mob went to his house and demanded. He begged he might send to the sheriff, but this was not permitted. How he escaped, or where he is gone, I know not; but just at the time I speak of they set fire to his house, broke in, and threw every piece of furniture they could find into the street, firing them also in an instant. The engines came, but were only suffered to preserve the private houses near the prison.

As I was standing near the spot, there approached another body of men, I suppose 500, and Lord George Gordon in a coach, drawn by the mob towards Alderman Bull's, bowing as he passed along. He is a lively-looking young man in appearance, and nothing more, though just now the reigning hero.

By eight o'clock, Akerman's house was in flames. I went close to it, and never saw any thing so dreadful. The prison was, as I said, a remarkably strong building; but, determined to force it, they broke the gates with crows and other instruments, and climbed up the outside of the cell part, which joins the two great wings of the building, where the felons were confined; and I stood where I plainly saw their operations. They broke the roof, tore away the rafters, and having got ladders they descended. Not Orpheus himself had more courage or better luck; flames all around them, and a body of soldiers expected, they defied and laughed at all opposition.

The prisoners escaped. I stood and saw about twelve women and eight men ascend from their confinement to the open air, and they were conducted through the street in their chains. Three of these were to be hanged on Friday. You have no conception of the phrensy of the multitude. This being done, and Akerman's house now a mere shell of brickwork, they kept a store of flame there for other purposes. It became red-hot, and the doors and windows appeared like the entrance to so many volcanoes. With some difficulty they then fired the debtor's prison – broke the doors – and they, too, all made their escape.

Tired of the scene, I went home, and returned again at eleven o'clock at night. I met large bodies of horse and foot soldiers coming to guard the Bank, and some houses of Roman Catholics near it. Newgate was at this time open to all; any one might get in, and, what was never the case before, any one might get out. I did both; for the people were now chiefly lookers on. The mischief was done, and the doers of it gone to another part of the town.

But I must not omit what struck me most. About ten or twelve of the mob getting to the top of the debtors' prison, whilst it was burning, to halloo, they appeared rolled in black smoke mixed with sudden bursts of fire – like Milton's infernals, who were as familiar with flame as with each other.

(Life 1901: 23–4)

22 SOPHIE VAN LA ROCHE, FROM *DIARY* (1786)

See Introduction, pp. 18–19. La Roche (1730–1807), the poet Wieland's erstwhile lover and lifelong friend, secured her own place in German literary history as its first woman novelist with *The History of Miss Sophie Sternheim* (1770) and other didactic–sentimental fiction showing the influence of Rousseau as well as Richardson. She travelled extensively in Europe in the mid-1780s, recording her impressions in the journal-letters to her grown-up children from which these passages derive. Her observations on London life may be those of a literary and political anglophile with, as her translator overstates it, 'a vision always blind to unpleasantness' (Roche 1933: 51), but this does not discredit her testimony to the resplendence and commercial sophistication of the chief shopping streets following the improvement schemes of the 1760s and 70s.

Sept. 11 – We strolled up and down lovely Oxford Street this evening, for some goods look more attractive by artificial light. Just imagine, dear children, a street taking half an hour to cover from end to end, with double rows of brightly shining lamps, in the middle of which stands an equally long row of beautifully lacquered coaches, and on either side of these there is room for two coaches to pass one another; and the pavement, inlaid with flagstones, can stand six people deep and allows one to gaze at the splendidly lit shop fronts in comfort. First one passes a watchmaker's, then a silk or fan store, now a silversmith's, a china or glass shop. The spirit booths are particularly tempting, for the English are in any case fond of strong drink. Here crystal flasks of every shape and form are exhibited: each one has a light behind it which makes all the different coloured spirits sparkle. Just as alluring are the confectioners and fruiterers, where, behind the handsome glass windows, pyramids of pineapples, figs, grapes, oranges and all manner of fruits are on show. We inquired the price of a fine pineapple, and did not think it too dear at 6s., or 3 fl.[1] Most of all we admired a stall with Argand and other lamps,[2] situated in a corner-house, and forming a really dazzling spectacle; every variety of lamp, crystal, lacquer and metal ones, silver and brass in every possible shade; large and small lamps arranged so artistically and so beautifully lit, that each one was visible as in broad daylight. There were reflecting lamps inside, which intensified the glare to such an extent that my eye could scarce stand it a moment: large pewter oil-vessels, gleaming like silver, were ranged there, and oil of every description, so that the lamp and the oil can be bought and taken home together if one likes, the oil in a beautiful glass flask, and the wick, too, in a dainty box. The highest lord and humble labourer may purchase here lamps of immense beauty and price or at a very reasonable figure, and both receive equally rapid and courteous attention. I stayed long enough to notice this, and was pleased with a system which supplied the common need – light – in this spot, whether for guineas or for pence, so efficiently.

Up to eleven o'clock at night there are as many people along this street as at Frankfurt during the fair, not to mention the eternal stream of coaches. The arrangement of the shops in good perspective, with their adjoining living-rooms, makes a very pleasant sight. For right through the excellently illuminated shop one can see many a charming family-scene enacted: some are still at work, others drinking tea, a third party is entertaining a friendly visitor; in a fourth parents are joking and playing with their children. Such a series of tableaux of domestic and busy life is hardly to be met with in an hour as I witnessed here. How rapidly I reviewed in the course of this evening countless daily tasks of countless busy folk. How heartily I desired that every artist craftsman and worker who had contributed to the production of this mass of works of art might enjoy a quiet supper and find new vigour in refreshing sleep.

Sept. 28 – To-day we visited Mr. Boydell's shop,[3] London's most famous print dealer. What an immense stock, containing heaps and heaps of articles! The shop is on the Strand, one of the city's most populous thoroughfares, and has a view either side.

Here again I was struck by the excellent arrangement and system which the love of gain and the national good taste have combined in producing, particularly in the elegant dressing of large shop-windows, not merely in order to ornament the streets and lure purchasers, but to make known the thousands of inventions and ideas, and spread good taste about, for the excellent pavements made for pedestrians enable crowds of people to stop and inspect the new exhibits. Many a genius is assuredly awakened in this way; many a labour improved by competition, while many people enjoy the pleasure of seeing something fresh – besides gaining an idea of the scope of human ability and industry.

I stayed inside for some time so as to watch the expressions of those outside: to a number of them Voltaire's statement – that they stare without seeing anything – certainly applied; but I really saw a great many reflective faces, interestedly pointing out this or that object to the rest.

(Roche 1933: 141–3, 237)

Notes

1 *and did ... 3 fl.*: London labourers and lower-paid craftsmen at this time earned about 15s. a week (Rudé 1971: 89).
2 *Argand ... lamps*: named after its French inventor, the Argand oil lamp had a cylindrical wick which produced a steadier flame, less smoke, and thus a much superior light.
3 *Boydell's*: John Boydell was an engraver and an art entrepreneur credited with establishing a school of English engravers and creating a European market for English prints. Served as Lord Mayor in 1790.

23   WILLIAM BLAKE, 'LONDON', *SONGS OF EXPERIENCE* (1794)

This famous masterpiece of fusion and compression has naturally received extensive exegesis; the readings of Glen (1976) and Thompson (1993: 174–94) are especially illuminating in locating the poem in the context of London radicalism, political and religious, in the 1790s, a decade of millenarian hopes and fears and of counter-revolutionary bans in the name of Church and King. Blake (1757–1827) lived and worked in the city for most of his life; 'London' offers an insider's nightmarish vision of inescapable, self-perpetuating oppression. The speaker is not, as the first two words deceptively suggest, a free-wheeling flaneur but someone condemned to go on 'marking' the ubiquitous marks of suffering and damnation. Similarly, the 'chartered' condition of the streets and river signifies not a general freedom but commercial privilege and expropriation. Buying and selling, the Mark of the Beast (Thompson 1993: 190), are also implicit in the grim parody of the Cries of London in subsequent verses, and human commerce yet more darkly figures (through the 'harlot's curse') in the culminating image of syndromic disease and death.

> I wander through each chartered street,
> Near where the chartered Thames does flow,
> And mark in every face I meet
> Marks of weakness, marks of woe.
>
> In every cry of every man,
> In every infant's cry of fear,
> In every voice, in every ban,[1]
> The mind-forged manacles I hear.
>
> How the chimney-sweeper's cry
> Every black'ning church appalls,[2]
> And the hapless soldier's sigh
> Runs in blood down palace walls;
>
> But most through midnight streets I hear
> How the youthful harlot's curse
> Blasts the new-born infant's tear
> And blights with plagues the marriage hearse.

10

(Blake 1868: 65)

Notes

1 *ban*: the modern sense is not excluded by the primary meaning of 'curse'; as 'bann' the word also anticipates 'the marriage hearse' (l. 16).
2 *appalls*: puts to shame, casts a pall over.

24 CHARLES LAMB, FROM 'A LONDONER', *MORNING POST* (1 FEBRUARY 1802)

Lamb (1775–1834) lived his whole life in London; most of the essays, letters and other writings for which he is remembered were done in his spare time during a long clerical career at East India House. In *The Spirit of the Age* Hazlitt referred to 'Elia' as Lamb's '*nom de guerre*' (Howe 1931–4: XI (1932), 178); the term is more appropriate to 'Londoner', under which identity two decades earlier Lamb championed the blessings of the city in repudiation of the Romantic cult of Nature currently being promoted by his friends, the Lake poets. Newlyn (1981) has skilfully charted the course of the personal environmentalist debate among this group from 1797 to 1802, pursued mainly in poems published by Wordsworth and Coleridge and in letters by Lamb to Wordsworth and others (Marrs 1975: I, 247–9, 265–9, 270–2) which vigorously rehearse the rhetorical strategies of this essay. As Newlyn points out (p. 426), in his use of the language of emotional nourishment and therapy Lamb 'is challenging Wordsworth in the Wordsworthian idiom'. His dissociation from 'puritanical aversion' to popular consumerist pleasures can similarly be interpreted as a pre-emptive strike against the dominant standpoint in Book VII of *The Prelude* (doc. 25).

I was born ... , bred, and have passed most of my time in a crowd. This has begot in me an entire affection for that way of life, amounting to an almost insurmountable aversion from solitude and rural scenes. ... I have no hesitation in declaring that a mob of happy faces crowding up at the pit door of Drury-Lane Theatre just at the hour of five give me ten thousand finer pleasures than I have ever received from all the flocks of silly sheep that have whitened the plains of Arcadia or Epsom Downs. This passion for crowds is nowhere feasted so full as in London. The man must have a rare recipe for melancholy who can be dull in Fleet Street. I am naturally inclined to hypochondria, but in London it vanishes, like all other ills. Often when I have felt a weariness or distaste at home, have I rushed out into her crowded Strand and fed my humour, till tears have wetted my cheek for inutterable sympathies with the multitudinous moving picture, which she never fails to present at all hours, like the shifting scenes of a skilful pantomime.

The very deformities of London, which give distaste to others, from habit do not displease me. The endless succession of shops, where Fancy (miscalled Folly) is supplied with perpetual new gauds and toys, excite in me no puritanical aversion. I gladly behold every appetite supplied with its proper food. ... I love the very smoke of London, because it has been the medium most familiar to my vision.

(Lamb 1929: II, 6–8)

25 WILLIAM WORDSWORTH, FROM *THE PRELUDE*, BOOK VII (1805)

This long, autobiographical poem remained unpublished and unnamed in Wordsworth's lifetime. His sister sometimes referred to it as 'the poem to Coleridge' – the 'Friend' addressed in line 592 below. The 1850 text published three months after his death is a revision of the first complete version, from which these excerpts are taken; most of Book VII, entitled 'Residence in London', was actually written in 1804. Wordsworth (1770–1850) had lived in the English capital in the first half of 1791 and again, after a year in France, in the first half of 1793. However, he had much more recently visited Bartholomew Fair in the company of Charles Lamb; on this and other aspects of the London sections of *The Prelude*, see Introduction, pp. 3, 5–6, 7–8, and the headnote to doc. 24.

> ... shall I, as the mood
> Inclines me, here describe, for pastime's sake

Plate 4 'Bartholomew Fair', T. Rowlandson and A. C. Pugin, in R. Ackermann, *The Microcosm of London*, 1809. Reproduced by permission of the Syndics of Cambridge University Library.

Some portion of that motley imagery,   150
A vivid pleasure of my youth, and now
Among the lonely places that I love
A frequent day-dream for my riper mind?
– And first the look and aspect of the place,
The broad highway appearance, as it strikes
On strangers, of all ages; the quick dance
Of colours, lights and forms; the Babel din;
The endless stream of men, and moving things,
From hour to hour the illimitable walk
Still among streets with clouds and sky above,   160
The wealth, the bustle and the eagerness,
The glittering chariots with their pampered steeds,
Stalls, barrows, porters; midway in the street
The scavenger, who begs with hat in hand,
The labouring hackney coaches, the rash speed
Of coaches travelling far, whirled on with horn

Loud blowing, and the sturdy drayman's team,
Ascending from some alley of the Thames
And striking right across the crowded Strand
Till the fore horse veer round with punctual skill: 170
Here there and everywhere a weary throng,
The comers and the goers face to face,
Face after face; the string of dazzling wares,
Shop after shop, with symbols, blazoned names,
And all the tradesman's honours overhead:
Here, fronts of houses, like a title-page
With letters huge inscribed from top to toe;
Stationed above the door, like guardian saints,
There, allegoric shapes, female or male,
Or physiognomies of real men,   180
Land-warriors, kings, or admirals of the sea,
Boyle, Shakespeare, Newton, or the attractive head
Of some Scotch doctor, famous in his day. . . .

O Friend! one feeling was there which belonged
To this great city, by exclusive right;
How often, in the overflowing streets,
Have I gone forwards with the crowd, and said
Unto myself, 'The face of every one
That passes by me is a mystery!'
Thus have I looked, nor ceased to look, oppressed
By thoughts of what and whither, when and how,
Until the shapes before my eyes became   600
A second-sight procession, such as glides
Over still mountains, or appears in dreams;
And all the ballast of familiar life,
The present, and the past; hope, fear; all stays,
All laws of acting, thinking, speaking man
Went from me, neither knowing me, nor known.
And once, far-travelled in such mood, beyond
The reach of common indications, lost
Amid the moving pageant, 'twas my chance
Abruptly to be smitten with the view   610
Of a blind Beggar, who, with upright face,
Stood, propped against a wall, upon his chest
Wearing a written paper, to explain
The story of the man, and who he was.

My mind did at this spectacle turn round
As with the might of waters, and it seemed
To me that in this label was a type,
Or emblem, of the utmost that we know,
Both of ourselves and of the universe;
And, on the shape of the unmoving man,
His fixèd face and sightless eyes, I looked
As if admonished from another world.

   Though reared upon the base of outward things,
These, chiefly, are such structures as the mind
Builds for itself; scenes different there are,
Full-formed, which take, with small internal help,
Possession of the faculties, – the peace
Of night, for instance, the solemnity
Of nature's intermediate hours of rest,
When the great tide of human life stands still;   620
The business of the day to come, unborn,
Of that gone by, locked up, as in the grave;
The calmness, beauty, of the spectacle,
Sky, stillness, moonshine, empty streets, and sounds
Unfrequent as in deserts; at late hours
Of winter evenings, when unwholesome rains
Are falling hard, with people yet astir,
The feeble salutation from the voice
Of some unhapy woman, now and then
Heard as we pass, when no one looks about,   640
Nothing is listened to. But these, I fear,
Are falsely catalogued; things that are, are not,
Even as we give them welcome, or assist,
Are prompt, or are remiss. What say you, then,
To times, when half the city shall break out
Full of one passion, vengeance, rage, or fear?
To executions, to a street on fire,
Mobs, riots, or rejoicings? From those sights
Take one, – an annual festival, the Fair
Holden where martyrs suffered in past time,   650
And named of St Bartholomew; there, see
A work that's finished to our hands, that lays,
If any spectacle on earth can do,
The whole creative powers of man asleep! –

For once, the Muse's help will we implore,
And she shall lodge us, wafted on her wings,
Above the press and danger of the crowd,
Upon some showman's platform. What a hell
For eyes and ears! what anarchy and din
Barbarian and infernal, – 'tis a dream,   660
Monstrous in colour, motion, shape, sight, sound!
Below, the open space, through every nook
Of the wide area, twinkles, is alive
With heads; the midway region, and above,
Is thronged with staring pictures and huge scrolls,
Dumb proclamations of the Prodigies;
And chattering monkeys dangling from their poles,
And children whirling in their roundabouts;
With those that stretch the neck and strain the eyes,
And crack the voice in rivalship, the crowd   670
Inviting; with buffoons against buffoons
Grimacing, writhing, screaming, – him who grinds
The hurdy-gurdy, at the fiddle weaves,
Rattles the salt-box, thumps the kettle-drum,
And him who at the trumpet puffs his cheeks,
The silver-collared Negro with his timbrel,
Equestrians, tumblers, women, girls, and boys,
Blue-breeched, pink-vested, and with towering plumes.
All moveables of wonder, from all parts,
Are here – Albinos, painted Indians, Dwarfs,   680
The Horse of knowledge, and the learned Pig,
The Stone-eater, the man that swallows fire,
Giants, Ventriloquists, the Invisible Girl,
The Bust that speaks and moves its goggling eyes,
The Wax-work, Clock-work, all the marvellous craft
Of modern Merlins, Wild Beasts, Puppet-shows,
All out-o'-the-way, far-fetched, perverted things,
All freaks of nature, all Promethean thoughts
Of man; his dulness, madness, and their feats
All jumbled up together to make up   690
This Parliament of Monsters. Tents and Booths
Meanwhile, as if the whole were one vast mill,
Are vomiting, receiving, on all sides,
Men, Women, three-years' Children, Babes in arms.

Oh, blank confusion! and a type not false
Of what the mighty City is itself
To all except a straggler here and there,
To the whole swarm of its inhabitants;
An undistinguishable world to men,
The slaves unrespited of low pursuits,   700
Living amid the same perpetual flow
Of trivial objects, melted and reduced
To one identity, by differences
That have no law, no meaning, and no end –
Oppression, under which even highest minds
Must labour, whence the strongest are not free.
But though the picture weary out the eye,
By nature an unmanageable sight,
It is not wholly so to him who looks
In steadiness, who hath among least things   710
An under-sense of greatest; sees the parts
As parts, but with a feeling of the whole.

(Wordsworth 1926: 224–6, 250–6)

26 [ROBERT SOUTHEY], FROM *LETTERS FROM ENGLAND* (1807)

This book purports to be a translation of the epistolary journal of a Spanish traveller, Don Manuel Alvarez Espriella, touring England from April 1802 to September 1803. Letter VIII (dated 30 April 1802) records the formal celebrations in London of the recently signed Treaty of Amiens which, however, was to bring peace between Britain and France for only a few months. Southey (1774–1843) was a prolific and versatile writer whose accomplishments have largely been eclipsed by his notoriety – especially at the hands of Byron and Hazlitt – as a politically renegade poet laureate. Yet Hazlitt it was who in *The Spirit of the Age* declared that 'Mr Southey's prose-style can scarcely be too much praised' and in whose portrait of his self-opinionated contrariness – 'Mr Southey walks with his chin erect through the streets of London and with an umbrella sticking out under his arm in the finest weather' (Howe 1931–4: XI (1932), 81, 84) – there is as much admiration as scorn. The Spanish Catholic persona adopted in *Letters from England* allows scope for such contrariness, evidenced here in the disparagement of London pageantry and illuminations.

The definitive treaty has arrived at last; peace was proclaimed yesterday, with the usual ceremonies, and the customary rejoicings have taken place. My expectations were raised to the highest pitch. I looked for a pomp and pageantry far surpassing whatever I had seen in my own country. Indeed every body expected a superb spectacle. The newspaper writers had filled their columns with magnificent descriptions of what was to be, and rooms or single windows in the streets through which the procession was to pass, were advertised to be let for the sight, and hired at prices so extravagant, that I should be suspected of exaggeration were I to say how preposterous.

The theory of the ceremony, for this ceremony, like an English suit at law, is founded upon a fiction, is, that the Lord Mayor of London, and the people of London, good people! being wholly ignorant of what has been going on, the king sends officially to acquaint them that he has made peace: accordingly the gates at Temple Bar, which divide London and Westminster, and which stand open day and night, are on this occasion closed; and Garter, king-at-arms, with all his heraldic peers, rides up to them and knocks loudly for admittance. The Lord Mayor, mounted on a charger, is ready on the other side to demand who is there. King Garter then announces himself and his errand, and requires permission to pass and pro-claim the good news; upon which the gates are thrown open. This, which is the main part of the ceremony, could be seen by only those persons who were contiguous to the spot, and we were not among the number. The apartment in which we were was on the Westminster side, and we saw only the heraldic part of the procession. The heralds and the trumpeters were certainly in splendid costume; but they were not above twenty in number, nor was there any thing to precede or follow them. The poorest brother-hood in Spain makes a better procession on its festival. In fact these func-tions are not understood in England. . . .

If, however, the ceremony of the morning disappointed me, I was amply rewarded by the illuminations at night. This token of national joy is not, as with us, regulated by law; the people, or the mob, as they are called, take the law into their own hands on these occasions, and when they choose to have an illumination, the citizens must illuminate to please them, or be content to have their windows broken; a violence which is winked at by the police, as it falls only upon persons whose politics are obnoxious. During many days, preparations had been making for this festivity, so that it was already known what houses and what public buildings would exhibit the most splendid appearance. M. Otto's, the French ambassador, surpassed all others, and the great object of desire was to see this. Between eight and nine the lighting-up began, and about ten we sallied out on our way to Portman Square, where M. Otto resided. . . .

The nearer we drew the greater was the throng. It was a sight truly sur-prising to behold all the inhabitants of this immense city walking abroad at midnight, and distinctly seen by the light of ten thousand candles. This was particularly striking in Oxford Street, which is nearly half a league in length; – as far as the eye could reach either way the parallel lines of light were seen narrowing towards each other. Here, however, we could still advance without difficulty, and the carriages rattled along unobstructed. But in the immediate vicinity of Portman Square it was very different. Never before had I beheld such multitudes assembled. The middle of the street was completely filled with coaches, so immoveably locked together, that many persons who wished to cross passed under the horses' bellies without fear, and without danger. The unfortunate persons within had no such means of escape; they had no possible way of extricating themselves, unless they could crawl out of the window of one coach into the window of another; there was no room to open a door. There they were, and there they must remain, patiently or impatiently; and there in fact they did remain the greater part of the night, till the lights were burnt out, and the crowd clearing away left them at liberty.

We who were on foot had better fortune, but we laboured hard for it. There were two ranks of people, one returning from the square, the other pressing on to it. Exertion was quite needless; man was wedged to man, he who was behind you pressed you against him who was before; I had nothing to do but to work out elbow room that I might not be squeezed to death, and to float on with the tide. . . .

[W]e entered the avenue immediately opposite to M. Otto's, and raising ourselves by the help of a garden-wall, overlooked the crowd, and thus obtained a full and uninterrupted sight, of what thousands and tens of thousands were vainly struggling to see. To describe it, splendid as it was, is impossible; the whole building presented a front of light. The inscription was Peace and Amity; it had been Peace and Concord, but a party of sailors in the morning, whose honest patriotism did not regard trifling differences of orthography, insisted upon it that they were not *conquered*, and that no Frenchman should say so; and so the word Amity, which can hardly be regarded as English, was substituted in its stead. . . .

Illuminations are better managed at Rome. Imagine the vast dome of St. Peter's covered with large lamps so arranged as to display its fine form; those lamps all kindled at the same minute, and the whole dome emerging, as it were, from total darkness, in one blaze of light. . . . This, and the fireworks from St. Angelo, which, from their grandeur, admit of no adequate description, as you may well conceive, effectually prevent those persons who have beheld them from enjoying the twinkling light of half-penny candles scattered in the windows of London. . . .

(Southey 1951: 54–8)

27 'PUBLIC ENTRY OF MR HUNT INTO LONDON', *THE STATESMAN* (13/14 SEPTEMBER 1819)

Henry 'Orator' Hunt's ceremonial return to the capital a month after the Peterloo Massacre might be seen as the high-water mark of popular constitutionalism, the staging of large but orderly open-air assemblies to press for universal manhood suffrage as an ancient constitutional right, in the tumultuous post-Napoleonic era. In pursuit of this strategy Hunt had already drawn large working-class London crowds at the Spa Fields meetings of 1816–17 and at Smithfield in July 1819 (see plate 5) before the 'tremendous moral and propaganda victory' (Belchem 1985: 5) of Peterloo elicited more broadly based sympathetic interest. This report on a remarkable piece of street-theatre appeared in a London daily newspaper displaying the slogan of popular constitutionalism on its masthead ('the Cause for which Hampden fell in the field and Sydney died on the scaffold'). It puts the vast crowd, momentarily unified in mood and purpose, centre-stage, heightening the drama of mass expectancy and participation with a breathless style of running commentary, especially in the first portion published on the day itself. However, the mood of optimistic unity was short-lived. The Six Acts, drastically curtailing constitutional freedoms, were passed two months later. Hunt, having fallen out with most other radical leaders, including those referred to in this report, James Watson and Arthur Thistlewood, and having utterly failed to bring the perpetrators of the massacre 'to condign punishment', was himself jailed for seditious assembly. Watson, too, was in jail by the end of the year and Thistlewood executed in 1820 as a Cato Street conspirator.

Plate 5 Smithfield Meeting, London 1819, Guildhall Library, Corporation of London.

Sept. 13

At one o'clock the procession for the public entry of Mr Hunt was marshalled in the Barnet Road, a little beyond the Holloway turnpike. The scarlet flag, inscribed 'Hunt, the heroic Champion of Liberty', is surmounted with the cap of liberty; and there is another scarlet flag inscribed 'Liberty or Death'. Mr Hunt was momentarily expected. He left Barnet at 12 o'clock, and was then on his way to join the procession. The numbers already collected are literally immense. The road is thronged with people; the trees, palings, houses, and churches are covered with spectators; every avenue from which a glimpse can be obtained is filled. In every direction the multitude is increasing. It seems to be a universal holiday, and every man waits for the arrival of Mr Hunt with feelings of indescribable interest. . . . On the carriage in which Messrs Watson and Thistlewood ride is a lad who bears on his head the scar of a long and deep sabre wound he received at Manchester the 16th August. The people . . . are not tumultuously disposed; but they require and expect that the perpetrators of these atrocities should be brought to condign punishment.

At length, at a few minutes before three, and after being announced by several horsemen who coursed at one another's heels, Mr Hunt's carriage approached. The road then became agitated with unusual bustle. . . . Mr Hunt might really be said to come 'like Ocean with all his waters'. A shout arose and was prolonged through an immense portion of the line of march. . . . After passing through the living lines which reached down to the crossroads, we took temporary leave of the procession as it set down the City Road like a vast tide, every part of that also being previously occupied by persons of all conditions and ages, within and without the houses, upon every part of the pavement and in all the avenues where even the hope of seeing him could be entertained.

Sept. 14

. . . Before Mr Hunt's arrival a huge dog was seen parading about, having round his neck a white collar bearing the inscription 'No Dog Tax', and a scarlet trophy fastened at each side of his head. This, we believe, was not intended for ridicule; at least it was viewed with approbation by an immense multitude, and the canine reformer passed through the crowd with the ease and carelessness of a dog who feels himself among friends. . . .

From the Angel . . . up to Highgate Hill, each side of the road, as well as the centre of the road, was so completely thronged as to render a passage extremely difficult. . . . The windows and balconies of the houses were filled with respectable females. . . . From Highgate the crowds came pouring down; the dust thickened; shouts and acclamations rent the air; laurels were seen in every hat; the windows presented a display of beauty scarcely ever before paralleled. . . . Triumph looked in every face. Military phrases were used in tones of sneering and contempt, and wherever the slightest disposition appeared to disorder, a general cry of 'Order!' was thundered out, until it passed through the crowd, and peace and quietness succeeded, as if the creation of some talismanic influence. . . .

About four, Mr Hunt reached the Angel Inn, and the *coup d'oeil* which presented itself at the confluence of the Pentonville, Islington and City roads completely sets description at defiance. The heat and the dust, and the almost overwhelming pressure of the increasing multitude did not seem to have the least effect on those who were assembled to witness a sight at once so novel and so imposing. . . . Amidst this assembly there was certainly much of poverty, much of borrowed finery, but still much more of apparent affluence and unsubduable spirit of freedom.

. . . In going along Sun Street etc. the band played 'The Exile of Erin' and 'Erin go Bragh' in which they were cordially joined by the immense crowd, while from many windows red flags were held out by most respectable females. The procession then went along Bishopsgate Street, and on arriving at the Mansion House the crowd gave three groans of the loudest nature we ever witnessed. . . .

(*The Statesman* 1819: Nos 4245–6)

28 PIERCE EGAN THE ELDER, FROM *LIFE IN LONDON* (1821)

Egan (1772–1849), an originator of 'sporting-life' literary journalism, first produced his best-known work, illustrated by the Cruikshank brothers (see plate 6), in monthly numbers (1820–1). The subtitle, 'the Day and Night Scenes of Jerry Hawthorn Esq. and his elegant friend Corinthian Tom, accompanied by Bob Logic, the Oxonian, in their Rambles and Sprees through the Metropolis', signals its influential fusion of two traditions of London writing: the pairing of sophisticated and uninitiated tourist (Tom and Jerry), and the round-the-clock kaleidoscope of metropolitan life (Introduction, pp. 2–3). Egan's treatment of 'SEEING LIFE' (p. 24) as an admirable field-sport for idle rich youths is reinforced by the typographically ludic display of local, class- and gender-specific slang. But though backward-looking in its recreational view of urban education and in its often unsympathetic attitude to those who are 'DOWN' (p. xiii), this quintessentially Regency work also anticipates the Victorian vogue for exploration of the city's lower depths and for the juxtaposition of social polarities. It should be added that sham mendicancy is a frequent topic, less lightheartedly treated, in commentaries on Victorian London.

'We have witnessed a great many *rich scenes*,' said the CORINTHIAN to JERRY, as they were chatting over a glass of wine, upon the removal of the tablecloth, 'since your arrival in London; but I have one in store for you, which I think will *equal* any of them, if not EXCEED them all.' 'Indeed,' answered JERRY;

Plate 6 'Tom and Jerry "Masquerading it" among the Cadgers in the Back Slums',
I. R. and G. Cruikshank, in P. Egan, *Life in London*, 1821. Reproduced by
permission of the Syndics of Cambridge University Library.

'what can that be?' 'It is a meeting of the *Cadgers*, to spend the evening, after
the *fatigues* of the day are over: but,' said TOM, 'it will be of no use, my dear
COZ, if you do not go in *character*. You will then find the *Grand Carnival*, or
the *Masquerade* at the Opera House, nothing to it, by comparison. *Disguise*, on
our parts, is absolutely necessary; for, if we were detected, I would not
answer for the consequences; therefore, we must at least assume the outward
appearance of *Beggars*. . . . Indeed, you ought not, JERRY, to return to
Hawthorn Hall without taking a *peep* at the *Cadgers*, at the *Noah's Ark*, to use
the slang of the *Oxonian*, in the *back slums*, in the *Holy Land*. It is a *rich* view
of Human Nature; and a fine page in the Book of Life; but it almost staggers
belief that mankind can be so debased; that *hypocrisy* should be so successful;
and that the fine feelings of the heart should become so *blunted* as to laugh at
the charitable and humane persons who have been imposed upon to relieve
their assumed wants, and to fatten on their daily crimes, without showing the
least remorse. But the Metropolis is so extensive, the population so immense,
and the opportunities occur so frequently to impose upon the credulity of
the passenger in his hasty walks through the streets of London, who has
scarcely time to "read as he runs," account, in *a great degree*, for the *Beggars*
escaping without detection.

To the great gratification of JERRY, LOGIC now joined our heroes; and the
TRIO started as soon as the darkness of the evening answered their purpose;
when it was not long before they entered the *back slums*, and found themselves in the midst of the *Cadgers*. . . . Although TOM was disguised as a *beggar*,

yet he did not lose the traces of a *gentleman*; according to the old adage, that a gentleman in rags does not forget his real character. JERRY did not make his look *beggarly* enough; but LOGIC *gammoned* to be the *cadger* in fine style, with his *crutch* and *specs*; indeed, if it had not been for the fun, flash, and confidence of the *Oxonian*, they must have completely failed in this expedition. *Peg*, the ballad-singer, all in tatters, and covered with various-coloured rags, yet her pretty face did not escape the roving eye of TOM, upon her winking and leering her ogles at him, and chaunting the ballad, 'Poverty's no sin,' in hopes to procure a new *fancy-man*. . . .

Quarrelsome old *Suke*, who has been *hobbling* all the day on her *crutches* through the streets, now descends the ladder quickly to join the party, and is *blowing-up* her *ould man* for not taking hold of her crutches, 'as he knows she doesn't vant 'em now.' Behind the stove, the row has become so great, from the copious draughts of liquor and jollity of the *Cadgers*, that the gin measure and glasses are thrown at each other; and their crutches and wooden legs are brought in contact to finish the *turn-up*, till they are again wanted to *cadge* with the next day. The black one-legged fiddler is *strumming* away to enliven the party; and the *peck* and *booze* is lying about in such lots, that it would supply numerous poor families if they had had the *office* given to them where to apply for it. . . .

Our heroes made their *lucky* as soon as they conveniently could, when LOGIC gave the *hint* to be off; and the TRIO congratulated themselves upon their safe arrival at *Corinthian House*, and also upon the enjoyment of such a portraiture of the versatility of the human character.

(Egan 1822: 342–7)

29 THOMAS DE QUINCEY, FROM *CONFESSIONS OF AN OPIUM-EATER* (1821)

This elliptical autobiographical account of youthful nocturnal vagrancy in redemptive association with an even younger yet 'noble-minded' prostitute, and of the subsequent search in vain for her 'through the mighty labyrinths of London', is the quintessence of urban Romanticism; its later nineteenth-century influence (intimated, as it were, in the final paragraph of this extract) is clearly evident in the work of, for example, Baudelaire (who translated it), Poe, Dickens, Munby and Gissing. When writing the *Confessions*, as on many other occasions during his career as a literary journalist, De Quincey (1785–1859) had been drawn back to London by acute insolvency and was living in hiding from creditors; in this instance, as Lindop (1981: 246) suggests, the current experience of marginality and isolation in the great city must have helped rekindle twenty-year-old memories of the same with imaginative intensity. *Confessions* appeared anonymously in two instalments in the *London Magazine*, an appropriate outlet given its 'policy of taking the metropolis itself as a subject' (Lindop 1981: 251). For De Quincey makes these street scenes integral to the work's thematic core: it is Oxford Street on a 'wet and cheerless' Sunday, two years after the episode below, 'that first brought me acquainted with the celestial drug' (De Quincey 1897: III, 380–1).

Being myself at that time of necessity a peripatetic, or a walker of the streets, I naturally fell in more frequently with those female peripatetics who are technically called street-walkers. Some of these women had occasionally taken my part against watchmen who wished to drive me off the steps of houses where I was sitting; others had protected me against more serious aggressions. But one amongst them, the one on whose account I have at all introduced this subject – yet no! let me not class thee, O noble-minded Ann –, with that order of women; let me find, if it be possible, some gentler name to designate the condition of her to whose bounty and compassion, ministering to my necessities when all the world stood aloof from me, I owe it that I am at this time alive. For many weeks I had walked at nights with this poor friendless girl up and down Oxford Street, or had rested with her on steps and under the shelter of porticos. She could not be so old as myself; she told me, indeed, that she had not completed her sixteenth year. . . .

One night, when we were pacing slowly along Oxford Street, and after a day when I had felt more than usually ill and faint, I requested her to turn off with me into Soho Square. Thither we went; and we sat down on the steps of a house, which to this hour I never pass without a pang of grief, and an inner act of homage to the spirit of that unhappy girl, in memory of the noble action which she there performed. Suddenly, as we sat, I grew much worse. I had been leaning my head against her bosom, and all at once I sank from her arms and fell backwards on the steps. . . . Then it was, at this crisis of my fate, that my poor orphan companion, who had herself met with little but injuries in this world, stretched out a saving hand to me. Uttering a cry of terror, but without a moment's delay, she ran off into Oxford Street, and in less time than could be imagined, returned to me with a glass of port wine and spices that acted upon my empty stomach (which at that time would have rejected all solid food) with an instantaneous power of restoration; and for this glass the generous girl without a murmur paid out of her own humble purse at a time, be it remembered, when she had scarcely wherewithal to purchase the bare necessaries of life, and when she could have no reason to expect that I should ever be able to reimburse her. O youthful benefactress! how often in succeeding years, standing in solitary places, and thinking of thee with grief of heart and perfect love – how often have I wished that . . . the benediction of a heart oppressed with gratitude . . . might have power given to it from above to chase, to haunt, to waylay, to pursue thee into the central darkness of a London brothel, or (if it were possible) into the darkness of the grave, there to awaken thee with an authentic message of peace and forgiveness, and of final reconciliation! . . .

[W]hen I kissed her at our final farewell, she put her arms about my neck, and wept without speaking a word. I hoped to return in a week at furthest,

and I agreed with her that on the fifth night from that, and every night afterwards, she would wait for me at six o'clock, near the bottom of Great Titchfield Street, which had formerly been our customary haven of rendezvous, to prevent our missing each other in the great Mediterranean of Oxford Street.
...

According to our agreement I sought her daily, and waited for her every night, so long as I stayed in London, at the corner of Titchfield Street; and during the last hours of my stay in London, I put into activity every means of tracing her that my knowledge of London suggested and the limited extent of my power made possible. . . . All was in vain. To this hour, I have never heard a syllable about her. This, amongst such troubles as most men meet with in this life, has been my heaviest affliction. If she lived, doubtless we must have been sometimes in search of each other at the very same moment through the mighty labyrinths of London; perhaps even within a few feet of each other – a barrier no wider in a London street, often amounting in the end to a separation for eternity! During some years I hoped that she *did* live; and I suppose that in the literal and unrhetorical use of the word *myriad*, I must, on my different visits to London, have looked into many myriads of female faces, in the hope of meeting Ann. I should know her again amongst a thousand, and if seen but for a moment. Handsome she was not, but she had a sweet expression of countenance and a peculiarly graceful carriage of the head. I sought her, I have said, in hope. So it was for years; but now I should fear to see her; and her cough, which grieved me when I parted with her, is now my consolation. I now wish to see her no longer, but think of her more gladly as one long since laid in the grave – in the grave, I would hope, of a Magdalen; taken away, before injuries and cruelty had blotted out and transfigured her ingenuous nature, or the brutalities of ruffians had completed the ruin they had begun.

So then, Oxford Street, stony-hearted step-mother! thou that listenest to the sighs of orphans, and drinkest the tears of children, at length I was dismissed from thee! The time was come that I no more should pace in anguish thy never-ending terraces, no more should wake and dream in captivity to the pangs of hunger. Successors too many to myself and Ann have doubtless since then trodden in our footsteps, inheritors of our calamities. Other orphans than Ann have sighed; tears have been shed by other children; and thou, Oxford Street, hast since those days echoed to the groans of innumerable hearts.

(De Quincey 1897: III, 360–2, 367–8, 374–6)

30 WILLIAM HAZLITT, FROM 'ON LONDONERS AND COUNTRY PEOPLE', *NEW MONTHLY MAGAZINE* (AUGUST 1823), *THE PLAIN SPEAKER* (1826)

See Introduction, pp. 5–9, 22. The great essayist Hazlitt (1778–1830) spent most of the last two decades of his unsettled life in London, having previously lived in Kent, Shropshire and Wiltshire, as well as the US. He was thus well qualified to treat the city versus country theme in a balanced way, but nearly all of this essay is about the Cockney, as defined in the first sentence of this extract. On this topic 'The Plain Speaker' deploys his characteristically terse and rapid style to devastating effect – until a rekindling of his longstanding hostility to Wordsworth's anti-urban conservatism occasions a remarkable shift in tone, style and perspective in the final paragraph.

The true Cockney has never travelled beyond the purlieus of the Metropolis, either in the body or the spirit. Primrose Hill is the Ultima Thule of his most romantic desires; Greenwich Park stands him in stead of the Vales of Arcady. Time and space are lost to him. He is confined to one spot, and to the present moment. He sees everything near, superficial, little, in hasty succession. The world turns round, and his head with it, like a roundabout at a fair, till he becomes stunned and giddy with the motion. Figures glide by as in a *camera obscura*.[1] There is a glare, a perpetual hubbub, a noise, a crowd about him; he sees and hears a vast number of things, and knows nothing. He is pert, raw, ignorant, conceited, ridiculous, shallow, contemptible. His senses keep him alive; and he knows, inquires and cares for nothing farther. He meets the Lord Mayor's coach, and without ceremony treats himself to an imaginary ride in it. He notices the people going to court or to a city-feast, and is quite satisfied with the show. He takes the wall of a Lord, and fancies himself as good as he. He sees an infinite quantity of people pass along the street, and thinks there is no such thing as life or a knowledge of character to be found out of London. 'Beyond Hyde Park all is a desert to him.' He despises the country, because he is ignorant of it, and the town, because he is familiar with it. He is as well acquainted with St. Paul's as if he had built it, and talks of Westminster Abbey and Poets' Corner with great indifference. The King, the House of Lords and Commons are his very good friends. . . . He is, in short, a great man by proxy, and . . . is surcharged with a sort of second-hand, vapid, tingling, troublesome self-importance. . . . *Your true Cockney is your only true leveller.* Let him be as low as he will, he fancies he is as good as anybody else. . . .

A real Cockney is the poorest creature in the world, the most literal, the most mechanical, and yet he too lives in a world of romance – a fairy-land of his own. . . . He is a shopman, and nailed all day behind the counter: but he sees hundreds and thousands of gay, well-dressed people pass – an endless phantasmagoria – and enjoys their liberty and gaudy fluttering pride. . . . Is he a tailor – that last infirmity of human nature? The stigma on his profession is lost in the elegance of the patterns he provides, and of the persons he adorns; and he is something very different from a mere country botcher. Nay, the very scavenger and nightman thinks the dirt in the street has something precious in it, and his employment is solemn, silent, sacred, peculiar to London! A barker in Monmouth Street, a slop-seller[2] in Radcliffe Highway, a tapster at a night-cellar, a beggar in St. Giles', a drab in Fleet Ditch, live in the eyes of millions, and eke out a dreary, wretched, scanty, or loathsome existence from the gorgeous, busy, glowing scene around them. It is a common saying among such persons that 'they had rather be hanged in London than die a natural death out of it anywhere else' – such is the force of habit and imagination. . . .

It is a strange state of society (such as that in London) where a man does not know his next-door neighbour, and where the feelings (one would think) must recoil upon themselves, and either fester or become obtuse. Mr Wordsworth, in the preface to his poem of *The Excursion*,[3] represents men in cities as so many wild beasts or evil spirits, shut up in cells of ignorance, without natural affections, and barricadoed down in sensuality and selfishness. . . . And it would be so, if men were merely cut off from intercourse with their immediate neighbours, and did not meet together generally and more at large. But man in London becomes, as Mr Burke has it, a sort of 'public creature.'[4] He lives in the eye of the world, and the world in his. . . . He sees the stream of human life pouring along the streets – its comforts and embellishments piled up in the shops – the houses are proofs of the industry, the public buildings of the art and magnificence of man; while the public amusements and places of resort are a centre and support for social feeling. . . . In London there is a *public*; and each man is part of it. We are gregarious and affect the kind. We have a sort of abstract existence; and a community of ideas and knowledge (rather than local proximity) is the bond of society and good-fellowship. This is one great cause of the tone of political feeling in large and populous cities. There is here a visible body-politic, a type and image of that huge Leviathan the State. We comprehend that vast denomination, the *People*, of which we see a tenth part daily moving before us; and by having our imaginations emancipated from petty interests and personal dependence, we learn to venerate ourselves as men, and to respect the rights of human nature. Therefore it is that the citizens and freemen of London and Westminster are patriots by prescription, philosophers and politicians by the right of their birthplace. In the country, men are no better than a herd of cattle or scattered deer. They have no idea but of individuals, none of rights or principles. . . .

(Howe 1931–4: XII (1931), 66–77)

Notes

1 *camera obscura*: a dark room into which images of the outside world are projected through a lens.
2 *slop-seller*: cheap-clothes merchant.
3 *The Excursion*: published 1814. Hazlitt reviewed it at length in *The Examiner* (August–October 1814).
4 *'public creature'*: Howe cites *Letter to a Noble Lord*, where Edmund Burke uses this term to describe his son's (unenviable) situation.

31 ROBERT MUDIE, FROM *BABYLON THE GREAT* (1825)

Mudie (1777–1842), the son of a Forfarshire weaver, became active in local journalism and reformist politics while teaching in Dundee. Moving to London in 1820 he preceded Dickens and Mayhew as a reporter on the *Morning Chronicle*, before becoming editor of the *Sunday Times*. His prodigious output as a miscellaneous writer included books on topography, natural history and popular science. Babylon/Babel being the metropolitan archetype of imperial grandeur, luxury, confusion and depravity, London was commonly referred to as 'the modern Babylon' throughout the nineteenth century. Mudie begins with a panoramic contemplation of Babylonian greatness from the dome of St Paul's, a by now conventional perspective (see Introduction, pp. 23–5) more immediately occasioned by a new wave of reconstruction (John Nash's West End) and of mushroom expansion in the 1820s (compare plate 7). He then offers a distinctively sanguine appraisal of the psychological and behavioural effects of the city's impersonal vastness.

London may be considered, not merely as the capital of England or the British Empire, but as the metropolis of the world – not merely as the seat

Plate 7 'London Going Out of Town – or – the March of Bricks and Mortar!', G. Cruikshank, 1829. © British Museum.

of a Government which extends its connexions and exercises its influence to the remotest points of the earth's surface . . . , but as being foremost and without a rival in every means of aggrandisement and enjoyment, and also of neglect and misery – of everything that can render life sweet and man happy, or that can render life bitter and man wretched . . . . Within a circumference, the radius of which does not exceed five miles, there are never fewer than a million and a half of human beings; and if the great bell of St Paul's were swung to the full pitch of its tocsin sound, more ears would hear it than could hear the loudest roaring of Etna or Vesuvius, or indeed the mightiest elemental crash that could happen at any other spot upon the earth's surface; and if one were to take one's station in the ball [sic] or the upper gallery of that great edifice, the wide horizon, crowded as it is with men and their dwellings, would form a panorama of industry and of life more astonishing than could be gazed upon from any other point. In the streets immediately below one, the congregated multitude of men, of animals, and of machines, diminished as they are by the distance, appear like streams of living atoms reeling to and fro; and as they are lost in the vapoury distances, rendered murky by the smoke of a million fires, the sublime but sad thought of the clashing and careering streams of life hurrying to and losing themselves in the impervious gloom of eternity, starts across the mind. Nor is the contemplation of the marvels of man's making, which that horizon displays, less wonderful than the multitudes and the movements of the men themselves . . . . Today one may discover a line of hovels; a month passes, and there is a rank of palaces. Now the eye may haply light upon a few spots of that delicious green which is the native vesture of Old England; but ere the moon has exhibited all the phases of her brief circle of change, the earth shall have been moulded into abodes for the ever-accumulating multitude. House after house, palace after palace, street after street, and square after square – it stretches on and on, till the eye fails in catching its termination, and the fancy easily pictures it as everywhere gliding into the infinitude of space . . . .

If any man be seized with an overweening conceit of himself, impressed with an idea of his transcendant importance or value to society, London will cure him, if his cure be not all the more desperate . . . . This tendency to restrain within narrow limits all the adventitious grounds of human vanity, and to drive man back for his notoriety upon that which belongs to him as man, is one of the most valuable features in the character of London. It gives a man fair play, clears the arena for him, and so places him that if he does not triumph the fault is wholly his own. Each individual feels that he can make no figure without the actual possession of those qualities to which he pretends; and that even then, if he is not courteous and polite, others will be, and desertion and neglect will be his fate . . . . Even those unfortunate females whose punishment is in all cases greater than their crimes and who, in by far the majority, are the victims of their own credulity and of man's cruelty, have the air of a wild and desolate politeness about them . . . . Those persons do let passers-by know what they are, but still, if modesty and politeness can be at all predicated of those poor outcasts, they are modest and polite; and notwithstanding all the dementing and demoralising circumstances to which they are exposed, they have still the bearing of women and even, in a great measure, that of ladies . . . .

But if you have come from a little society where external courtesy is the sign of cordiality of heart, you will be sadly out in Babylon. The Babylonian smile and bow and welcome are the genuine smile and bow and welcome of the counter. They are levelled not at you but at your purse. The man varnishes his speech for the same purpose that he varnishes his sign-board, and arranges his smiles just as he arranges the goods in his shop-window – for the purpose of attracting customers; and he . . . cares no more for you than the gown or the gallipot upon his shelves, and would look with all the complacency in the world upon you taking the air upon the little platform in front of Newgate . . . .

But if such a society be unfavourable to the existence of the more intense feelings – if it tend to make people cold and heartless, it is not without its advantages. Where the heart is deeply affected, the observation never can be very vigorous; and for this reason, a man may know more and judge better, not only of all external matters, all subjects of speculation and criticism, but of human nature in general and human character in particular instances, while a mere spectator amid the crowds of London, than if he were in a place where every face that he met sent a pulse through his heart and brought a glow over his cheek . . . .

(Mudie 1825: 2–5, 54–7, 81–2)

32 HEINRICH HEINE, FROM *ENGLISH FRAGMENTS* (1828)

Heine (1797–1856), the German poet, spent four months in England in 1827. Far from mitigating the anti-British prejudices of this hero-worshipper of Napolean, the visit reinforced them; the counter-revolutionary and commercial power which, in Heine's eyes, had destroyed the dream of pan-European liberation at Waterloo, he found writ large in the architectural and social character of the London streets. He then sought escape not in futuristic visions of political freedom but in nostalgia for the tranquil conservatism of his homeland, as an environment less inimical to poetry than London's mechanistic frenzy. Yet the latter's alleged oppression of the poetic imagination is belied by the memorable vision of a 'stone forest' of houses tiled by 'newly extracted bleeding teeth'. The first three paragraphs below are taken from a translation of the *Memoirs*, in which Heine reproduced this passage verbatim; the remainder, from an older, inferior translation of *English Fragments*, is not in the *Memoirs*.

I have seen the most remarkable phenomenon that the world has to show to the amazed mind of man. I have seen it and am still amazed. In my memory there remains the stone forest of houses and in between the surging stream of vivid human faces, with all their gay passions, with all their horrible flurry of love and hunger and hate – I mean London.

Send a philosopher to London: but on pain of your life, not a poet! Send a philosopher thither and set him at the corner of Cheapside, and he will learn more there than from all the books of the last Leipzig fair; and as the waves of human beings roar about him there will arise before him a sea of new thoughts, the eternal spirit which hovers over the place will waft him up and suddenly reveal to him the most hidden secrets of the social order, and he will hear with his ears and see with his eyes the beating pulse of the world – for if London is the right hand of the world, the active, strong right hand, then that street which leads from the Exchange to Downing Street must be regarded as the pulse of the world.

But do not send a poet to London! The mere seriousness of everything, the colossal uniformity, the machine-like movement, the shrillness even of joy – this over-driven London oppresses fancy and rends the heart. And if you send a German poet thither, a dreamer who stands before everything he sees – ragged beggar-woman or gleaming goldsmith's shop – oh, then he will be in a bad way and he will be jostled on all sides and trampled underfoot with a mild 'God damn!' . . .

(Heine 1910: I, 192–3)

How much more pleasant and homelike it is in our dear Germany! With what dreaming comfort, in what Sabbath-like repose all glides along here! Calmly the sentinels are changed, uniforms and houses shine in the quiet sunshine, swallows flit over the flag-stones, fat court-councillor-esses smile from the windows, while along the echoing streets there is room enough for the dogs to sniff at each other, and for men to stand at ease and chat about the theatre . . . .

I had made up my mind in advance not to be astonished at that immensity of London of which I had heard so much . . . . I anticipated great palaces and saw nothing but mere small houses. But their very uniformity and their limitless extent impress the soul wonderfully. These houses of brick, owing to the damp atmosphere and coal smoke, are all of a uniform colour, that is to say of a brown olive green, and are all of the same style of building, generally two or three windows wide, three storeys high and finished above with small red tiles, which remind one of newly extracted bleeding teeth, while the broad and accurately squared streets which these houses form, seem to be bordered by endlessly long barracks . . . .

The stranger who wanders through the great streets of London and does not chance right into the regular quarters of the multitude sees little or nothing of the fearful misery existing there. Only here and there, at the mouth of some dark alley, stands a ragged woman with a suckling babe at her weak breast, and begs with her eyes. Perhaps if those eyes are still beautiful, we glance into them and are shocked at the world of wretchedness visible within . . . .

(Heine 1879: 417–19)

33   THOMAS DE QUINCEY, FROM 'THE NATION OF LONDON', *AUTOBIOGRAPHICAL SKETCHES* (1834, 1853)

Originally published in 1834 as the second of twenty-five autobiographical papers De Quincey wrote for *Tait's Magazine*, this is a classic treatment of the newcomer's psychological shock on entering the metropolis and encountering the street crowds as a solitary stranger. On the visit recalled here the 15-year-old De Quincey was in fact accompanied by a tutor and a younger boy; the testimony to a 'sense of desertion and utter loneliness' among 'a pageant of phantoms' doubtless draws upon his later experiences in London, especially the episode famously reconstructed in the *Confessions* (doc. 29), and also upon Wordsworth's *Prelude* VII (see doc. 25 and Lindop 1981: 250, 331–2).

It was a most heavenly day in May of this year (1800) when I first beheld and first entered this mighty wilderness, the city – no! not the city, but the nation – of London. Often since then, at distances of two and three hundred miles or more from this colossal emporium of men, wealth, arts, and intellectual power, have I felt the sublime expression of her enormous magnitude in one simple form of ordinary occurrence – viz., in the vast droves of cattle, suppose upon the great north roads, all with their heads directed to London, and expounding the size of the attracting body, together with the force of its attractive power, by the never-ending succession of these droves, and the remoteness from the capital of the lines upon which they were moving. A suction so powerful, felt along radii so vast, and a consciousness, at the same time, that upon other radii still more vast, both by land and by sea, the same suction is operating, night and day, summer and winter, and hurrying for ever into one centre the infinite means needed for her infinite purposes, and the endless tributes to the skill or to the luxury of her endless population, crowds the imagination with a pomp to which there is nothing corresponding upon this planet, either amongst the things that have been, or the things that are . . . .

Already at three stages' distance (say, 40 miles from London), upon some of the greatest roads, the dim presentiment of some vast capital reaches you obscurely, and like a misgiving. This blind sympathy with a mighty but unseen object, some vast magnetic range of Alps, in your neighbourhood, continues to increase, you know not how . . . .

Finally, for miles before you reach a suburb of London such as Islington, for instance, a last great sign and augury of the immensity which belongs to the coming metropolis forces itself upon the dullest observer, in the growing sense of his own utter insignificance. Everywhere else in England, you yourself, horses, carriage, attendants (if you travel with any), are regarded with attention, perhaps even curiosity: at all events you are seen. But, after passing the final post-house on every avenue to London, for the latter ten or twelve miles, you become aware that you are no longer noticed: nobody sees you; nobody hears you; nobody regards you; you do not even regard yourself. In fact, how should you at the moment of first ascertaining your own total unimportance in the sum of things – a poor shivering unit in the aggregate of human life? Now, for the first time, whatever manner of man you were or seemed to be at starting, squire or 'squireen', lord or lordling, and however related to that city, hamlet, or solitary house, from which yesterday or to-day you slipped your cable – beyond disguise you find yourself but one wave in a total Atlantic, one plant (and a parasitical plant besides, needing alien props) in a forest of America.

These are feelings which do not belong by preference to thoughtful people – far less to people merely sentimental. No man ever was left to himself for the first time in the streets, as yet unknown, of London, but he must have been saddened and mortified, perhaps terrified, by the sense of desertion and utter loneliness which belong to his situation. No loneliness can be like that which weighs upon the heart in the centre of faces never-ending, without voice or utterance for him; eyes innumerable, that have 'no speculation' in their orbs which *he* can understand; and hurrying figures of men and women weaving to and fro, with no apparent purposes intelligible to a stranger, seeming like a mask of maniacs, or, oftentimes, like a pageant of phantoms. The great length of the streets in many quarters of London; the continual opening of transient glimpses into other vistas equally far-stretching, going off at right angles to the one which you are traversing; and the murky atmosphere which, settling upon the remoter end of every long avenue, wraps its termination in gloom and uncertainty; all these are circumstances aiding that sense of vastness and illimitable proportions which for ever brood over the aspect of London in its interior.

(De Quincey 1896: I, 178–82)

34 FRANCIS PLACE, 'THE STREET CHARING CROSS', *AUTOBIOGRAPHY* (1835)

Place (1771–1854) was active in radical politics and reform movements from the 1790s to the 1840s. He orchestrated the successful campaign for legalisation of trades unions in 1824, and as a disciple of Bentham and Malthus pioneered the promotion of contraceptive practice. His extensive writings, most of them (including the *Autobiography*) not published until the late twentieth century (if then), together with his large collection of press cuttings and other contemporary documents, constitute a priceless archive for social historians of the period. They provide detailed evidence of the often sordid environment and cultural practices in the working-class London of his youth – all overtly intended to demonstrate, as in the passage below, the march of progress in subsequent decades. But as Thale observes, 'his six volumes of data on the deplorable moral conditions of the eighteenth century could only have been assembled by a man who felt considerable fascination for these conditions' (Place 1972: xxv). Known as 'the radical tailor of Charing Cross', Place lived for thirty-two years at No. 16; he here offers an inductive sociological history of the street unmatched in detail before Booth's surveys (doc. 72) at the end of the century.

The state of London may be somewhat guessed at by a short description of the fine open street from the statue at Charing Cross to the commencement of Parliament Street. On the eastern side and not far from Northumberland House was Johnson's Court. There were 13 houses in this court, all in a state of great delapidation; in every room in every house, excepting one only, lived one or more common prostitutes of the most wretched description, such as cannot now be seen in any place. The house excepted was a kind of public-house and a crimping-house[1] of the very worst sort. [[2]I remember the gutting of this crimping-house: a poor young man had been crimped and confined in one of the garrets; here he fell sick with the smallpox, and in his delirium broke the bars of his window, ran out upon the top of the house and along the top of another house, from which he fell naked into the street. A mob collected and destroyed everything the house contained. This put an end to the trade of crimping there, and the house was afterwards occupied like the others.] The place could not be outdone in infamy and indecency by any place in London. The manner in which many of the drunken, filthy young prostitutes behaved is not describable nor would it be believed were it described.

A little lower down was the long-celebrated brothel, the Rummer Tavern. It was a large back-house, now occupied by Mr Clowes as a printing-office, and there were doors through the walls at the back part of my house which communicated with the Rummer. They both had signs, and the large iron bolts which held them are still in my house, projecting from the wall. For some years after I took my house there was an immense wooden rummer[3] some five feet high fixed against the front of the next house, a silversmith's shop, behind which was the Rummer Tavern . . . . At the next house, No. 17, was a small back-house, to which access was gained by a very narrow passage – this was a crimping-house and low brothel. [Mr. Thomas, the butcher who kept No. 17, says that when he first took the house he has seen as many as 13 sedan chairs in the middle of the day, belonging to noblemen and gentlemen, waiting outside the Rummer for their masters. The arms of the owners were on the chairs and the chairmen wore their liveries.] Behind No. 22 was another such house occupied in the same way. Behind No. 28 was another; this was an authorised crimping-public-house and had a large Union Jack standing out from the house in front. At No. 19 was a barber's shop, with a striped poll in front. Below No. 30 were some three or four houses with their gable ends towards the street. Their ground floors were about six steps below the foot pavement; they were very old and inhabited by very low, dirty people.

No. 24 was a dirty gin-shop, as was also another house a few doors lower down; those were frequented by prostitutes and soldiers. I can remember the crimping-house, No. 28, being gutted, and a drummer who was active in the Riot[4] being hanged in front of the house in the open street. Scotland Yard, where Whitehall Place now stands, was covered in part with old wooden buildings, one of which was used as a kind of barrack or guard-house for soldiers. This place was called the Tilt-Yard. Along the front of Privy Gardens . . . there was an old wall, against which, early in the morning and late in the evening, saloop[5] was sold. In the daytime the wall was covered with ballads and pictures; some of these were such as could not now be exhibited anywhere. Miserable daubs, but subjects of the grossest nature. At night there were a set of prostitutes along this wall, so horridly ragged, dirty and disgusting that I doubt much there are now any such in any part of London. These miserable wretches used to take any customer who would pay them twopence, behind the wall.

On the opposite side of the way was a range of miserable-looking, low buildings with high, tiled roofs; there were government offices and [sic] reached from Downing Street to the old Treasury. From the place where these ended, along the front of the Treasury and the Horse Guards, the soldiers going on guard in the morning were shaved, weather permitting – had their heads well greased and flowered, and their pigtails tied . . . . Immediately in front of the Horse Guards were a range of apple stalls, and at . . . noon every day two very large stalls were set up for the sale of 'bow-wow pie'. This pie was made of meat, very highly seasoned. It had a thick crust around the inside and over the very large, deep, brown pans which held it. A small plate of this pie was sold for three-halfpence, and was usually eaten on the spot, by what sort of people and amidst what sort of language they who have known what low life is may comprehend, but of which they who do not must remain ignorant . . . .

It seems almost incredible that such a street could be in the condition described, but so it was: people were not then offended with grossness, dirtiness, vulgarity, obscenity and atrocious language. I can myself remember every fact I have mentioned. I need hardly notice how highly respectable the street is now . . . .

(Place 1972: 227–30)

Notes

1 *crimping-house*: a house used to confine men decoyed for service in army or navy.
2 *[. . .]*: in this passage signifies marginalia in Place's manuscript.
3 *rimmer*: a drinking-glass.
4 *Riot*: i.e., the Gordon Riots of 1780 (see doc. 21).
5 *saloop*: 'a hot drink made of powdered salep or sassafras, milk and sugar' (Place 1972: 229).

PART III
'THE ATTRACTION OF REPULSION'
The Mid-Nineteenth Century

35 CHARLES DICKENS, FROM *NICHOLAS NICKLEBY* (1839), CHAPTER 32

See Introduction, p. 5. In 1858 Walter Bagehot memorably wrote of Dickens (1812–70) that 'he describes London like a special correspondent for posterity' (Bagehot 1911: II, 176), and posterity has gratefully concurred. Yet Bagehot's observation, prompted by the idea that London's newspaper-like miscellaneity was ideally conducive to the flowering of Dickens' 'unsymmetrical genius' (1911: II, 169), is only partly true in the sense intended. Even in the early work, as this passage well illustrates, some control of the journalistic relish for promiscuous detail is exercised in the novelist's pursuit of pattern and relationship. The effect here of dazzling, kinetic profusion is eventually superseded in the final paragraph by a series of paradigmatic contrasts, at once traditional and contemporary, 'to give new point and purpose to the shifting scene'.

They rattled on through the noisy, bustling, crowded streets of London, now displaying long double rows of brightly-burning lamps, dotted here and there with the chemists' glaring lights, and illuminated besides with the brilliant flood that streamed from the windows of the shops, where sparkling jewellery, silks and velvets of the richest colours, the most inviting delicacies, and most sumptuous articles of luxurious ornament, succeeded each other in rich and glittering profusion. Streams of people apparently without end poured on and on, jostling each other in the crowd and hurrying forward, scarcely seeming to notice the riches that surrounded them on every side; while vehicles of all shapes and makes, mingled up together in one moving mass like running water, lent their ceaseless roar to swell the noise and tumult.

As they dashed by the quickly-changing and every-varying objects, it was curious to observe in what a strange procession they passed before the eye. Emporiums of splendid dresses, the materials brought from every quarter of the world; tempting stores of everything to stimulate and pamper the sated appetite and give new relish to the oft-repeated feast; vessels of burnished gold and silver, wrought into every exquisite form of vase, and dish, and goblet; guns, swords, pistols, and patent engines of destruction; screws and irons for the crooked, clothes for the newly-born, drugs for the sick, coffins for the dead, and churchyards for the buried – all these jumbled each with the other and flocking side by side, seemed to flit by in motley dance like the

105

fantastic groups of the old Dutch painter,[1] and with the same stern moral for the unheeding restless crowd.

Nor were there wanting objects in the crowd itself to give new point and purpose to the shifting scene. The rags of the squalid ballad-singer fluttered in the rich light that showed the goldsmith's treasures, pale and pinched-up faces hovered about the windows where was tempting food, hungry eyes wandered over the profusion guarded by one thin sheet of brittle glass – an iron wall to them; half-naked shivering figures stopped to gaze at Chinese shawls and golden stuffs of India. There was a christening party at the largest coffin-maker's, and a funeral hatchment had stopped some great improvements in the bravest mansion. Life and death went hand in hand; wealth and poverty stood side by side; repletion and starvation laid them down together.

(Dickens 1876: 206–7)

Notes

1 *the old Dutch painter.* Hans Holbein the Younger, whose series of woodcuts entitled *The Dance of Death* is referred to here, was actually German.

36 FLORA TRISTAN, FROM *LONDON JOURNAL* (1840), CHAPTERS 8 AND 10

See Introduction, p. 19. Tristan (1803–44) was born in Paris, the technically illegitimate daughter of a Spanish-Peruvian nobleman who died when she was only 4 years old. Thus began a tragically brief life full of personal calamity and courageous adventure – emblematised in the title of another of her travel books, *Peregrinations of a Pariah* (though she attracted devotion as well as opprobrium along the way). Tristan was a socialist and feminist whose vision of non-violent revolution she was heroically striving to realise on an arduous speaking tour of industrial centres throughout France at the time of her death from typhoid fever. The *London Journal*, an account of her fourth visit in 1839, does not, as the French title *Promenades dans Londres* might suggest, recommend sightseeing itineraries for the strolling tourist. Instead, personal testimony fuels a passionate critique of capitalist exploitation in 'the monster city'.

Around seven or eight in the evening and accompanied by two men armed with canes, I went to visit the new district on either side of the long, broad street called Waterloo Road, at the end of Waterloo Bridge. The district is populated almost entirely by prostitutes and people who live off prostitution. It would be extremely dangerous to walk there alone in the evening. It was a very warm evening; the women were looking out of windows or seated at their doorsteps, laughing and jesting with their fancy men. They were half-dressed; several were bare to the waist. They were revolting, disgusting, and the cynical and criminal expressions on the fancy men's faces were frightening . . . . We walked about all the streets near Waterloo Road and sat down on the bridge to watch another spectacle. Around eight or nine o'clock, the Waterloo Road women pass by in groups on their way to the West End. They carry on their trade during the night and come back around eight or nine in the morning . . . .

After the theatre, the women go to the 'finishes'. These are low taverns or large and luxurious public house where people go to finish off the night . . . . What goes on in these places ought to be seen. It reveals England's moral state better than anything one could say. These luxurious taverns have a look all to their own. The habitués of these palaces seem to be creatures of the night. They go to bed when the sun begins to lighten the east and awaken when it sets. From the outside, the gin-palaces appear to be shut up; they give the impression of silence and sleep. But scarcely has the doorkeeper opened the little door reserved for initiates than one is dazzled by the brilliance of hundreds of gas lights. On the second floor there is a huge saloon divided into two lengthwise. On one side there is a row of tables separated by wooden partitions, as in all English restaurants. On each side of the tables there are sofa-like benches. On the other side there is a platform where the prostitutes display themselves in their finest attire. Their words and glances are calculated to arouse men. When one responds they lead the amorous gentleman off to one of the tables laden with cold meats, hams, fowls, pastries, and all kinds of wines and cordials . . . .

Around midnight, the habitués begin to arrive. Several of these taverns are meeting places for society; it is where the elite of the aristocracy gather. At first the young lords lie on the sofa-like benches, and they smoke and jest with the women. Then after several libations, the alcoholic vapours of champagne and madeira go to their heads. The illustrious scions of English nobility, the honourable Members of Parliament take off their coats, waistcoats and braces. They make themselves at home in a public tavern as if they were in their private boudoir. There is no reason for them not to feel quite at home; after all they pay a high price for the right to show their contempt. As for the contempt they inspire, they could not care less. The pace of the orgy increases; it reaches its peak between four and five o'clock in the morning.

It takes a good deal of courage to sit through it all, a silent spectator of what goes on! . . .

The visitor cannot venture into Bainbridge Street, that dark and narrow alley, without a feeling of trepidation. Scarcely has he gone ten paces when he is overcome by a foul stench. The alley, entirely taken up by the great coal warehouse, is impassable. On the right we found another alley, this one not even paved and full of nauseating, stagnant pools of greasy, soapy water and other filth . . . . Oh how difficult it was to overcome my loathing and gather up sufficient courage to proceed through the mire and nastiness! In St Giles one feels asphyxiated by the stench; there is no air to breathe nor daylight to find one's way. The wretched inhabitants must wash their own rags, and they hang them out to dry on poles that stretch from one side of the alley to the other, so that fresh air and sunlight are completely blocked out. Foul odours rise from the mire at your feet, and dirty water drips upon your head from the paupers' rags above. The ravings of a demented imagination could not equal the dreadful reality of such horrors! When I reached the end of the street, which is not very long, I felt my resolve beginning to abandon me; my strength is not equal to my courage; my stomach was churning and my temples throbbed. I was about to give up the idea of venturing any farther into the Irish quarter, when suddenly I remembered that these were human beings, my fellow men, all about me, and that for hundreds of years they had suffered in silence the agony to which, in the space of ten short minutes, my frailty had succumbed! I overcame my distress, the promptings of my heart came to the rescue, and I once again felt up to the task I had set myself, to examine these evils one by one. Oh what ineffable compassion then filled my heart, and what dark terror!

Imagine men, women, children, all barefoot, ploughing through the nasty, filthy mire. Some were leaning against the wall for lack of a place to sit, others were squatting on the ground, there were children lying about in the mud like pigs. No, unless one has seen it with his own eyes, it is impossible to imagine such squalid indigence, such utter debasement, nor a more total degradation of the human creature! . . .

(Tristan 1980: 74–7, 134–5)

37   WILLIAM MAKEPEACE THACKERAY, FROM 'GOING TO SEE A MAN HANGED', *FRASER'S MAGAZINE* (AUGUST 1840)

Thackeray (1811–63) published this remarkable essay in *Fraser's* after *Blackwood's* had turned it down. Its challengingly radical, modern ring derives from three related components: the case for democracy explicit in an appreciative close-up view of the common people in the vast crowd; the 'democratic' empathy with the hanged man, Courvoisier, a French servant who had brutally murdered his master, Lord William Russell; and the resultant sense of conviction about the wrongness, not merely of public executions, but of capital punishment itself. As Gattrell's informative and finely judicious discussion makes clear (1994: 294–7), Thackeray's stance here – like the 90 votes for William Ewart's abolitionist motion alluded to in the first sentence of the essay – reflects a generally reformist climate which was similarly short-lived: in common with Dickens and other notable contemporaries, Thackeray soon changed his mind about capital punishment, and public executions remained a frequent occurrence until 1868. But this historically disappointing context does not detract from the innovative power of a brilliantly paced, sharply and sensitively observed crowd scene.

X —,[1] who had voted with Mr Ewart for the abolition of the punishment of death, was anxious to see the effect on the public mind of an execution, and asked me to accompany him to see Courvoisier killed. We . . . determined to mingle with the crowd at the foot of the scaffold, and take up our positions at a very early hour . . . .

Throughout the whole four hours . . . the mob was extraordinarily gentle and good-humoured. At first we had leisure to talk to the people about us; and I recommend X —'s brother senators of both sides of the House to see more of this same people and to appreciate them better . . . . I declare that I have never been in a great London crowd without thinking of what they call the two 'great' parties in England with wonder . . . . Ask yonder ragged fellow, who has evidently frequented debating-clubs, and speaks with good sense and shrewd good-nature. He cares no more for Lord John than he does for Sir Robert;[2] and, with due respect be it said, would mind very little if both of them were ushered out by Mr Ketch and took their places under yonder black beam. What are the two great parties to him and those like him? Sheer wind, hollow humbug, absurd claptraps; a silly mummery of dividing and debating, which does not in the least, however it may turn, affect his condition . . . . He is a *democrat*, and will stand by his friends, as you by yours; and they are twenty millions, his friends, of whom a vast minority now, a majority a few years hence, will be as good as you . . . .

What is the meaning of this unconscionable republican tirade – *apropos* a hanging? Such feelings, I think, must come across any man in a vast multitude like this. What good sense and intelligence have most of the people by whom you are surrounded! How much sound humour does one hear bandied about from one to another! A great number of coarse phrases are used that would make ladies in drawing-rooms blush, but the morals of the men are good and hearty . . . . The crowd has grown very dense by this time, it is about six o'clock, and there is great heaving, and pushing, and swaying to and fro; but round the women the men have formed a circle and keep them as much as possible out of the rush and trample. In one of the houses near us, a gallery has been formed on the roof. Seats were here let and a number of persons of various degrees were occupying them. Several tipsy, dissolute-looking young men of the Dick Swiveller[3] cast, were in this gallery. One was lolling over the sunshiny tiles, with a fierce sodden face, out of which came a pipe and which was shaded by long matted hair, and a hat cocked very much on one side. This gentleman was one of a party which had evidently not been to bed on Sunday night but had passed it in

109

some of those delectable night-houses in the neigbourhood of Covent Garden. The debauch was not over yet, and the women of the party were giggling, drinking and romping, as is the wont of these delicate creatures: sprawling here and there, and falling upon the knees of one or other of the males. Their scarves were off their shoulders, and you saw the sun shining down upon the bare white flesh, and the shoulder-points glittering like burning-glasses. The people about us were very indignant at some of the proceedings of this debauched crew, and at last raised up such a yell as frightened them into shame, and they were more orderly for the remainder of the day . . . .

The character of the crowd was as yet, however, quite festive. Jokes bandying about here and there, and jolly laughs breaking out. Some men were endeavouring to climb up a leaden pipe on one of the houses. The landlord came out and endeavoured with might and main to pull them down. Many thousand eyes turned upon this contest immediately. All sorts of voices issued from the crowd and uttered choice expressions of slang. When one of the men was pulled down by the leg, the waves of this mob-ocean laughed innumerably; when one fellow slipped away, scrambled up the pipe and made good his lodgement on the shelf, we were all made happy and encouraged him by loud shouts of admiration . . . .

It was past seven now; the quarters rang and passed away; the crowd began to grow very eager and more quiet, and we turned back every now and then and looked at St Sepulchre's clock. Half an hour, twenty-five minutes. What is he doing now? He has his irons off by this time. A quarter: he's in the press-room now, no doubt. Now at last we had come to think about the man we were going to see hanged. How slowly the clock crept over the last quarter! Those who were able to turn round and see (for the crowd was now extraordinarily dense) chronicled the time, eight minutes, five minutes; at last – ding, dong, dong, dong! – the bell is tolling the chimes of eight . . . .

As the clock began to strike an immense sway and movement swept over the whole of that vast dense crowd. They were all uncovered directly, and a great murmur arose, more awful, bizarre and indescribable than any sound I had ever before heard. Women and children began to shriek horridly. I don't know whether it was the bell I heard, but a dreadful quick, feverish kind of jangling noise mingled with the noise of the people and lasted for about two minutes . . . . Courvoisier bore his punishment like a man and walked very firmly. He was dressed in a new black suit, as it seemed; his shirt was open. His arms were tied in front of him. He opened his hands in a helpless kind of way, and clasped them once or twice together. He turned his head here and there, and looked about him for an instant with a wild, imploring look. His mouth was contracted into a sort of pitiful smile. He went and placed himself at once under the beam, with his face towards St Sepulchre's. The tall, grey man in black twisted him round swiftly in the other direction, and drawing from his pocket a nightcap pulled it tight over the patient's head and face. I am not ashamed to say that I could look no more, but shut my eyes as the last dreadful act was going on which sent this wretched, guilty soul into the presence of God . . . .

I must confess . . . that the sight has left on my mind an extraordinary feeling of terror and shame. It seems to me that I have been abetting an act of frightful wickedness and violence, performed by a set of men against one of their fellows, and I pray God that it may soon be out of the power of any man in England to witness such a hideous and degrading sight. Forty thousand persons (say the Sheriffs), of all ranks and degrees, mechanics, gentlemen, pickpockets, members of both Houses of Parliament, street-walkers, newspaper-writers, gather together before Newgate at a very early hour; the most part of them give up their natural quiet night's rest in order to partake of this hideous debauchery, which is more exciting than sleep, or than wine, or the last new ballet, or any other amusement they can have. Pickpocket and Peer each is tickled by the sight alike, and has that hidden lust after blood which influences our race . . . .

I fully confess that I came away down Snow Hill that morning with a disgust for murder, but it was for *the murder I saw done*. As we made our way through the immense crowd, we came upon two little girls of eleven and twelve years; one of them was crying bitterly and begged, for heaven's sake, that someone would lead her from that horrid place. This was done and the children were carried into a place of safety. We asked the elder girl – and a very pretty one – what brought her into such a neighbourhood. The child grinned knowingly and said, 'We've koom to see the mon hanged!' Tender law, that brings out babes upon such errands and provides them with such gratifying moral spectacles! . . .

(Thackeray 1903: 90, 95–100, 104–6, 109)

Notes

1   *X—*: Richard Monkton Milnes (1809–85), minor literary figure as well as reforming politician.
2   *Lord John . . . Sir Robert*: Russell and Peel, current leaders of, respectively, the Whigs and the Tories.
3   *Dick Swiveller*: character in Dickens' *The Old Curiosity Shop*, currently (July 1840) appearing in serial form.

38 CHARLES DICKENS, FROM *MASTER HUMPHREY'S CLOCK* (1841)

On panoramas, including this one, see Introduction, Section VIII, especially p. 24; and on Dickens, see headnote to doc. 36. Though not visually panoramic, the passage offers a moral–philosophical overview of London from its prime location for literal panoramas, the dome of St Paul's. The emphasis, as so often in Dickens, is upon two related characteristics: the atomised structure of life in the city and, partly in consequence of that, a largely unperceived juxtaposition of extremes. Equally characteristic of early Dickens, however, is the concluding note of more optimistic exhortation, even though this involves reversing the meaning of the 'Heart of London' trope: having treated the clock's mechanical ticking as an emblem of city-dwellers' self-absorption, the meditation ends by attributing to it a more reassuringly heart-like concern to promote the communal values of an organic society. *Master Humphrey's Clock* was a periodical issued in both weekly and monthly parts from April 1840 to November 1841, written entirely by Dickens and carrying both *The Old Curiosity Shop* and *Barnaby Rudge* in serial form. This passage was written as part of the bridging material between the two novels.

It is night. Calm and unmoved amidst the scenes that darkness favours, the great heart of London throbs in its Giant breast. Wealth and beggary, vice and virtue, guilt and innocence, repletion and the direst hunger, all treading on each other and crowding together, are gathered round it. Draw but a little circle above the clustering housetops, and you shall have within its space everything, with its opposite extreme and contradiction, close beside. Where yonder feeble light is shining, a man is but this moment dead. The taper at a few yards' distance is seen by eyes that have this instant opened on the world. There are two houses separated by but an inch or two of wall. In one, there are quiet minds at rest; in the other, a waking conscience that one might think would trouble the very air. In that close corner where the roofs shrink down and cower together as if to hide their secrets from the handsome street hard by, there are such dark crimes, such miseries and horrors, as could be hardly told in whispers. In the handsome street, there are folks asleep who have dwelt there all their lives, and have no more knowledge of these things than if they had never been, or were transacted at the remotest limits of the world, – who, if they were hinted at, would shake their heads, look wise, and frown, and say they were impossible, and out of Nature, – as if all great towns were not. Does not this Heart of London, that nothing moves, nor stops, nor quickens, – that goes on the same let what will be done, – does it not express the City's character well?

The day begins to break, and soon there is the hum and noise of life. Those who have spent the night on doorsteps and cold stones crawl off to beg; they who have slept in beds come forth to their occupation, too, and business is astir. The fog of sleep rolls slowly off, and London shines awake. The streets are filled with carriages, and people gaily clad. The jails are full, too, to the throat, nor have the workhouses or hospitals much room to spare. The courts of law are crowded. Taverns have their regular frequenters by this time, and every mart of traffic has its throng. Each of these places is a world, and has its own inhabitants; each is distinct from, and almost unconscious of the existence of any other. There are some few people well to do, who remember to have heard it said, that numbers of men and women – thousands, they think it was – get up in London every day, unknowing where to lay their heads at night; and that there are quarters of the town where misery and famine always are. They don't believe it quite, – there may be some truth in it, but it is exaggerated, of course. So, each of these thousand worlds goes on, intent upon itself, until night comes again, – first with its lights and pleasures, and its cheerful streets; then with its guilt and darkness.

Heart of London, there is a moral in thy every stroke! as I look on at thy indomitable working, which neither death, nor press of life, nor grief, nor gladness out of doors will influence one jot, I seem to hear a voice within thee which sinks into my heart, bidding me, as I elbow my way among the crowd, have some thought for the meanest wretch that passes, and, being a man, to turn away with scorn and pride from none that bear the human shape.

(Dickens 1892: 644–5)

Plate 8 View from St Paul's, Looking South-West, c. 1890, *The Queen's London.*

113

39 JOHN FISHER MURRAY, FROM *THE WORLD OF LONDON* (1843), CHAPTERS 1, 3, 4, 16

Murray (1811–65) was an Irishman, the most notable of whose miscellaneous writings were studies of metropolitan life: a group of humorous sketches of London life first published in *Blackwood's* in the 1830s; a satirical novel about fashionable Dublin, *The Viceroy* (1841); and two pairs of volumes called *The World of London*, from the first of which these extracts are taken. Murray writes observantly about street-life, and with keen intelligence regarding the social psychology of metropolitan living: see Introduction, p. 6, on his use in this connection of the evocative phrase, 'the attraction of repulsion'. Despite a race-consciousness apparent from the first chapter onwards, the strongly anti-semitic description of the Jewish quarter may still come as a shock; in this regard, however, Murray's is not an unrepresentative voice in the early Victorian period.

Not even in their native lands do the various races of men who huddle together in the world of London preserve more strictly their idiosyncracies, their national peculiarities, their marked expression of face, tone of voice, manners, customs, religion, prejudices, passions, and all the items that together make up the national character, than in London . . . . *There*, let a man be of what humour he may, he will meet with men of his humour; let a man be of what country he may, he will meet with men of his country; and as a state of solitude in crowds is a state of torture, it is not to be wondered at that the solitary man finds sympathy in the society of other solitary men, or that an exiled people clings fondly to the countenance and support of compatriots who feel with them the like wants and the like necessities . . . .

A solitude of society is the character of London loneliness. It is a solitude without desolation, an isolated aggregation: a solitude wherein we are perpetually cheating ourselves with the belief that we are sociable. Nothing can be farther from the truth: the attraction of London life is an attraction of repulsion. The power of plunging and being lost in an ocean of human beings is ever at hand, and the possession of that power generates an indifference to the use of it; this indifference becomes at length a habit . . . .

It would scarcely be credited that in splendid London, women are subjected to various kinds of severe and repulsive toil, that if such things were related of Turks or Hottentots, we should set them down as so many proofs of inherent barbarism among the people where such usages had place. For example, the porterage of meat at the wholesale markets, as Newgate and Leadenhall, is performed by women, many of them old. You will see these wretched creatures stagger under the weight of a side of beef or, having an entire sheep upon their heads, conveying their burdens to the butchers' carts drawn up in the vicinity of the market. Surely this is man's work. And surely, if women are driven by hard necessity to such masculine toil, it must argue something rotten in the state of that society where such extreme necessity is suffered to exist. Another melancholy and revolting spectacle is that of women and children of all ages, up to the middle in the vast laystalls wherein are collected the removed filth of the metropolis, riddling and sifting the materials of which these mountains of *dust*, as it is technically called, are composed, begrimed with irremovable skins of dirt and looking more like damned souls toiling in some infernal prison-house than creatures who are heirs to an eternal heritage of Heaven!

The Jewish Quarter ... is bounded to the north by High Street, Spital-fields; to the east by Middlesex Street, popularly known and called Petticoat Lane; to the south by Leadenhall Street, Aldgate, and the hither end of Whitechapel; to the west by Bishopgate Street. This is literally the New Jerusalem: here we Christians are foreigners, strangers in a strange land; here, over the doors, are inscribed pot-hooks and vowel points, indicative to those who understand them that Moses Abrahams furnisheth 'slops' for home consumption and exportation – this we naturally conclude to be the meaning from the articles exhibited in the windows, for though the sign be Hebrew to them we need hardly say that it is *Greek* to us. Within the area bounded as above described, but especially about Bevis Marks, Houndsditch, St Mary Axe and Petticoat Lane, you might readily imagine yourself transported to Frankfort, Warsaw or any place enjoying a superabundant Jewish popula-tion. Here, every face is of the shape and somewhat of the complexion of a

Plate 9 Petticoat Lane, mid-nineteenth century (?), Thornbury and Walford 1873–8, Vol. II.

turkey egg; every brow pencilled in an arch of exact ellipse; every nose modelled after the proboscis of a Toucan. Locks as bushy and black as those of Absalom abound, and beards of the patriarchal ages. Here and hereabouts, Isaac kills beef and mutton according to the old dispensation; Jacob receives accidental silver spoons and consigns gold watches, now warranted never more to lose a second, to the crucible, kept always at white heat in his little dark cellar and *no questions asked.*

The avidity with which this, in one sense, primitive people pursues gain is not wonderful when we reflect that gain is all that the, till lately, unrelenting persecution of the Christian has left them to pursue . . . . To the pursuit of gain all their energies are directed with an intensity, unscrupulosity and perseverance unknown to and unattempted by any Christian people. Money they must and will have; . . . the lowest depths of knavery, chicanery and extortion are practised by some to accomplish this the end of their existence. For this the infamous 'crimp' grasps the hard earnings of the unsuspecting seaman as soon as he steps upon his native shore, and then spurns him naked in the street; for this the marine store-dealers and receivers open their seminaries of theft; for this the current coin of the realm is clipped, and ingots and sovereigns perspire; for this the pander entraps and the bawd opens wide the gates that lead to everlasting death, trafficking in Christian flesh for purposes worse than the worst of slavery . . . .

[W]e must candidly confess that when we see the daughter of a Christian man patrolling the streets, decorated in the trumpery properties of a Jewish brothel, while the devil's dam, in the shape of a hideous Hebrew hag, follows the poor unfortunate like the shadow of death to clutch the wages of her shame, we really think a Christian government might, without any hazard of public odium, string up at the doors of their own dens Mother Abrahams, Mother Isaacs and Mother Jacobs. But after all, perhaps it is better as it is. If this abominable traffic *must* be connived at, it is better that those should have a monopoly who have nothing in common with us, save that which the weasel has in common with its prey: those who have made a god of mammon, worshipping the golden calf with the tenfold idolatry of their fathers. There are various kinds of industry – the industry of enterprise, the industry of saving, the industry of toil. The industrial characteristic of the Jew is industry of over-reaching: other men are content to do business, the Jew must do *you.* . . .

(Murray 1843: I, 22–3, 52–3, 63–4, 251–5)

40 EDGAR ALLAN POE, FROM 'A MAN OF THE CROWD' (1840, REVISED 1845)

This story was first published in *Burton's Gentlemen's Magazine* of Philadelphia, one of several periodicals of which Poe (1809–49) became editor as well as main contributor. It was a key text for its first French translator, Charles Baudelaire (see Benjamin 1983: 48–53, 128–31); the great Parisian poet's own evocations of street-crowd experience, in their turn a major influence upon later English urban writing, likewise display both compulsive fascination and neurotic alienation. Poe had never revisited England since his schooldays at Stoke Newington on the outskirts of London; his admiration for De Quincey and Dickens as well as the need for effects of the densest populousness may account for the choice of a London setting. The story has an epigraph from La Bruyère meaning 'This great misfortune of not being able to be alone.' Prior to the concluding paragraphs given below, the crowd-watching narrator has described being seized with 'a craving desire . . . to know more' of 'a decrepid old man' (pp. 334–5) whom he has then followed for several hours.

A loud-toned clock struck eleven, and the company were fast deserting the bazaar. A shop-keeper, in putting up a shutter, jostled the old man, and at the instant I saw a strong shudder come over his frame. He hurried into the street, looked anxiously around him for an instant, and then ran with incredible swiftness through many crooked and people-less lanes, until we emerged once more upon the great thoroughfare whence we had started – the street of the D— Hotel. It no longer wore, however, the same aspect. It was still brilliant with gas; but the rain fell fiercely, and there were few persons to be seen. The stranger grew pale. He walked moodily some paces up the once populous avenue, then, with a heavy sigh, turned in the direction of the river, and, plunging through a great variety of devious ways, came out, at length, in view of one of the principal theatres. It was about being closed, and the audience were thronging from the doors. I saw the old man gasp as if for breath while he threw himself amid the crowd; but I thought that the intense agony of his countenance had, in some measure, abated. His head again fell upon his breast; he appeared as I had seen him at first. I observed that he now took the course in which had gone the greater number of the audience – but, upon the whole, I was at a loss to comprehend the waywardness of his actions.

As he proceeded, the company grew more scattered, and his old uneasiness and vacillation were resumed. For some time he followed closely a party of some ten or twelve roisterers; but from this number one by one dropped off, until three only remained together, in a narrow and gloomy lane little frequented. The stranger paused, and, for a moment, seemed lost in thought; then, with every mark of agitation, pursued rapidly a route which brought us to the verge of the city, amid regions very different from those we had hitherto traversed. It was the most noisome quarter of London, where everything wore the worst impress of the most deplorable poverty, and of the most desperate crime. By the dim light of an accidental lamp, tall, antique, worm-eaten, wooden tenements were seen tottering to their fall, in directions so many and capricious that scarce the semblance of a passage was discernible between them. The paving-stones lay at random, displaced from their beds by the rankly growing grass. Horrible filth festered in the dammed-up gutters. The whole atmosphere teemed with desolation. Yet, as we proceeded, the sound of human life revived by sure degrees, and at length large bands of the most abandoned of a London populace were seen reeling to and fro. The spirits of the old man again flickered up, as a lamp which is near its death-hour. Once more he strode onward with elastic tread. Suddenly a corner was turned, a blaze of light burst upon our sight, and we stood before one of the huge suburban temples of Intemperance – one of the palaces of the fiend, Gin.

It was now nearly day-break; but a number of wretched inebriates still pressed in and out of the flaunting entrance. With a half shriek of joy the old man forced a passage within, resumed at once his original bearing, and stalked backward and forward, without apparent object, among the throng. He had not been thus long occupied, however, before a rush to the doors gave token that the host was closing them for the night. It was something even more intense than despair that I then observed upon the countenance of the singular being whom I had watched so pertinaciously. Yet he did not hesitate in his career, but, with a mad energy, retraced his steps at once, to the heart of the mighty London. Long and swiftly he fled, while I followed him in the wildest amazement, resolute not to abandon a scrutiny in which I now felt an interest all-absorbing. The sun arose while we proceeded, and, when we had once again reached that most thronged mart of the populous town, the street of the D— Hotel, it presented an appearance of human bustle and activity scarcely inferior to what I had seen on the evening before. And here, long, amid the momently increasing confusion, did I persist in my pursuit of the stranger. But, as usual, he walked to and fro, and during the day did not pass from out the turmoil of that street. And, as the shades of the second evening came on, I grew wearied unto death, and, stopping fully in front of the wanderer, gazed at him steadfastly in the face. He noticed me not, but resumed his solemn walk, while I, ceasing to follow, remained absorbed in contemplation. 'This old man,' I said at length, 'is the type and the genius of deep crime. He refuses to be alone. *He is the man of the crowd.* It will be in vain to follow; for I shall learn no more of him, nor of his deeds. The worst heart of the world is a grosser book than the 'Hortulus Animæ,'[1] and perhaps it is but one of the great mercies of God that *es lässt sich nicht lesen.*'[2]

(Poe 1884: I, 337–40)

Notes

1 '*Hortulus Animae*': 'The *Hortulus Animae cum Oratiunculis Aliquibus Superadditis* [of Grüninger]' (Poe's note).
2 *es . . . lesen*: 'it does not permit itself to be read' – the narrator's own translation in the story's first sentence, which as often in Poe prefigures the last one.

41 G. W. M. REYNOLDS, FROM *THE MYSTERIES OF LONDON*, SERIES 1 (1845), CHAPTERS 42 AND 43

Reynolds (1814–79) was probably the most prolific of all Victorian writers, producing tens of millions of words as popular novelist and journalist. He was also active for a time in Chartist politics, chairing large meetings in Trafalgar Square and on Kennington Common in 1848. *The Mysteries of London* (two series) and its sequel, *The Mysteries of the Court of London* (four series), appeared without intermission in 624 weekly penny numbers and twelve volumes between 1844 and 1856, with sales of up to 40,000 a number. Mayhew (1967: I, 25) found these to be the most popular fiction read aloud to illiterate costermongers, partly on political grounds. The francophile Reynolds was quick to adopt the 'urban mysteries' genre inaugurated by Eugène Sue in *Les Mystères de Paris* (1843), and to maximise its appeal to a new mass readership in England with a fervid mix of political polemic, social realism, prurient voyeurism and gothic melodrama. These formal discontinuities are underscored by a dual vision of the city as impenetrably labyrinthine and as polarised between equally depraved

Plate 10 'Over London – By Rail', G. Doré, *London: A Pilgrimage*, 1872.

extremes of wealth and poverty (Humpherys 1983: 74). In the episode partly reproduced here, the hero Richard Markham ventures into the East End to meet his blackmailer and eternal foe, the Resurrection Man. In a chance encounter beforehand with
another acquaintance, Markham secures documentary proof of his innocence,
enabling him to announce to his blackmailer (just before the second passage below):
'Our ways lie in different directions both at present and in future. Farewell.'

There is not probably in all London ... so great an amount of squalid misery and fearful crime huddled together as in the joint districts of Spitalfields
and Bethnal Green. Between Shoreditch Church and Wentworth Street the
most intense pangs of poverty, the most profligate morals, and the most odi-
ous crimes rage with the fury of a pestilence. ...

The Eastern Counties' Railway intersects Spitalfields and Bethnal Green.
The traveller upon this line may catch, from the windows of the carriage in
which he journeys, a hasty but alas! too comprehensive glance of the
wretchedness and squalor of that portion of London. He may actually obtain
a view of the interior and domestic misery peculiar to the neighbourhood; he
may penetrate with his eyes into the secrets of those abodes of sorrow, vice
and destitution. In summertime the poor always have their windows open,
and thus the hideous poverty of their rooms can be readily descried from the
summit of the arches on which the railroad is constructed.

And in those rooms may be seen women half naked, some employed in
washing the few rags which they possess, others ironing the linen of a more
wealthy neighbour, a few preparing the sorry meal, and numbers scolding,
swearing and quarrelling. At many of the windows men out of work, with
matted hair, black beards and dressed only in filthy shirts and ragged trousers,
lounge all the day long smoking. ... Around the doors children, ... shoeless,
dirty and uncared for, throng in numbers – a rising generation of thieves and
vagabonds. ...

It was now midnight, and the streets were nearly deserted. The lamps, few
and far between, only made darkness visible instead of throwing a useful
light upon the intricate maze of narrow thoroughfares. Markham's object
was to reach Shoreditch as soon as possible, for he knew that opposite the
church there was cab-stand where he might procure a vehicle to take him
home. ...

He soon perceived that he had mistaken his way, and at length found himself floundering about in a long, narrow street, unpaved, and here and there
almost blocked up with heaps of putrescent filth. There was not a lamp in
this perilous thoroughfare; no moon on high irradiated his path; black night
enveloped everything above and below in total darkness.

Once or twice he thought he heard footsteps behind him, and then he
stopped, hoping to be overtaken by someone of whom he might inquire his

way. But either his ears deceived him or else the person whose steps he heard stopped when he did.

There was not a light in any of the houses on either side, and not a sound of revelry or sorrow escaped from the ill-closed casements.

Richard was bewildered, and to speak truly he began to be alarmed. He remembered to have read of the mysterious disappearance of persons in the east end of the metropolis, and also of certain fell deeds of crime which had been lately brought to light in the very district where he was now wandering; and he could not help wishing that he was in some more secure and less gloomy region.

He was groping his way along, feeling with his hands against the houses to guide him – now kneedeep in some filthy puddle, now stumbling over some heap of slimy dirt, now floundering up to his ankles in the mud – when a heavy and crushing blow fell upon his hat from behind.

He staggered and fell against the door of a house. Almost at the same instant that door was thrust open, and two powerful arms hurled the prostrate young men down three or four steps into a passage. The person who thus ferociously attacked him leapt after him, closing the door violently behind him. . . .

Richard's first idea was to rise and attempt an escape by the front door; but before he had time to consider it even for a moment, the murderous ruffian struck a light in the room, which . . . was immediately illuminated by a powerful glare. . . .

Markham was about to start from his prostrate position when the interior of that room was thus abruptly revealed to him; but for a few moments the spectacle which met his sight paralysed every limb, and rendered him breathless, speechless and motionless with horror.

Stretched upon a shutter, which three chairs supported, was a corpse – naked, and of that blueish or livid colour which denotes the beginning of decomposition!

Near this loathsome object was a large tub full of water; and to that part of the ceiling immediately above it were affixed two large hooks, to each of which hung thick cords.

In one corner of the room were long flexible iron rods, spades, pickaxes, wooden levers, coils of thick rope, trowels, saws, hammers, huge chisels, skeleton keys, &c.

But how great was Richard's astonishment when, glancing from the objects just described towards the villain who had hurled him into that den of horrors, his eyes were struck by the sombre and revolting countenance of the Resurrection Man. . . .

(Reynolds n.d.: I, 118, 122–3)

42 CHARLES DICKENS, FROM *DOMBEY AND SON* (1848), CHAPTER 6

Dickens (on whom see headnote to doc. 35) lived as a boy (1822–4) in Camden Town, the location of 'Staggs's Gardens'; he later (1836–7) observed the construction of one of the earliest passenger railway lines, the London and Birmingham, through the same suburb. A decade afterwards, in his first and most conspicuously railway-age novel, the physical and communal upheaval which this construction involved is powerfully rendered. Contextual evidence, including later passages of the same novel, indicates that the second paragraph below is not intended to be ironic. Staggs's Gardeners, unlike many nineteenth-century Londoners in actuality, suffer only temporary displacement; by Chapter 15 their squalid district has been transformed into one of 'wholesome comforts and conveniences', and among other progressive effects is the diehard chimney-sweep's conversion, albeit opportunistic, to 'the cleansing of railway chimneys by machinery'!

The first shock of a great earthquake had, just at that period, rent the whole neighbourhood to its centre. Traces of its course were visible on every side. Houses were knocked down; streets broken through and stopped; deep pits and trenches dug in the ground; enormous heaps of earth and clay thrown up; buildings that were undermined and shaking, propped by great beams of wood. Here, a chaos of carts, overthrown and jumbled together, lay topsy-turvy at the bottom of a steep unnatural hill; there, confused treasures of iron soaked and rusted in something that had accidentally become a pond. Everywhere were bridges that led nowhere; thoroughfares that were wholly impassable; Babel towers of chimneys, wanting half their height; temporary wooden houses and enclosures, in the most unlikely situations; carcases of ragged tenements, and fragments of unfinished walls and arches, and piles of scaffolding, and wildernesses of bricks, and giant forms of cranes, and tripods straddling above nothing. There were a hundred thousand shapes and substances of incompleteness, wildly mingled out of their places, upside down, burrowing in the earth, aspiring in the air, mouldering in the water, and unintelligible as any dream. Hot springs and fiery eruptions, the usual attendants upon earthquakes, lent their contributions of confusion to the scene. Boiling water hissed and heaved within dilapidated walls; whence, also, the glare and roar of flames came issuing forth; and mounds of ashes blocked up rights of way, and wholly changed the law and custom of the neighbourhood.

In short, the yet unfinished and unopened Railroad was in progress; and, from the very core of all this dire disorder, trailed smoothly away, upon its mighty course of civilisation and improvement.

But as yet, the neighbourhood was shy to own the Railroad. One or two bold speculators had projected streets; and one had built a little, but had stopped among the mud and ashes to consider farther of it. A bran-new Tavern, redolent of fresh mortar and size, and fronting nothing at all, had taken for its sign The Railway Arms; but that might be rash enterprise – and then it hoped to sell drink to the workmen. . . .

The general belief was very slow. There were frowzy fields, and cow-houses, and dunghills, and dustheaps, and ditches, and gardens, and summer-houses, and carpet-beating grounds, at the very door of the Railway. Little tumuli of oyster shells in the oyster season, and of lobster shells in the lob-ster season, and of broken crockery and faded cabbage leaves in all seasons, encroached upon its high places. Posts, and rails, and old cautions to tres-passers, and backs of mean houses, and patches of wretched vegetation, stared it out of countenance. Nothing was the better for it, or thought of being so. If the miserable waste ground lying near it could have laughed, it would have laughed it to scorn, like many of the miserable neighbours.

Staggs's Gardens was uncommonly incredulous. It was a little row of houses, with little squalid patches of ground before them, fenced off with old doors, barrel staves, scraps of tarpaulin, and dead bushes; with bottom-less tin kettles and exhausted iron fenders, thrust into the gaps. Here, the Staggs's Gardeners trained scarlet beans, kept fowls and rabbits, erected rot-ten summer-houses (one was an old boat), dried clothes, and smoked pipes. Some were of opinion that Staggs's Gardens derived its name from a deceased capitalist, one Mr. Staggs, who had built it for his delectation. Others, who had a natural taste for the country, held that it dated from those rural times when the antlered herd, under the familiar denomination of Staggses, had resorted to its shady precincts. Be this as it may, Staggs's Gardens was regarded by its population as a sacred grove not to be withered by railroads; and so confident were they generally of its long outliving any such ridiculous inventions, that the master chimney-sweeper at the corner, who was under-stood to take the lead in the local politics of the Gardens, had publicly declared that on the occasion of the Railroad opening, if ever it did open, two of his boys should ascend the flues of his dwelling, with instructions to hail the failure with derisive jeers from the chimney-pots.

(Dickens 1877a: 33–4)

43 ANGUS REACH, FROM 'THE LOUNGER IN REGENT STREET', *GAVARNI IN LONDON* (1849)

See Introduction, pp. 6–7. Despite the brevity of his life, Reach (1821–56) achieved prominence in mid-century journalism, where he was prolific and versatile. In the *Morning Chronicle*'s large-scale investigation of 'Labour and the Poor' from 1849 (see doc. 44), he reported on conditions in the provincial manufacturing districts. He was also on the staff of *Punch*, and wrote for many other periodicals. *Gavarni in London* contained articles by various hands to accompany a set of sketches of high and low life in the English capital by the famous French graphic artist.

It is the beginning of the evening in the City – and therefore high noon in the West. A bright summer sun is warmly white upon the terraced and stuccoed ranges of Regent Street. The flaring, dusty thoroughfare is swarming with flashing equipages, and pouring crowds of gay pedestrians. The ample wooden pavement is divided into two long lines of moving vehicles. How they sweep gaudily on – a changing, shifting panorama of glittering panels and glancing wheels, and sleek-pacing horses, and overpowering footmen, and delicious peeps into the dim cushioned interiors, where the eye loses itself in half-seen, half-missed, visions of fair faces and rich tresses, and reclining forms dressed in cool muslins, or lost in the massive folds of costly shawls. And the broad, clean, white *pavé!* How it swarms with that continuous procession of gaily-dressed women and men. How, as you glance along it, the multitude – the shifting, rushing, rolling multitude – becomes one dazzling, puzzling, confounding chaos of faces and forms, and hats and bonnets, and paletots and visites, and moustaches and curls – all jumbled up together – all mixing – all blending – and all forming one confounding, bewildering, bewitching whole – which, as you contemplate it, makes the eye dazzle and the brain ache!

It is high noon in Regent Street. At every shop-door the big-calved, gaudy-plushed footmen cluster. By every lamp-post the dealers in poodles and terriers and spaniel pups congregate. Men with pen-knives, which seem all blades, abound. Along the kerb-stone, itinerant vendors of prints, and stain-cleaning pastes, and mosaic gold chains, and studs, display their merchandise; and round the corner, near the tavern door, the Italian boy grinds his piano-organ in dumb show. Happily, the music of the wheels drowns the noise of the instrument. . . .

Yes – once more we repeat, it is high noon in the West. Regent Street is at its fullest, and its brightest, and its gayest; and the Regent Street Lounger is abroad with the butterflies! Now, therefore, to plunge into his habits and characteristics.

The Regent Street Lounger must not be confounded with other loungers who occasionally lounge in Regent Street. He is not the Lounger of the Lowther Arcade – or of the steam-boat piers – or of the stage doors – or of the piazzas of Covent Garden, or the central fruity and flowery tunnel thereof. He is not even the Lounger of the Quadrant.[1] Hard as inferior philosophers may find it to believe, the Lounger of the Quadrant is a different being from the Lounger of Regent Street. The former is a mosaic edition of the latter. He shuns the glare of the open street, and finds comfort in the subdued light of the colonnade. His smartness is often alloyed by seediness. His hat has more jauntiness in its set than nap in its texture. His linen is questionable, and his general air is mildewy. He haunts dim cigar shops, and glides furtively into fifth-rate billiard rooms. Often the Quadrant Lounger is a foreigner. Then he smokes cigarettes, and has brown fingers heavy with dim rings; and if you look to his broad feet, you are instantly transported in imagination to Boulogne-sur-Mer, Rue de l'Ecu – the shop where they are always selling bankrupt stocks of divers-coloured boots, with pearl buttons which don't button, and little toe-tips of varnished leather, at the reasonable rate of four francs a-pair. . . .

The Regent Street Lounger knows Town. He is of it, perhaps on it. He may not perhaps approach the inner penetralia of West-End life, but he hangs upon its outward development. If he cannot ride in the coronetted carriage, he will at least be within sound of the wheels. If he does not know the peer, he knows the peer's liveries. Try him – cross-question him. Not a carriage which rolls along the wood, or waits along the kerb, but he can tell the occupant of. He is learned in hammer-cloths, elaborate on crests, and can discern the strawberry leaf on the panel even when the two sleek and glossy horses, with their foaming mouths and high action, being put to their mettle by the fat be-wigged coachman, seem to shoot past like a rocket.

The Regent Street Lounger cares little about the shops. The people are his study. He is not like the more easterly tribes of Loungers. He never stops to listen to a man whistling canary notes with a quill in a tin jug of water. An excavated gas-pipe has no charms for him. He can withstand the temptation of an omnibus horse which has slipped on the wooden pavement, and he pays not the most remote attention to the gentleman who disposes of favourite lyric poetry at six yards a-penny; on the contrary, he paces easily yet jauntily on from the baker's at the corner of Glasshouse Street to the music-shop which marks the confluence of Regent and Oxford Streets. These are the general frontiers of his lounging dominions. And he traverses his kingdom with a certain observant thoughtfulness. Not a lady escapes the ordeal. His eye falls listlessly, yet searchingly, on face and form, and toilet and dress – from the saucy little boot to the flutter of the parasol fringe. He has a keen appreciation of visites, and entertains deep theories on the handling and disposing of shawls. Gentlemen fare no better. He divides them into two classes – the 'good style of men' and 'the bad style of men'. The mere harmless, pitiful little gent does not even excite his contempt. He is philosophic, and knows that we are all mortal – little minnows and big whales. . . .

(Smith 1849: 70–3)

Note

1 *The Quadrant*: adjunct of Regent Street, with a shady reputation for gaming and prostitution, in consequence of which it was demolished by Act of Parliament shortly after this article was written.

44 HENRY MAYHEW, FROM 'LABOUR AND THE POOR: THE METROPOLITAN DISTRICTS, LETTER I', *MORNING CHRONICLE* (1849, 1862)

On Mayhew and panoramas, including this passage, see Introduction, pp. 23–5. One of seventeen children of a London solicitor, and now the best known of four literary brothers, Mayhew (1812–87) had a long but chequered career, much of it shrouded in bohemian obscurity. He was one of the founders of *Punch* in 1841, and the author (sometimes collaboratively) of numerous farces, novels and other minor works, most of which give little inkling of his remarkable powers as an investigative and documentary writer on the London working class. These he developed as the *Morning Chronicle*'s 'Metropolitan Correspondent', contributing twice-weekly letters between October 1849 and December 1850 on the (mostly deplorable) conditions of work and standards of living of employees in many of the capital's major areas of trade and manufacture. A distinction is often drawn between the Mayhew of the *Chronicle* and 'the somewhat quainter . . . Mayhew of the London street folk' (Thompson 1971: 49) in the immediately subsequent *London Labour and the London Poor*. Yet when this passage, a prelude to the former project, closes in from its initially distant overview, it is that 'quainter' street-world of vagrants, scavengers, and the watercress girl of doc. 45 which is strikingly prefigured. Mayhew, typically, recycled the passage more than once; the 1862 version used here differs slightly from the text of 1849.

Those who have seen London only in the day-time, with its flood of life pouring through the arteries to its restless heart, know it not in *all* its grandeur. They have still, in order to comprehend the multiform sublimity of the great city, to contemplate it by night, afar off from an eminence. As noble a prospect as any in the world, it has been well said, is London viewed from the suburbs on a clear winter's evening. Though the stars be shining in the heavens, there is another firmament spread out below with its millions of bright lights glittering at the feet. Line after line sparkles like the trails left by meteors, and cutting and crossing one another till they are lost in the haze of distance. Over the whole, too, there hangs a lurid cloud, bright as if the monster city were in flames, and looking from afar like the sea at dusk, made phosphorescent by the million creatures dwelling within it.

Again, at night it is, that the strange anomalies of London life are best seen. As the hum of life ceases, and the shops darken, and the gaudy gin palaces thrust out their ragged and squalid crowds to pace the streets, London puts on its most solemn look of all. On the benches of the parks, in the niches of the bridges, and in the litter of the markets, are huddled together the homeless and the destitute. The only living things that haunt the streets are the poor wretched Magdalens, who stand shivering in their finery, waiting to catch the drunkard as he goes shouting homewards. There, on a door-step, crouches some shoeless child, whose day's begging has not brought it enough to purchase even the penny night's lodging that his young companions in beggary have gone to. Where the stones are taken up and piled high in the road, while the mains are being mended, and the gas streams from a tall pipe, in a flag of flame, a ragged crowd are grouped round the glowing coke fire – some smoking, and others dozing beside it.

Then, as the streets grow blue with the coming light, and the church spires and roof-tops stand out against the clear sky with a sharpness of out-line that is seen only in London before its million chimneys cover the town with their smoke – then come sauntering forth the unwashed poor; some with greasy wallets on their backs to hunt over each dust-heap, and eke out life by seeking refuse bones, or stray rags and pieces of old iron; others, whilst on their way to their work, are gathered at the corner of some street round the early breakfast-stall, and blowing saucers of steaming coffee, drawn from tall tin cans that have the red-hot charcoal shining crimson through the holes in the fire-pan beneath them; whilst already the little slat-tern girl, with her basket slung before her, screams, 'Water-*creases!*' through the sleeping streets.

(Mayhew and Binny 1968: 29)

45 HENRY MAYHEW, FROM 'WATERCRESS GIRL', *LONDON LABOUR AND THE LONDON POOR*, VOL. 1 (1851, 1861)

On Mayhew, see headnote to doc. 44. Immediately after leaving the *Morning Chroni-cle* in December 1850, he began independently issuing his studies of street-folk in two-penny weekly parts; the bound parts appeared in two volumes during the next fif-teen months, and most of this material appears unaltered in the expanded edition of 1861–2. Though often poorly organised and edited, *London Labour and the London Poor* is a rich treasure-house for students of Victorian culture and social history, and the selection of a single (and abridged) example an invidious task for the anthologist. This passage effectively illustrates some of Mayhew's distinctive qualities as literary artist and pioneer oral historian: following brief but sharply focused introductory com-ments by the investigator, the subject's idiomatic 'statement' (with the interviewer's questions edited out but deducible) provides a dramatic rendition of her presence, character and biography; meanwhile, intimations emerge of a subcultural hinterland – mostly but not entirely bleak – of education, familial roles and ethnic relationships. Steedman's analysis of her 'obsession' with Mayhew's watercress girl (1992: 193–202) is very suggestive regarding the historiography of childhood and its cultural and psychological implications.

The little watercress girl who gave me the following statement, although only eight years of age, had entirely lost all childish ways, and was indeed, in thoughts and manner, a woman. There was something cruelly pathetic in hearing this infant, so young that her features had scarcely formed themselves, talking of the bitterest struggles of life with the calm earnestness of one who had endured them all. I did not know how to talk with her. . . . All her knowledge seemed to begin and end with water-cresses and what they fetched. She knew no more of London than that part she had seen on her rounds. . . . Her little face, pale and thin with privation, was wrinkled where the dimples ought to have been, and she would sigh frequently. . . .

The poor girl, although the weather was severe, was dressed in a thin cotton gown, with a threadbare shawl wrapped round her shoulders. She wore no covering to her head, and the long rusty hair stood out in all directions. When she walked she shuffled along, for fear that the large carpet slippers that served her for shoes should slip off her feet.

'I go about the streets with water-creases crying, "Four bunches a penny, water-creases." I am just eight years old – that's all, and I've a big sister, and a brother and a sister younger than I am. On and off, I've been very near a twelvemonth in the streets. . . . My mother learned me to needle-work and to knit when I was about five. I used to go to school too, but I wasn't there long. I've forgot all about it now, it's such a time ago; and mother took me away because the master whacked me. . . . What do you think? He hit me three times, ever so hard, across the face with his cane, and made me go dancing downstairs. . . .

'The creases is so bad now that I haven't been out with 'em for three days. They're so cold, people won't buy 'em; for when I goes up to them, they say, "They'll freeze our bellies." . . . In summer there's lots, and 'most as cheap as dirt; but I have to be down at Farringdon Market between four and five, or else I can't get any creases, because everyone almost – especially the Irish – is selling them, and they're picked up so quick. Some of the saleswomen – we never calls 'em ladies – is very kind to us children, and some of them altogether spiteful. The good one will give you a bunch for nothing when they're cheap; but the others, cruel ones, if you try to bate them a farden less than they ask you, will say, "Go along with you, you're no good." I used to go down to market along with another girl, as must be about fourteen 'cos she does her back hair up. When we've bought a lot, we sits down on a doorstep and ties up the bunches. We never goes home to breakfast till we've sold out; but if it's very late, then I buys a penn'orth of pudden, which is very nice with gravy. I don't know hardly one of the people as goes to Farringdon to talk to; they never speak to me, so I don't speak to them. We children never play down there 'cos we're thinking of our living. No, people never pities me in the street – excepting one gentleman, and he says, says he, "What do you do out so soon in the morning?" But he gave me nothink – he only walked away.

'It's very cold before winter comes on reg'lar – specially getting up of a morning. I gets up in the dark by the light of a lamp in the court. When the snow is on the ground there's no creases. I bears the cold – you must. So I puts my hands under my shawl, though it hurts 'em to take hold of the creases, especially when we takes 'em to the pump to wash 'em. No, I never see any children crying – it's no use.

'Sometimes I make a great deal of money. One day I took 1s. 6d., and the creases cost 6d.; but it isn't often I get such luck as that. I oftener makes 3d, or 4d. than 1s., and then I'm at work crying, "Creases, four bunches a penny, creases!" from six in the morning to about ten. What do you mean by mechanics? – I don't know what they are. The shops buy most of me. Some of 'em says, "Oh! I ain't a-goin' to give a penny for these," and they want 'em at the same price as I buys 'em at.

'I always give mother my money, she's so very good to me. She don't often beat me; but when she do, she don't play with me. She's very poor and goes out cleaning rooms sometimes, now she don't work at the fur. I ain't got no father, he's a father-in-law. No, mother ain't married again – he's a father-in-law. He grinds scissors, and he's very good to me. No, I don't mean by that that he says kind things to me, for he never hardly speaks. When I gets home after selling creases I stops at home. I puts the room to rights; mother don't make me do it, I does it myself. I cleans the chairs, though there's only two to clean. I takes a tub and scrubbing-brush and flannel, and scrubs the floor – that's what I do three or four times a week.
. . .

'On a Friday night, . . . I goes to a Jew's house till eleven o'clock on Saturday night. All I has to do is to snuff the candles and poke the fire. You see they keep their Sabbath then, and they won't touch anything; so they give me my wittals and $1\frac{1}{2}$ d., and I does it for 'em. I have a reg'lar good lot to eat. Supper of Friday night, and tea after that, and fried fish of a Saturday morning, and meat for dinner, and tea, and supper, and I like it very well.

'Oh yes, I've got some toys at home. I've a fire-place, and a box of toys, and a knife and fork, and two little chairs. The Jews gave 'em to me where I go to on a Friday, and that's why I said they were very kind to me. . . .

'I am a capital hand at bargaining – but only at buying watercreases. They can't take me in. If the woman tries to give me a small handful of creases, I says, "I ain't a-goin' to have that for a ha'porth," and I go to the next basket, and so on all round. I know the quantities very well. . . . I can't read or write, but I knows how many pennies goes to a shilling, why, twelve of course, but I don't know how many ha'pence there is, though there's two to a penny. When I've bought 3d. of creases, I ties 'em up into as many little bundles as

I can. They must look biggish or the people won't buy them, some puffs them out as much as they'll go. All my money I earns I puts into a club and draws it out to buy clothes with. It's better than spending it in sweet-stuff, for them as has a living to earn. Besides it's like a child to care for sugar-sticks, and not like one who's got a living and vittals to earn. I ain't a child, and I shan't be a woman till I'm twenty, but I'm past eight I am. . . .'

(Mayhew 1967: I, 151–2)

46   ALFRED, LORD TENNYSON, *IN MEMORIAM* VII (1850)

In Memoriam comprises 131 poems (flanked by 'Prologue' and 'Epilogue') of varying length but unvarying stanzaic form, which Tennyson (1809–92) composed between 1833 – when his close friend and prospective brother-in-law, Arthur Hallam, died suddenly at the age of 22 – and 1850 – when the collection was anonymously published. The published sequence charts the gradual, multiplex process of coming to terms with loss and mortality; in VII, though one of the last sections to be written, early sensations of total bereavement are dramatised in the speaker's address to his dead friend's city residence (Hallam lived in Wimpole Street), which he haunts with a survivor's irrational guilt feelings. Harsh sound patterns and bleak street imagery in the final lines indicate that at this stage the normal continuance of life around constitutes a painful affront rather than a comfort. However, when the speaker returns to the same scene in the pendant poem, CXIX, he finds it transfigured into a quasi-pastoral dawn landscape.

> Dark house, by which once more I stand
>   Here in the long unlovely street,
>   Doors, where my heart was used to beat
> So quickly, waiting for a hand,
>
> A hand that can be clasped no more –
>   Behold me, for I cannot sleep,
>   And like a guilty thing[1] I creep
> At earliest morning to the door.
>
> He is not here; but far away
>   The noise of life begins again,   10
>   And ghastly through the drizzling rain
> On the bald street breaks the blank day.

(Tennyson 1905: 12)

Note

1   *like . . . thing*: the echo of *Hamlet* I i 148 reinforces the haunted-house motif, but with an ironic reversal: the ghost is the survivor rather than the deceased.

47   CHARLOTTE BRONTË, FROM *VILLETTE* (1853), CHAPTER 6

It is unclear how literally autobiographical this episode is. Brontë (1816–55) first went via London to study in 'Villette' (i.e., Brussels) in 1842, accompanied by her sister Emily; she repeated the journey alone the following year. In any case, the passage below has obvious pertinence to recent debates about the nineteenth-century *flâneuse*. It is also thematically significant in a novel whose title proclaims the urban environment to be of central importance. The freedom in which the narrator-agent, Lucy Snowe, here briefly exults proves much less readily attainable in Villette itself, where her dominant experiences are of confinement and surveillance. Near the end, however, Lucy does enjoy a comparable – and decisive – sense of liberation in her remarkable noctambulation amid the crowds and illuminations of fête-night (Ch. 38).

The next day was the first of March, and when I awoke, rose and opened my curtain, I saw the risen sun struggling through fog. Above my head, above the house-tops, co-elevate almost with the clouds, I saw a solemn, orbed mass, dark blue and dim – THE DOME. While I looked, my inner self moved; my spirit shook its always-fettering wings half loose; I had a sudden feeling as if I, who had never yet truly lived, were at last about to taste life: in that morning my soul grew as fast as Jonah's gourd.

'I did well to come,' I said, proceeding to dress with speed and care. 'I like the spirit of this great London which I feel around me. Who but a coward would pass his whole life in hamlets, and for ever abandon his faculties to the eating rust of obscurity?' . . .

Having breakfasted, out I went. Elation and pleasure were in my heart: to walk alone in London seemed of itself an adventure. . . . Prodigious was the amount of life I lived that morning. Finding myself before St Paul's, I went in; I mounted to the dome: I saw thence London, with its river and its bridges and its churches; I saw antique Westminster, and the green Temple Gardens, with sun upon them, and a glad, blue sky of early spring above; and between them and it, not too dense a cloud of haze.

Descending, I went wandering whither chance might lead, in a still ecstacy of freedom and enjoyment; and I got – I know not how – I got into the heart of city life. I saw and felt London at last: I got into the Strand; I went up Cornhill; I mixed with the life passing along; I dared the perils of crossing. To do this, and to do it utterly alone, gave me, perhaps an irrational, but a real pleasure. Since those days, I have seen the West End, the parks, the fine squares; but I love the city far better. The city seems so much more in earnest: its business, its rush, its roar are such serious things, sights, and sounds. The city is getting its living – the West End but enjoying its pleasure. At the West End you may be amused, but in the city you are deeply excited. . . .

(Bell 1855: 43–4)

48 CHARLES DICKENS, FROM *BLEAK HOUSE* (1853), CHAPTER 11

On Dickens, see headnote to doc. 35. The first word of this novel is 'LONDON', and the opening description of its muddy streets on a foggy November day is justly famous; almost as well known are the depictions of the fever-infested slum, Tom-All-Alone's, in Chapters 16 and 46. I have chosen instead an excerpt from the inquest scene which follows the discovery of the corpse of 'Nemo', a destitute, opium-addicted law-writer, in his rented room in Krook's Rag-and-Bottle Shop. In its overall purport the episode is as much part of Dickens' darkening social vision as are the passages referred to above. Yet this piece of Bakhtinian carnivalesque evokes the street-culture of the working-class community of Cook's (in actuality Took's) Court in generous and lively detail, and shows the novelist's comic powers to be undiminished.

By this time the news has got into the court. Groups of its inhabitants assemble to discuss the thing; and the outposts of the army of observation (principally boys) are pushed forward to Mr. Krook's window, which they closely invest. A policeman has already walked up to the room, and walked down to the door, where he stands like a tower, only condescending to see the boys at the base occasionally; but whenever he does see them, they quail and fall back. Mrs. Perkins, who has not been for some weeks on speaking terms with Mrs. Piper, in consequence of an unpleasantness originating in young Perkins having 'fetched' young Piper 'a crack', renews her friendly intercourse on this auspicious occasion. The potboy at the corner, who is a privileged amateur, as possessing official knowledge of life, and having to deal with drunken men occasionally, exchanges confidential communications with the policeman, and has the appearance of an impregnable youth, unassailable by truncheons and unconfinable in station-houses. People talk across the court out of window, and bare-headed scouts come hurrying in from Chancery Lane to know what's the matter. The general feeling seems to be that it's a blessing Mr. Krook warn't made away with first, mingled with a little natural disappointment that he was not. In the midst of this sensation, the beadle arrives.

The beadle, though generally understood in the neighbourhood to be a ridiculous institution, is not without a certain popularity for the moment, if it were only as a man who is going to see the body. The policeman considers him an imbecile civilian, a remnant of the barbarous watchmen-times; but gives him admission, as something that must be borne with until Government shall abolish him. The sensation is heightened, as the tidings spread from mouth to mouth that the beadle is on the ground, and has gone in.

By-and-bye the beadle comes out, once more intensifying the sensation, which has rather languished in the interval. He is understood to be in want of witnesses, for the Inquest to-morrow, who can tell the Coroner and Jury anything whatever respecting the deceased. Is immediately referred to innumerable people who can tell nothing whatever. Is made more imbecile by being constantly informed that Mrs. Green's son 'was a law-writer his-self, and knowed him better than anybody' – which son of Mrs. Green's appears, on inquiry, to be at the present time aboard a vessel bound for China, three months out, but considered accessible by telegraph, on application to the Lords of the Admiralty. Beadle goes into various shops and parlours, examining the inhabitants; always shutting the door first, and by exclusion, delay, and general idiotcy, exasperating the public. Policeman seen to smile to pot-boy. Public loses interest, and undergoes reaction. Taunts the beadle, in shrill youthful voices, with having boiled a boy; choruses fragments of a popular song to that effect, and importing that the boy was made into soup for the workhouse. Policeman at last finds it necessary to support the law, and seize the vocalist; who is released upon the flight of the rest, on condition of his getting out of this then, come! and cutting it – a condition he immediately observes. So the sensation dies off for the time. . . .

Next day the court is all alive – is like a fair, as Mrs. Perkins, more than reconciled to Mrs. Piper, says, in amicable conversation with that excellent woman. The Coroner is to sit in the first-floor room at the Sol's Arms, where the Harmonic Meetings take place twice a-week, and where the chair is filled by a gentleman of professional celebrity, faced by Little Swills, the comic vocalist, who hopes (according to the bill in the window) that his friends will rally round him, and support first-rate talent. The Sol's Arms does a brisk stroke of business all the morning. Even children so require sustaining, under the general excitement, that a pieman who has established himself for the occasion at the corner of the court, says his brandy-balls go off like smoke. What time the beadle, hovering between the door of Mr. Krook's establishment and the door of the Sol's Arms, shows the curiosity in his keeping to a few discreet spirits, and accepts the compliment of a glass of ale or so in return.

At the appointed hour arrives the Coroner, for whom the Jurymen are waiting, and who is received with a salute of skittles from the good dry skittle-ground attached to the Sol's Arms. The Coroner frequents more public-houses than any man alive. The smell of sawdust, beer, tobacco-smoke, and spirits, is inseparable in his vocation from death in its most awful shapes. He is conducted by the beadle and the landlord to the Harmonic Meeting Room, where he puts his hat on the piano, and takes a Windsor-chair at the head of a long table, formed of several short tables put together, and ornamented with glutinous rings in endless involutions, made by pots and glasses. As many of the Jury as can crowd together at the table sit there. The rest get among the spittoons and pipes, or lean against the piano. Over the Coroner's head is a small iron garland, the pendant handle of a bell, which rather gives the Majesty of the Court the appearance of going to be hanged presently.

Call over and swear the Jury! While the ceremony is in progress, sensation is created by the entrance of a chubby little man in a large shirt-collar, with a moist eye, and an inflamed nose, who modestly takes a position near the door as one of the general public, but seems familiar with the room too. A whisper circulates that this is Little Swills. It is considered not unlikely that he will get up an imitation of the Coroner, and make it the principal feature of the Harmonic Meeting in the evening.

(Dickens 1873: 73–4)

49 HERMAN MELVILLE, FROM *ISRAEL POTTER: HIS FIFTY YEARS OF EXILE* (1855), CHAPTER 24

Israel Potter was first published in *Putnam's Magazine* (1854–5). On a visit to London some five years before, Melville (1819–91) wrote in his journal (9 November 1849): 'Went down to the bridges to see the people crowding there. . . . [T]he thought struck me again that a fine thing might be written about a Blue Monday in November London – a city of Dis (Dante's)' (Hayford *et al.* 1989: 14). Potter was a historical figure, an American soldier taken prisoner in the War of Independence and condemned thereby to nearly half a century in and around the country of the enemy, most of it as a poor chair-mender in the London streets. Melville radically transforms his source material, a first-person account of Potter's life published in 1824 (Hayford *et al.* 1982: 286–394); the earlier version contains no parallel to this London Bridge scene, a major contribution to the 'Dantesque London' tradition and an illustration of how the novelist gives his subject mythic status.

It was late on a Monday morning, in November – a Blue Monday – a Fifth of November – Guy Fawkes' Day! – very blue, foggy, doleful and gunpowdery, indeed, as shortly will be seen, – that Israel found himself wedged in among the greatest every-day crowd which grimy London presents to the curious stranger. That hereditary crowd – gulf-stream of humanity – which, for continuous centuries, has never ceased pouring, like an endless shoal of herring, over London Bridge.

On his route from Brentford to Paris, Israel had passed through the capital, but only as a courier. So that now, for the first, he had time to linger and loiter, and lounge – slowly absorb what he saw – meditate himself into boundless amazement. For forty years he never recovered from that surprise – never, till dead, had done with his wondering.

Hung in long, sepulchral arches of stone, the black, besmoked bridge seemed a huge scarf of crape, festooning the river across. Similar funereal festoons spanned it to the west, while eastward, towards the sea, tiers and tiers of jetty colliers lay moored, side by side, fleets of black swans.

The Thames, which far away, among the green fields of Berks, ran clear as a brook, here, polluted by continual vicinity to man, curdled on between rotten wharves, one murky sheet of sewerage. Fretted by the ill-built piers, awhile it crested and hissed, then shot balefully through the Erebus arches, desperate as the lost souls of the harlots, who, every night, took the same plunge. Meantime, here and there, like awaiting hearses, the coal-scows drifted along, poled broadside, pell-mell to the current.

And as that tide in the water swept all craft on, so a like tide seemed hurrying all men, all horses, all vehicles on the land. As ant-hills, the bridge arches crawled with processions of carts, coaches, drays, every sort of wheeled, rumbled thing, the noses of the horses behind touching the backs of the vehicles in advance, all bespattered with ebon mud, ebon mud that stuck like Jews' pitch. At times the mass, receiving some mysterious impulse far in the rear, away among the coiled thoroughfares out of sight, would start forward with a spasmodic surge. It seemed as if some squadron of centaurs, on the thither side of Phlegethon, with charge on charge, was driving tormented humanity, with all its chattels, across.

Whichever way the eye turned, no tree, no speck of any green thing was seen; no more than in smithies. All laborers, of whatsoever sort, were hued like the men in foundries. The black vistas of streets were as the galleries in coal mines; the flagging, as flat tomb-stones minus the consecration of moss; and worn heavily down, by sorrowful tramping, as the vitreous rocks in the cursed Gallipagos, over which the convict tortoises crawl.

As in eclipses, the sun was hidden; the air darkened; the whole dull, dismayed aspect of things, as if some neighboring volcano, belching its premonitory smoke, were about to whelm the great town, as Herculaneum and Pompeii, or the Cities of the Plain. And as they had been upturned in terror towards the mountain, all faces were more or less snowed, or spotted with soot. Nor marble, nor flesh, nor the sad spirit of man, may in this cindery City of Dis abide white. . . .

As retired at length, midway, in a recess of the bridge, Israel surveyed them, various individual aspects all but frighted him. Knowing not who they were; never destined, it may be, to behold them again; one after the other, they drifted by, uninvoked ghosts in Hades. . . .

Arrived, in the end, on the Middlesex side, Israel's heart was prophetically heavy; foreknowing, that being of this race, felicity could never be his lot.

(Hayford *et al.* 1982: 158–60)

50 CHARLES DICKENS, FROM 'A NIGHTLY SCENE IN LONDON', *HOUSEHOLD WORDS* (26 JANUARY 1856)

See Introduction, pp. 12–13. Despite or rather because of its relatively austere style, this is perhaps Dickens' most moving treatment of destitution in the London streets.

On the fifth of last November, I, the Conductor of this journal, accompanied by a friend well known to the public, accidentally strayed into Whitechapel. It was a miserable evening; very dark, very muddy, and raining hard.

There are many woeful sights in that part of London, and it has been well-known to me in most of its aspects for many years. We had forgotten the mud and rain in slowly walking along and looking about us, when we found ourselves, at eight o'clock, before the Workhouse.

Crouched against the wall of the Workhouse, in the dark street, on the muddy pavement-stones, with the rain raining upon them, were five bundles of rags. They were motionless, and had no resemblance to the human form. Five great beehives, covered with rags – five dead bodies taken out of graves, tied neck and heels, and covered with rags – would have looked like those five bundles upon which the rain rained down in the public street.

'What is this!' said my companion. 'What *is* this!'

'Some miserable people shut out of the Casual Ward, I think,' said I.

We had stopped before the five ragged mounds, and were quite rooted to the spot by their horrible appearance. Five awful Sphinxes by the wayside, crying to every passer-by, 'Stop and guess! What is to be the end of a state of society that leaves us here!'

As we stood looking at them, a decent working-man, having the appearance of a stone-mason, touched me on the shoulder.

'This is an awful sight, sir,' said he, 'in a Christian country!'

'God knows it is, my friend,' said I.

'I have often seen it much worse than this, as I have been going home from my work. I have counted fifteen, twenty, five-and-twenty, many a time. It's a shocking thing to see.'

'A shocking thing, indeed,' said I and my companion together. . . .

We went to the ragged bundle nearest to the Workhouse-door, and I touched it. No movement replying, I gently shook it. The rags began to be slowly stirred within, and by little and little a head was unshrouded. The head of a young woman of three or four and twenty, as I should judge; gaunt with want, and foul with dirt; but not naturally ugly.

'Tell us,' said I, stooping down. 'Why are you lying here?'

'Because I can't get into the Workhouse.'

She spoke in a faint dull way, and had no curiosity or interest left. She looked dreamily at the black sky and the falling rain, but never looked at me or my companion.

'Were you here last night?'

'Yes. All last night. And the night afore too.'

'Do you know any of these others?'

'I know her next but one. She was here last night, and she told me she come out of Essex. I don't know no more of her.'

'You were here all last night, but you have not been here all day?'

'No. Not all day.'

'Where have you been all day?'

'About the streets.'

'What have you had to eat?'

'Nothing.'

'Come!' said I. 'Think a little. You are tired and have been asleep, and don't quite consider what you are saying to us. You have had something to eat to-day. Come! Think of it!'

'No I haven't. Nothing but such bits as I could pick up about the market. *Why, look at me!*'

She bared her neck, and I covered it up again.

'If you had a shilling to get some supper and a lodging, should you know where to get it?'

'Yes. I could do that.'

'For God's sake get it then!'

I put the money into her hand, and she feebly rose up and went away. She never thanked me, never looked at me – melted away into the miserable night, in the strangest manner I ever saw. I have seen many strange things, but not one that has left a deeper impression on my memory than the dull impassive way in which that worn-out heap of misery took that piece of money, and was lost.

One by one I spoke to all the five. In every one, interest and curiosity were as extinct as in the first. They were all dull and languid. No one made any sort of profession or complaint; no one cared to look at me; no one thanked me. When I came to the third, I suppose she saw that my companion and I glanced, with a new horror upon us, at the two last, who had dropped against each other in their sleep, and were lying like broken images. She said, she believed they were young sisters. These were the only words that were originated among the five.

And now let me close this terrible account with a redeeming and beautiful trait of the poorest of the poor. When we came out of the Workhouse, we had gone across the road to a public house, finding ourselves without silver, to get change for a sovereign. I held the money in my hand while I was speaking to the five apparitions. Our being so engaged, attracted the attention of many people of the very poor sort usual to that place; as we leaned over the mounds of rags, they eagerly leaned over us to see and hear; what I had in my hand, and what I said, and what I did, must have been plain to nearly all the concourse. When the last of the five had got up and faded away, the spectators opened to let us pass; and not one of them, by word, or look, or gesture, begged of us. Many of the observant faces were quick enough to know that it would have been a relief to us to have got rid of the rest of the money with any hope of doing good with it. But, there was a feeling among them all, that their necessities were not to be placed by the side of such a spectacle; and they opened a way for us in profound silence, and let us go. . . .

I know that the unreasonable disciples of a reasonable school, demented disciples who push arithmetic and political economy beyond all bounds of sense (not to speak of such a weakness as humanity), and hold them to be all-sufficient for every case, can easily prove that such things ought to be, and that no man has any business to mind them. Without disparaging those indispensable sciences in their sanity, I utterly renounce and abominate them in their insanity; and I address people with a respect for the spirit of the New Testament, who do mind such things, and who think them infamous in our streets.

(Dickens 1914: 572–6)

51   CHARLES MANBY SMITH, FROM 'LAGSMANBURY', *THE LITTLE WORLD OF LONDON* (1857)

Most of what is known about the life of Smith (1804–80) is derived from his autobiographical *The Working Man's Way in the World* (1853), which deals mainly with his experiences as a journeyman printer, first in Bristol and later in Paris and London. *The Little World of London*, his second book of essays on lowish life and culture, includes well-informed pieces on, for example, the distribution of books and periodicals from Paternoster Row, and the production of street-literature in Seven Dials. 'Lagsmanbury' illustrates the common Victorian practice in urban-topographical journalism of thinly veiling the identity of a street or precinct, especially a disreputable one, under an emblematic name. Lagsmanbury is actually Bedfordbury, dismissed by Sala (1971 [1859]: 164) as 'a devious, slimy little reptile of a place', which came out on to New Street between Leicester Square and Covent Garden.

Like a rotten core beneath the bloom of ripe fruit – like a treacherous and villanous heart under a hypocritical aspect – like anything and everything that is evil and bad, yet clings to the semblance of decency and goodness – is Lagsmanbury. . . . You shall pass a hundred times within a few paces of the boundaries of the Lagsman's domain without discovering it or suspecting its existence – for it lies between two well-frequented thoroughfares of respectable and official character, and can be entered through either only by the narrow approach of a covered-way. . . .

Three or four acres are probably the utmost extent of the whole area, and this is traversed from north to south by a narrow winding lane, at least twice the length of the distance, as the crow flies, between its termini: like a long snake in a short bottle, it has to double upon itself to keep within its bounds. The sinuous course of the lane saves it from being used as a short cut by pedestrians, and thus helps to keep the company within select; another cause conducing to the same result is the fact that Lags Lane is rarely passable to people of the outer world, unless at an early hour. From twenty to thirty small courts and *impasses* disembogue into it, and of whatever is ejected and rejected from them all it is necessarily the receptacle, gathering its deposits the whole day long. . . .

[T]he resident population of Lagsmanbury at the present moment consists of a low class of labourers, chiefly Irish, who get an honest living by the work of their hands, and a predatory class, still lower, who never work, but live by the exercise of their wits in the prosecution of any artifice or imposture – or, their wits failing them, by any species of depredation they can find or make an opportunity to commit. The contact of these two classes is, of course, the last thing that is desirable; but how it is to be avoided is not plain. Among the Lagsmen, what is noticeable is the determination of those who live by their honest labour, and against whom no suspicion rests, to keep themselves and their families distinct and separate from their contaminated or suspected neighbours. To do this as effectually as may be, they have taken possession of certain of the entire courts, into which they admit only those who can give a satisfactory account of themselves – and have surrendered other quarters as entirely to those who have no such account to give. . . .

The migratory class of vagabonds who honour Lagsmanbury with their presence at irregular and uncertain intervals embraces the whole catalogue of poverty-stricken professional nomads that are seen in London streets. A good proportion of these are men who travel with 'properties' of some kind or other, and for whom the accommodation of the common cheap lodging-houses and 'kens' would not suffice. There are the acrobats and conjurors, with their gymnastic apparatus and juggling paraphernalia, their big drums, long swords, golden balls, daggers, tinsel robes, the lamplighter's ladder, and the little donkey. . . . There are the dog-leaders and dancers with their melancholy troops. There are the wandering bands of boy-Germans, with their burden of battered brass. There is the player on the bells, whose apparatus runs upon wheels, and has to be stabled like a beast. There are the grinders of monster organs as big as caravans. There are the Punch and Judy men with their travelling stages. . . . There is the travelling rat-catcher and rat-fighter, with his traps and ferrets, and dogs and whiskered menageries. There is . . . the poor Jew picture-dealer, with his collection of moonlights and Dutch metal; the belated hawker of plants, shrubs, and flowers, 'all a-growing and a-blowing'; the omnium stall-keeper, with his sta-tionary stage or rambling hand-cart; and the travelling razor-grinder, with his rickety equipage. . . .

'Shinders's' is a pretty extensive caravanserai, occupying the whole area and buildings of Allsaints Court. It is said, with what truth we know not, that Shinders himself is a retired bear-leader, who formerly piped a bruin through every county in England, but who retired, when bears went out of fashion, into Lagsmanbury, and set about gaining a living by providing for others that accommodation he had often stood in need of himself. Be this as it may, he has long enjoyed the reputation of being the father of this peculiar class, and under the endearing cognomen of Daddy Shinders, is known far and wide. . . .

The sun may be shining and scorching aloft ever so hot, but the air of All-saints is cool and moist, and fragrant with the odour of damp linen, combining unmistakably with the reek of tobacco and the flavour of 'entire'. The flagstones of the court exude a soapy ooze, which glistens in a deep umbrageous gloom, through which the fiery sun casts not a single ray. The reason is that at this season of the year it is always washing-day at Shinders's, and the trophies of the tub are hanging out aloft upon innumerable lines stretched across from house to house, from poles thrust forth from the windows, and from stays and tight-ropes rigged from the roofs and chimneys on both sides of the way.

(Smith 1857: 135–6, 139–41)

52 NATHANIEL HAWTHORNE, FROM *THE ENGLISH NOTEBOOKS* (6 AND 8 DECEMBER 1857)

When Hawthorne (1804–64) took up the post of American Consul in Liverpool in 1853, he had never before been abroad. The journal he kept during his four years in Britain contains numerous accounts of urban exploration, Hawthorne having become an inveterate street-wanderer in both Liverpool and London, susceptible to the modern city's 'attraction of repulsion', as these entries show. While their twin motifs of mud and fog make them reminiscent of the celebrated opening to Dickens' *Bleak House*, touches of other-worldly vision confirm a closer affinity with Hawthorne's compatriot, admirer and fellow-allegorist, Melville (see doc. 49).

I have walked the streets a great deal in the dull November days, and always take a certain pleasure in being in the midst of human life – as closely encompassed by it as it is possible to be, anywhere in this world; and, in that way of viewing it, there is a dull and sombre enjoyment always to be had in Holborn, Fleet Street, Cheapside, and the other thronged parts of London. It is human life; it is this material world; it is a grim and heavy reality. I have never had the same sense of being surrounded by materialisms, and hemmed in with the grossness of this earthly life, anywhere else; these broad, thronged streets are so evidently the veins and arteries of an enormous city. London is evidenced in every one of them, just as a Megatherium is in each of its separate bones, even if they be small ones. Thus I never fail of a sort of self-congratulation in finding myself, for instance, passing along Ludgate Hill; but, in spite of this, it is really an ungladdened life, to wander through these huge, thronged ways, over a pavement foul with mud, ground into it by a million of footsteps; jostling against people who do not seem to be individuals but all one mass, so homogeneous is the street-walking aspect of them; the roar of vehicles pervading me, wearisome cabs and omnibuses; everywhere, the dingy brick edifices heaving themselves up, and shutting out all but a strip of sullen cloud that serves London for a sky; – in short, a general impression of grime and sordidness, and, at this season, always a fog scattered along a vista of streets, sometimes so densely as almost to spiritualize the materialism and make the scene resemble the other world of worldly people, gross even in ghostliness. . . .

I went home by way of Holborn; and the fog was denser than ever – very black, indeed, more like a distillation of mud than anything else; the ghost of mud, the spiritualized medium of departed mud, through which the departed citizens of London probably tread in the Hades whither they are translated. So heavy was the gloom, that gas was lighted in all the shop-windows; and the little charcoal furnaces of the women and boys roasting chestnuts threw a ruddy misty glow around them. And yet I liked it. This fog seems an atmosphere proper to huge, grimy London; as proper as that light, neither of the sun nor moon, is to the New Jerusalem. . . .

(Hawthorne 1941: 607, 616)

53 'ANOTHER UNFORTUNATE', FROM LETTER TO *THE TIMES* (24 FEBRUARY 1858)

The late 1850s saw a marked increase in public discussion of prostitution. There were several investigative studies, Acton's (1857) being the most notable, and these appeared in the context of demands for draconian measures to control the insanitary effects of the Great Social Evil (resulting in the Contagious Diseases Act of 1864) and to reduce the massed ranks of its practitioners (including children) in the streets of central London, especially around the Haymarket (see doc. 55). Another Unfortunate was responding to a fellow-prostitute who, in two letters signed 'One More Unfortunate' (*Times*, 4 and 11 February 1858), had described herself as a well-brought-up ex-governess deeply ashamed of her fallen condition. Another Unfortunate's remarkable '*je ne regrette rien*' retort, à la Mrs Warren, prompted a *Times* leader the next day (25 February, p. 12) to declare: 'We have never been very hopeful upon the subject, but what little expectation one might have entertained was sadly dashed by [this] letter. . . . This is certainly a new view of the Great Social Evil.' For this leader-writer (and his readers) the disturbing novelty of Another Unfortunate's views probably lay as much in their radical social criticism as in their moral unorthodoxy; *The Times* deserves credit for having published them at such great length (greater than I have space to reproduce in full).

Sir, – Another 'Unfortunate', but of a class entirely different from the one who has already instructed the public in your columns, presumes to address you.

I am a stranger to all the fine sentiments which still linger in the bosom of your correspondent. I have none of those youthful recollections which, contrasting her early days with her present life aggravate the misery of the latter. My parents did not give any education; they did not instil into my mind virtuous precepts nor set me a good example. . . .

As long as they lived I looked up to them as my parents. I assisted them in their poverty, and made them comfortable. They looked on me and I on them with pride, for I was proud to be able to minister to their wants; and as for shame, although they knew perfectly well the means by which I obtained money, I do assure you, Sir, that by them, as by myself, my success was regarded as the reward of a proper ambition, and was a source of real pleasure and gratification. . . .

My father's most profitable occupation was brickmaking. . . . My mother worked with him in the brickfield, and so did I and a progeny of brothers and sisters. . . . We all slept in the same room. There were few privacies, few family secrets in our house. . . .

Our neighbourhood furnished many subjects to the treadmill, the hulks, and the colonies, and some to the gallows. We lived with the fear of these things, and not with the fear of God before our eyes.

I was a very pretty child, and had a sweet voice; of course I used to sing. Most London boys and girls of the lower classes sing. 'My face is my fortune, kind Sir, she said' was the ditty on which I bestowed most pains, and my father and mother would wink knowingly as I sang it. . . .

I was a fine, robust, healthy girl, 13 years of age. I had larked with the boys of my own age. I had huddled with them, boys and girls together, all night long in our common haunts. I had seen much and heard abundantly of the mysteries of the sexes. To me such things had been matters of common sight and common talk. For some time I had trembled and coquetted on the verge of a strong curiosity, and a natural desire, and without a particle of affection, scarce a partiality. I lost – what? not my virtue, for I never had any. . . .

Opportunity was not long wanting to put my newly acquired knowledge to profitable use. In the commencement of my fifteenth year one of our beribanded visitors took me off, and introduced me to the great world, and thus commenced my career as what you better classes call a prostitute. I cannot say that I felt any other shame than the bashfulness of a noviciate introduced to strange society. . . .

I speak for others as well as for myself, for the very great majority, nearly all of the real undisguised prostitutes in London, spring from my class, and are made by and under pretty much such conditions of life as I have narrated, and particularly by untutored and unrestrained intercourse of the sexes in early life. We come from the dregs of society, as our so-called betters term it. What business has society to have dregs – such dregs as we? You railers of the Society for the Suppression of Vice, you the pious, the moral, the respectable, as you call yourselves, who stand on your smooth and pleasant side of the great gulf you have dug and keep between yourselves and the dregs, why don't you bridge it over, or fill it up, and by some humane and generous process absorb us into your leavened mass, until we become interpenetrated with goodness like yourselves? Why stand on your eminence shouting that we should be ashamed of ourselves? What have we to be ashamed of, we who do not know what shame is – the shame you mean? . . .

Hurling big figures at us, it is said that there are 80,000 of us in London alone – which is a monstrous falsehood – and of this 80,000, poor hard-working sewing girls, sewing women, are numbered in by thousands and called indiscriminately prostitutes; writing, preaching, speechifying, that they have lost their virtue too.

It is a cruel calumny to call them in mass prostitutes; and, as for their virtue, they lose it as one loses his watch who is robbed by the highway thief. Their virtue is the watch, and society is the thief. These poor women toiling on starvation wages, while penury, misery, and famine clutch them by the throat and say, 'Render up your body or die.' . . .

(*The Times*, 24 February 1858: 12)

54   GEORGE AUGUSTUS SALA, FROM *TWICE ROUND THE CLOCK* (1859)

Sala (1828–95) was a veritable monarch of 'New Grub Street', disavowing any claims to literary distinction but proud of his extraordinarily high levels of productivity and remuneration as a journalist. Born in London, he grew up with little formal schooling in theatrical bohemia, the son of a widowed singer and actress. After editing *Chat*, a half-penny weekly, at the age of 20, he became a Dickens protégé on the staff of *Household Words*, eventually graduating to leader-writing on the *Daily Telegraph* (3,000 words a day). With *Twice Round the Clock*, first serialised in *The Welcome Guest*, Sala clinched recognition as a specialist in journalistic *flânerie*. He himself stressed 'that the idea of thus chronicling, hour by hour, the shifting panorama of London life was not original' (Sala 1895: I, 392), and in the Preface acknowledged a direct debt to *Low-Life* (see doc. 15). On the other hand, as this extract shows, Sala was anxious *not* to acknowledge a stronger taste for low life than mid-Victorian propriety and the audience of 'a magazine of recreative reading for all' (*The Welcome Guest*'s subtitle) might approve. The Victoria Theatre, already popularly known as the Old Vic by that time, was indeed a place of some notoriety, not only with regard to the social character of its clientele but to dangerous levels of over-crowding: in December 1858, just after Sala's account of 'the great gulf stream of this human ocean' pouring out first appeared, a false alarm of fire prompted a stampede in which many died (Thornbury & Walford 1873–8: VI, 394).

Here we are, at the corner of New Cut. It is Nine o'Clock precisely . . . , and while the half-price is pouring into the Victoria Theatre, the whole price . . . is pouring out with equal and continuous persistence, and are deluging the

New Cut. . . . There are not many gradations of rank among the frequenters of the Victoria Theatre. Many of the occupants of the boxes sat last night in the pit, and will sit tomorrow in the gallery, according to the fluctuations of their finances. . . . And the same equality and fraternity are manifest when the audience pour forth at half-price to take their beer. . . . [T]he great gulf stream of this human ocean flows towards a gigantic 'public' opposite the Victoria, . . . which continually drives a roaring trade.

I wish that I had a more savoury locality to take you to than the New Cut. I acknowledge frankly that I don't like it. We have visited many queer places in London together, of which, it may be, the fashionables of the West End have never heard; but they all had some out-of-the-way scraps of Bohemianism to recommend them. I can't say the same for the New Cut. It isn't picturesque, it isn't quaint, it isn't curious. It has not even the questionable merit of being old. It is simply Low. It is sordid, squalid, and, the truth must out, disreputable. The broad thoroughfare which, bordered with fitting houses, would make one of the handsomest streets in London, is gorged with vile, rotten tenements, occupied by merchants who oft-times pursue the very contrary to innocent callings. Everything is second-hand, except the leviathan gin-shops, which are ghastly in their newness and richness of decoration. The broad pavement presents a mixture of Vanity Fair and Rag Fair. It is the paradise of the lowest of costermongers, and often the saturnalia of the most emerited thieves. Women appear there in their most unlovely aspect: brazen, slovenly, dishevelled, brawling, muddled with beer or fractious with gin. The howling of beaten children and kicked dogs, the yells of ballad-singers, 'death and fire-hunters', and reciters of sham murders and elopements; the bawling recitations of professional denunciators of the Queen, the Royal family and the ministry; the monotonous *jödels* of the itinerant hucksters; the fumes of the vilest tobacco, of stale corduroy suits, of oilskin caps, of mildewed umbrellas, of decaying vegetables, of escaping (and frequently surreptitiously tapped) gas, of deceased cats, of ancient fish, of cagmag meat, of dubious mutton pies, and of unwashed, soddened, unkempt humanity: all these make the night hideous and the heart sick. The New Cut is one of the most unpleasant samples of London you could offer to a foreigner. . . . Here, there is mixed with the poverty a flaunting, idle, vagabond, beggarly-fine don't-care-a-centishness. Burkins in hold in Pentonville for his sins assures the chaplain that the wickedness of the New Cut is due solely to the proximity of the 'Wictoriar Theayter, that 'aunt of disypashion and the wust of karackters.' For my part, I think that if there were no such safety-valve as a theatre for the inhabitants of the 'Cut', it would become a mere Devil's Acre, a Cour des Miracles,[1] a modern edition of the Whitefriars Alsatia;[2] and that the Cutites would fall to plundering, quarrelling and fighting, through sheer *ennui*. It is horrible, dreadful, we know, to have such a place; but then consider – the population of London is fast advancing towards three millions, and the wicked people must live somewhere – under a strictly constitutional government. There is a despot, now, over the water,[3] who would make very short work of the New Cut. He would see, at a glance, the capacities of the place; in the twinkling of a decree the rotten tenements would be doomed to destruction; houses and shops like palaces would line the thoroughfare; trees would be planted along the pavement; and the Boulevard de Lambeth would be one of the stateliest avenues in the metropolis. But Britons never will be slaves, and we must submit to thorns (known as 'vested interests') in the constitutional rose, and pay somewhat dear for our liberty as well as for our whistle.

(Sala 1971: 272–5)

Notes

1 *Cour des Miracles*: lawless area in the medieval Paris of Hugo's *Notre-Dame de Paris* (1831), II, 6.
2 *Whitefriars Alsatia*: for centuries a sanctuary for debtors and frequently riotous criminals adjacent to the Temple, the legal quarter of central London.
3 *There . . . water*: Under Napoleon III, Baron Haussmann's radical reconstruction of Paris in the 1850s and 1860s included the building of wide boulevards and much slum clearance.

55 FYODOR DOSTOYEVSKY, FROM *WINTER NOTES ON SUMMER IMPRESSIONS* (1863)

Dostoyevsky (1821–81) travelled through Western Europe in the summer of 1862, staying longest in Paris and spending just one week in London, where he visited the exiled radical, Alexander Herzen. This account was first published as a series of articles in his own review, *Vremya* ('Time'). Although most of *Summer Impressions* is about France, the intense alienation Dostoyevsky experienced in the West is nowhere more strongly articulated than in the chapter on London called 'Baal' (the Old Testament's false god of the flesh). While partly influenced by Herzen, who was himself to write powerfully about 'wandering lonely about London' (Herzen 1968: 431), these pages sketch out themes and ideas regarding materialistic urban society and its victims which were to resonate in Dostoyevsky's own later fictional masterpieces.

One . . . night – it was getting on for two o'clock in the morning – I lost my way and for a long time trudged the streets in the midst of a vast crowd of gloomy people, asking my way almost by gestures, because I do not know a word of English. I found my way, but the impression of what I had seen tormented me for three days afterwards. The populace is much the same anywhere, but there all was so vast, so vivid that you almost physically felt things which up till then you had only imagined. In London you no longer see the populace. Instead, you see a loss of sensibility, systematic, resigned and encouraged. And you feel, as you look at all those social pariahs that it will be a long time before the prophecy is fulfilled for them. . . .

Anyone who has ever visited London must have been at least once in the Haymarket at night. It is a district in certain streets of which prostitutes swarm by night in their thousands. Streets are lit by jets of gas – something completely unknown in our country. At every step you come across magnificent public houses, all mirrors and gilt. They serve as meeting places as well as shelters. It is a terrifying experience to find oneself in that crowd. And what an odd amalgam it is. You will find old women there and beautiful women at the sight of whom you stop in amazement. There are no women in the world as beautiful as the English.

The streets can hardly accommodate the dense, seething crowd. The mob has not enough room on the pavements and swamps the whole street. All this mass of humanity craves for booty and hurls itself at the first comer with shameless cynicism. Glistening, expensive clothes and semi-rags and sharp differences in age – they are all there. A drunken tramp shuffling along in this terrible crowd is jostled by the rich and titled. You hear curses, quarrels, solicitations and the quiet, whispered invitation of some still bashful beauty. . . .

In the Haymarket I noticed mothers who brought their little daughters to make them ply that same trade. Little girls aged about twelve seize you by the arm and beg you to come with them. I remember once amidst the crowd of people in the street I saw a little girl not older than six, all in rags, dirty, barefoot and hollow-cheeked; she had been severely beaten and her body, which showed through the rags, was covered with bruises. She was walking along, as if oblivious of everybody and everything, in no hurry to get anywhere and, Heaven knows why, loafing about in that crowd; perhaps she was hungry. Nobody was paying any attention to her. But what struck me most was the look of such distress, such hopeless despair on her face that to see that tiny bit of humanity already bearing the imprint of all that evil and despair was somehow unnatural and terribly painful. She kept on shaking her tousled head as if arguing about something, gesticulated and spread her little hands and then suddenly clasped them together and pressed them to her little bare breast. I went back and gave her sixpence. She took the small silver coin, gave me a wild look full of frightened surprise, and suddenly ran off as fast as her legs could carry her, as if afraid that I should take the money away from her. Jolly scenes, altogether. . . .

(Dostoyevsky 1955: 61–6)

56 A. J. MUNBY, FROM 'DIARIES' (1863–4)

Nine volumes of poetry by Munby (1828–1910) were published in his lifetime, but it was not until 1972 that even a sampling of his major literary enterprise, the private diaries compiled over nearly forty years and running to millions of words, appeared in Hudson's fine selection-cum-biography. This has given Munby a somewhat equivocal celebrity as the 'man of two worlds': a civil servant in the Ecclesiastical Commission and Latin teacher at the Working Men's College who numbered such cultural luminaries as Ruskin, Rossetti, F. D. Maurice, Browning and Swinburne among his friends and acquaintances; and the secret husband of a servant girl, pursuing an obsessive interest in working women in general. The Mayhew-like scale and value of the diary record regarding this latter concern is now gaining appreciation. But there has been much less attention paid to Munby's equally remarkable powers in describing public events, especially crowd scenes as in the first two passages below (see Introduction, pp. 10–11, and plates 12 and 13). Passage [c] invites comparison with document 50.

[a] *10 March [1863]*. . . . We got to town about nine, & saw the brown sky over London lit up with reflected light. I buttoned up my coat and plunged into the crowd at London Bridge. The bridge itself, with its parapets topped with tripods of burning incense and statues with rings of light round the pedestals and tall pennons that waved dimly above, was very beautiful: a lane of brilliant fantastic colour, and full of eager struggling human beings; and on either side, far down, the dark water of the Thames, its ripples faintly gleaming here & there, but still and solemn everywhere. Life, bustling and blazing for awhile; and the great mute eternity lying unheeded below it.

The dome of Paul's too was visible in the night, with a lurid zone of red lights across it; and from the top of the Monument a stream of electric flame shot across the sky before us. The whole effect was not unlike one of Martin's wildest pictures. I went on with the stream, under the illuminated triumphal arch at the north end of the bridge; up to the Mansion House, which with the Bank & Exchange made a splendid group, the façade of each being traced in light; along the midst of Cheapside, S. Paul's Churchyard, and Ludgate Hill. Almost every house was lighted up: the streets were as bright as day: pavement & roadway were packed with a dense mass of people, slowly but freely moving on foot between two rows of helpless and motionless vehicles. Men of all classes, and women of the lower and lower middle, made up the crowd; and more women than men: but the ladies – luckless beings – were rooted in omnibus & carriage.

On Ludgate Hill, a young woman, bonnetless & dishevelled, was carried past me on a stretcher upon men's shoulders. Drunk, I thought: *dead*, it afterwards proved; for she was one of the six poor creatures who were crushed to death near that very spot and time. A minute or two after, I was in the middle of the press that killed them. A tremendous throng, at the four streets; two broad *torrents* of people, meeting and striving among a confused mass of carriages.

Plate 11 'London Bridge on the Night of the Marriage of the Prince and Princess of Wales', W. Holman Hunt, 1863–6. Reprinted by permission of the Ashmolean Museum, Oxford.

I saw no one hurt; but the crush was severe and increasing, and I had only one free arm, having my knapsack with me; so with much difficulty I retreated, and went round by the passages into the quieter stream that filled Fleet Street; and so to Temple Bar, which stood up against the dark, one sheet of dazzling gold tissue and of crimson.

It had taken me about an hour and a half to reach it: writhing and squeezing, one of many atoms, through a crowd that was at every point dense enough to hide every stone of the street from one who had seen it above. And such a crowd extended also to Paddington, to Brompton, to Camberwell: two millions and a half of souls, they say. Yet a more orderly quiet & goodnatured assemblage I never saw: even in that fierce crush, there was no rioting nor illwords nor drinking. . . .

[b] *11 April [1864]*. . . . All the afternoon, the neighbourhood of Whitehall was in a bustle; bells ringing, music playing, everyone getting ready to witness the entry of Garibaldi into London. . . .

By four o'clock the crowd was impassably dense as far as one could see, from Trafalgar Square to Parliament Street. It was a crowd composed mainly of the lowest classes; a very shabby and foul smelling crowd; and the women of it, young and old, were painfully ugly and dirty & tawdry: indeed in all the

Plate 12 'Garibaldi's Visit to London: Arrival at Charing Cross',
Illustrated London News, 1864.

evening I only saw two who could be looked at without pity or disgust; and
they were stout yellow haired lasses, costergirls, with bare heads and broad
shoulders; in short cotton frocks, and picturesque red & yellow kerchiefs
across the bosom.

Yet for three hours, from four till seven – for I stood on the steps of a
tobacconist's shop all that time – this coarse mob behaved with the utmost
good humour and peacefulness, though their patience must have been taxed
to the utmost. . . . The procession, such as it was, came in sight at 5, and went
on continuously till 5.50. Then it suddenly ended, *re infectâ*[1] . . . . Then at last
the rest of the procession struggled up: more banners of Odd Fellows and
the like, more carriages and cabs, filled with working men and foreigners,
who looked all unused to the luxury of riding; more trades unions on foot,
from all parts of London; a young lady on horseback (who was she?) riding
calmly alone; a small bodyguard of Garibaldians; and the General himself,
seated on the box of a barouche, in brown wideawake[2] and what looked like
a blue blouse. The excitement had been rapidly rising, and now, when this
supreme moment came, it resulted in such a scene as can hardly be witnessed
twice in a lifetime. That vast multitude rose as one man from their level attitude of expectation: they leapt into the air, they waved their arms and hats
aloft, they surged & struggled round the carriage, they shouted with a mighty
shout of enthusiasm that took one's breath away to hear it: and above them

149

on both sides thousands of white kerchiefs were waving from every window and housetop.

There was an ardour and a sort of deep pathetic force about this sound that distinguished it plainly from the shouts of simple welcome which I heard given last year to the Princess Alexandra. . . .

This of today has been the greatest demonstration by far that I have beheld or, probably, shall behold. No soldier was there, no official person: no King nor government nor public body got it up or managed it: it was devised & carried out spontaneously by men and women simply as such; and they often of the lowest grade. It was the work of the rough but lawabiding English people, penetrated with admiration for something divine, and expressing themselves as usual in a clumsy earnest orderly way. Contemptible as a pageant, it is invaluable for its political and moral significance, and for the good that it reveals in the makers of it, and for the good they themselves receive by reverencing a guileless person. . . .

[c] *15 July [1864]*. . . . Walking through S. James's Park about 4 p. m., I found the open spaces of sward on either side the path thickly dotted over with strange dark objects. They were human beings; ragged men & ragged women; lying prone & motionless, not as those who lie down for rest & enjoyment, but as creatures worn out and listless. A park keeper came up: who are these? I asked. 'They are men out of work,' said he, 'and unfortunate girls; servant girls, many of them, what has been out of place and took to the streets, till they've sunk so low that they can't get a living by prostitution. It's like this every day, till winter comes; and then what they do *I* don't know. They come as soon as the gate opens; always the same faces: they bring broken victuals with 'em, or else goes to the soup kitchen in Vinegar (?) Yard; and except for that, they lie about here all day. The girls herd with the men, whether they know 'em or not: and at night they leave, and sleep on steps or anywhere, and comes back next morning. It's a disgrace, Sir (said he), to go on in a city like this; and foreigners to see it, too! Why Sir, these unfortunates are all over the place: the ground (he added with a gesture of disgust) is *lousy* with them.' I looked and looked; it was Dante and Virgil gazing on the damned; and still they did not move. The men were more or less tattered, but their dress was working dress, & so did not seem out of place. But the girls were clothed in what had once been finery: filthy draggled muslins; thin remnants of gay shawls, all rent and gaping; crushed and greasy bonnets of fashionable shape, with sprigs of torn flowers, bits of faded velvet, hanging from them. Their hands and faces were dirty & weatherstained; and they lay, *not* (as far as I saw) herding with the men, but singly or in little groups; sprawling about the grass in attitudes ungainly, and unfeminine, and bestial. . . . Every

pose expressed an absolute degradation and despair: and the silence & dead-
ness of the prostrate crowd was appalling. I counted these miserable lazza-
roni, as I went along; and on one side only of the path ... there were *one
hundred and five* of them. 105 forlorn and foetid outcasts – women, many of
them – grovelling on the sward, in the bright sunshine of a July afternoon,
with Carlton House Terrace and Westminster Abbey looking down at them,
and infinite welldrest citizens passing by on the other side. ...

(Munby 1993: 18, 29–33; 24, 85–98; 26, 42–7)

Notes

1   *re infectâ*: with the business incomplete.
2   *wideawake*: wide-brimmed felt hat.

57   ROBERT BUCHANAN, FROM 'NELL' (1866)

Now best remembered for his critical assault on the Pre-Raphaelites in 'The Fleshly
School of Poetry' (*Contemporary Review*, 1871), Buchanan (1841–1901) wrote numerous poems, novels and plays as well as essays. The son of a Glaswegian tailor who
ran several socialist journals, he came to London in 1860 ambitious to produce poetry
with a contemporary resonance and accessible style; these ambitions clearly inform
London Poems, the collection in which this dramatic monologue appeared. The titular
speaker describes to Nan, a neighbour in 'Camden Court', her experiences and feelings prior to her partner's execution for murder, presumably at Newgate. Buchanan
does not here attempt to heighten authenticity with dialectal speech (a feature of his
poems with a Scottish setting), and the effect of plain diction is sometimes mere flat-
ness. On the other hand, Nell's nocturnal trudge through the city streets is documented with a topographical specificity which is much rarer in poetry than in prose
fiction of the period, where the hybrid form of realistic melodrama was well established
(see, for example, doc. 41).

VI

... That night before he died,
I didn't cry – my heart was hard and dried;
But when the clocks went 'one', I took my shawl
   To cover up my face, and stole away,
And walked along the moonlight streets, where all
   Looked cold and still and grey, –
Only the lamps o' London here and there
   Scattered a dismal gleaning;
And on I went, and stood in Leicester Square,
   Just like a woman dreaming: 10
But just as 'three' was sounded close at hand,
   I started and turned east, before I knew, –
Then down Saint Martin's Lane, along the Strand,

And through the toll-gate, on to Waterloo.
How I remember all I saw, although
   'Twas only like a dream! –
The long still lines o' lights, the chilly gleam
   Of moonshine on the deep black stream below;
While far, far away, along the sky
   Streaks soft as silver ran,   20
And the pale moon looked paler up on high,
   And little sounds in far-off streets began!
Well, I stood, and waited, and looked down,
And thought how sweet 'twould be to drop and drown,
Some men and lads went by,
   And I turned round, and gazed, and watched 'em go,
Then felt that they were going to see him die,
   And drew my shawl more tight, and followed slow.
How clear I feel it still!
   The streets grew light, but rain began to fall;   30
I stopped and had some coffee at a stall,
   Because I felt so chill;
A cock crew somewhere, and it seemed a call
   To wake the folk who kill!
The man who sold the coffee stared at me!
I must have been a sorry sight to see!
   More people passed – a country cart with hay
Stopped close beside the stall, – and two or three
   Talked about *it*! I moaned, and crept away!

VII

Ay, nearer, nearer to the dreadful place,   40
   All in the falling rain,
I went, and kept my shawl upon my face,
   And felt no grief or pain –
Only the wet that soaked me through and through
   Seemed cold and sweet and pleasant to the touch –
It made the streets more drear and silent, too,
   And kept away the light I feared so much.
Slow, slow the wet streets filled, and all were going,
   Laughing and chatting, the same way,
And greyer, sadder, lighter, it was growing,   50
   Though still the rain fell fast and darkened day!
Nan! – every pulse was burning – I could feel

My heart was made o' steel –
As, crossing Ludgate Hill, where many stirred,
   I saw Saint Paul's great clock and heard it chime,
And hadn't power to count the strokes I heard,
   But strained my eyes and saw it was not time;
Ah! then I felt I dared not creep more near,
   But went into a lane off Ludgate Hill,
And sitting on a doorstep, I could hear   60
   The people gathering still!
And still the rain was falling, falling,
   And deadening the hum I heard from *there*;
And wet and stiff, I heard the people calling,
   And watched the rain-drops glistening down my hair,
My elbows on my knees, my fingers dead, –
My shawl thrown off, now none could see, – my head
   Dripping and wild and bare.
I heard the murmur of a crowd of men,
   And next, a hammering sound I knew full well,   70
For something gripped me round the heart! – and then
   There came the solemn tolling of a bell!
O Lord! O Lord! how could I sit close by
And neither scream nor cry?
As if I had been stone, all hard and cold,
   But listening, listening, listening, still and dumb,
While the folk murmured, and the death-bell tolled,
   And the day brightened, and his time had come. . . .
. . . . Till – Nan! – all else was silent, but the knell
Of the slow bell!   80
And I could only wait, and wait, and wait,
   And what I waited for I couldn't tell, –
At last there came a groaning deep and great –
Saint Paul's struck 'eight' –
   I screamed, and seemed to turn to fire, and fell!

                      (Buchanan 1866: 156–9)

58   MATTHEW ARNOLD, 'WEST LONDON' (1867)

This is one of a pair of sonnets – the other being 'East London' – which Arnold
(1822–88) wrote in or around 1863. They have been dismissed as formulaic and conventional (Stange 1973: II, 485; Thesing 1982: 76); yet, among the handful of Arnold
poems with an urban theme or setting, 'West London' is the only one presenting a day-
time (and precisely located) street-scene, and it is this very quotidian quality which
constitutes the poem's originality and effectiveness.

Crouched on the pavement, close by Belgrave Square,
A tramp I saw, ill, moody, and tongue-tied.
A babe was in her arms, and at her side
A girl; their clothes were rags, their feet were bare.

Some labouring men, whose work lay somewhere there,
Passed opposite; she touched her girl, who hied
Across, and begged, and came back satisfied.
The rich she had let pass with frozen stare.

Thought I: 'Above her state this spirit towers;
She will not ask of aliens, but of friends,   10
Of sharers in a common human fate.

'She turns from the cold succour, which attends
The unknown little from the unknowing great,
And points us to a better time than ours.'

(Arnold 1890: 181)

59   ANON., THREE 'BROADSIDES', *CURIOSITIES OF STREET LITERATURE* (1871)

These samples of street literature (on which see Introduction, pp. 16–17 and Neuburg 1977: 123–43) are taken from Charles Hindley's compilation in facsimile form of such material 'which but for him would have disappeared' (Neuburg 1977: 125). The first two appear in a group classified as 'Political Litanies, &c', the third in a division called 'Ballads on a Subject'. All three have a strongly topical ring while good-humouredly satirising those in authority: Sir Richard Mayne, Metropolitan Police Chief, is targeted in every case.

a) The Reform League was an inter-class pressure group campaigning for manhood suffrage; its president was Edward Beales, a barrister. The League had been barred from meeting in Hyde Park in July 1866; some of its locked-out supporters then provoked outrage by breaking down railings (see plate 14). In the following spring the government again banned a meeting in the Park called by the League, and drafted in thousands of troops, police and special constables to enforce the edict. After further legal advice, however, they allowed the peaceable gathering of some 150,000 people to go ahead. According to *The Times* (7 May), 'ballad singers without number' entertained those who were too far away to hear the speeches (Harrison 1965: 94) – doubtless with just such impromptu effusions of exultation as this one. The government's humiliating *volte-face* resulted in the resignation of the Home Secretary, Spencer Walpole, but Harrison's argument (1965: 100) that this defeat significantly influenced the surprisingly large franchise extension in the Second Reform Bill passed shortly afterwards has been disputed by other historians.

b) As we know from Mayhew in particular, there was a huge variety of street occupations in Victorian London, including many different kinds of trading by pavement stall-holders. The Metropolitan Streets Act of 1867 threatened to end the relative permissiveness of the legal authorities in this area by, for example, 'forbidding the placing of goods anywhere on the street for purposes other than loading and unload-

154

ing' (Winter 1993: 109); the original double-columned broadside form is neatly exploited to parody the Act. After considerable agitation against the new legislation, the Home Secretary introduced an Amendment Bill exempting all costermongers, hawkers and itinerant dealers from liability. In consequence, as Winter shows, the numbers involved in street trading as a proportion of the central London population actually increased substantially in the later nineteenth century.

c) The 1860s saw the launch, and in some cases completion, of a number of major engineering projects in London to try to ease traffic congestion and emulate Paris in metropolitan renovation (see doc. 54). One of the most ambitious (more than six years' work) and expensive (well over £2 million) was the Holborn Viaduct, opened by the Queen on the same day (6 November 1869) as the new Blackfriars Bridge. The ballad, no doubt composed beforehand for sale among the vast crowds on the day itself, is gently satirical about Victoria's prolonged avoidance of public appearances since the death of her husband in 1861; the references to her 'coming on a veloci-pede' ironically comment on her physical inactivity on such occasions and are borne out by reports on this one, when she remained seated in her carriage through-out. The City dignatories are treated with more contemptuous mockery.

[a] The Reform Demonstration in Hyde Park, May 6th, 1867

Good people come listen, I'll tell of a lark,
That happened on Monday, the 6th, in Hyde Park,
For brave Edmund Beales and his friends they did start,

Plate 13 'The Mob Pulling Down the Railings in Park Lane',
Illustrated London News, 1866.

155

To meet the working men there.
They reached there at six o'clock, gallant and right,
   And when in so boldly did shout,
We're here my brave boys, and we'll show them this night
   We'll speak, and they shan't turn us out.

So remember, my boys, 'twas a glorious sight,
In Hyde Park, on the 6th, it was right against might,
With Beales for our leader, we beat them that night,
   At last working men they are free.

Now Dickey M– to his friend Walley said,
If you go to Hyde Park pray mind your poor head,
And I'm sure I expect to be taken home dead,
   And for me it will not be a lark.
Now don't go says Walley, to you I declare,
   Against us you know they've a spite,
The people mean business, so I shan't go there,
   Not in Hyde Park, on that Monday night.

In busses the Poleaxes hurried along,
And when they arrived they were five thousand strong,
But during the night you couldn't see one,
   Interfere with our friends in Hyde Park.
I heard that one said to his mate, 'Bill, I say,
   If they have a row, I'll be off quick,
For I got in a bother the last reform day,
   And they measured my head with a brick.'

Now Government frightened on Monday they were,
Some constables special in then they did swear,
Their staffs they did hide, when in the Park there,
   They thought that they would have to fight.
One went home enraged, says he, 'I'll have a row –
   Since to Hyde Park I've been on the march,
I am almost a boiling – we have been I vow,
   Like dummies stuck on the Marble Arch.'

So the Franchise for ever, we've beat them, hurra!
Long life to brave Beales, and Reformers, I say,
United let's be, and we'll yet gain the day,
   And always remember Hyde Park.
We do not want SPECIAL duty to be done,
   Our rights! it is all that we ask,

To meet with each other when labour is done,
And speak out our minds in the Park.

[b] The New Streets Act

The First Clause in this truly farcical and singular Act is relating to all 'regular' but not 'running' dustmen –

That it be enacted that no dustman or scavenger shall dare to sing out dust oh! in a falsetto voice, between the hours of 10 in the morning and 7 in the evening; and that all housekeepers or lodgers shall place all their cabbage stumps, potatoe peels, or fish bones into a frying-pan, dustpan, box or basket, chamber utensil, or any other utensil that is at hand, and place them neatly along the kerb, so that children may play at leap-frog on their way to school.

2. That no persons shall under any pretence leave any goods in the streets for more than sixteen seconds and a half; and any baker resting his basket for a longer space of time, shall for the first offence, forfeit his basket, and for the second, be compelled to stand three hours in a flour sack.

3. That no ox, pig, or ass, or any other kind of donkey shall be driven through the streets without an order from Scotland yard, or the Police Commissioners may detain them for ther own use.

And it is enacted that on and after the first day of November no cabman shall ply for hire, unless his cab shall be illuminated; and moreover, it is expected that each cabman shall be furnished with a transparent hat, each hat to have a life-like photographic likeness of Sir R– M– stuck in the centre.

4. That no 'bus driver or conductor shall allow more than twenty-four volunteers to ride on the roof at one time, and any female with a crinoline more than twelve yards round shall not be allowed as an inside passenger; and any person with more than thirteen stone of useless fat, shall not be considered as a single fare. And it is expected that each 'bus will be provided with a truck to transport all such live lumber to their destination.

5. No walking sandwich will be allowed to parade the streets, and no pavement to be disfigured with, 'read Fun or Tommyhawk.' And any dandy seen strutting about in one of Moses's Guinea Overcoats, will be considered as a walking advertisement, and will be punished as the law directs. No play bills, show bills, sale bills, nor bills of any kind be seen in the public streets, and any quack doctor's butler who shall be seen giving out bills relative to extraordinary cures of incurable cures shall be treated as a treasonable offender.

6. All carts, go-carts, or donkey carts, must keep a correct line, at least four inches and a half from the kerb, and all nursemaids who are seen out with a

perambulator with more than two soldiers as an escort, shall forfeit their last quarter's wages.

7. And be it enacted that any pug-dog, lap-dog, poodle-dog, bull-dog, who shall be found lurking about the street without being well muzzled, so as to prevent them from picking up the stray bones; and such dogs not giving their names and address to the police will be treated as bad characters, and will be taken into custody, – that is if the police can catch them – and be detained until their parents or friends can be found.

8. And further that such dogs shall board and lodge at the nearest station-house for three days free of expence, and provided with such food a medical inspector shall think fit, but if not owned at the end of that time they shall be treated as outcasts and executed accordingly; and their bodies sold for what they will fetch, the proceeds to go towards a fund for the relief of decayed pie shop keepers.

9. No shoeblack will be allowed to polish up your understandings, nor use the words, 'shine your boots, sir,' without being duly licensed according to Act of Parliament. And no costermonger, or costermonger's apprentice, shall dare to cry 'ten a penny walnuts,' within four feet of the footway; and any donkey braying without an order from the Commissioners shall be taken into custody, and fed upon cabbage stumps for one month.

10. With a view to suppressing all gaming, all betting men are forbidden to meet more than three together in public thoroughfares, but may victimise as many as they like in the back streets.

11. No owners of soup or cook shops shall dare to sell any stocking pudding that has not got at least two plums and a half in a square inch, or they will be compelled to swallow three quarts of double size every day for a fortnight. No confectioner shall make or cause to be made, any lollipops or sugar sticks measuring more than six inches in length, and any children sucking any of larger dimensions in the public streets will be considered as causing an obstruction, and punished accordingly.

12. This Act is favourable to all cats as we find they are not mentioned, so they are empowered to plunder our cupboards, and seranade us with their nightly gambols on the tiles.

13. No boy under twenty years of age will be allowed to trundle a hoop upon the footpath, except between the hours of twelve at night and six in the morning.

14. No lady after the passing of this Act must wear a bonnet larger than the bottom of a halfpenny bun, lest they should be afflicted with the brain fever, nor have more hair sticking out behind than would stuff a moderate side pillow-case.

15. No gent shall be allowed to wear whiskers that shall extend more than

four inches and a half from his face under the pain of being close shaved with a carpenter's hand-saw.

16. And all mothers will be compelled to keep a supply of soothing syrup on hand, as no child will be allowed to cry during the prescribed hours; and this Clause refers to all persons addicted to snoring, who are hereby cautioned not to lay on their backs, for fear they should disturb the public peace.

17. And as no one can be convicted unless seen by a policeman, the public are requested to wait till that gentlemen is out of sight before they violate any part of this Act.

18. And as evil doers will be punished by Mayne force, a placard to that effect will be stuck on each lamp-post. So much for the New Police Act.

God save the People!

[c] Opening of the Viaduct by the Queen

Come lads and lasses, be up in a jiffy,
The Queen is about to visit the City,
That her visits are so scarce, we think it a pity,
    She will open the Viaduct and Bridge.
With the Lord Mayor Elect like a porpoise,
Big round as an elephant is his old corpus,
To see this great sight nothing shall stop us,
    Gog and Magog shall dance with the Queen.

Oh dear, what can the matter be,
The Queen she is coming on a velocipede,
How nicely she treads it with high heels and buckles. –
She will open the Viaduct and Bridge.

The Mayor, Mr Lawrence will take off his hat,
He would like to be Whittington without the cat,
There's old Alderman Besley, all blubber and fat,
    They are going to welcome the Queen,
Girls of the period, of every station,
With hair down their backs of all occupations,
That would frighten Old Nick out of this nation,
It's all just to please our good Queen.

All the good clothes that is got upon tally,
They'll put on this day as they look at the valley,
Dusty Bob, Tom and Jem, and African Sally,
    These bye-gones will visit the Queen.
All the old horses will jump for joy,

'Twas up Holborn Hill that did them annoy,
I remember truck dragging when I was a boy,
   Good luck to the Viaduct and Bridge.
There will be all nations ashore and afloat,
Old Jack Atcheler will cut his throat,
No horses are killed, no cat's meat afloat,
   All through this great Viaduct and Bridge.
The cabman will dance in every passage,
Cow Cross is done up, you wont get a sassage,
   You can travel the Viaduct like a telegraph message,
   Now they've opened the Viaduct & Bridge.

The banners and flags will go in rotation,
Emblems of things of every nation,
The workmen of England and emigration,
   And old Besley fighting for Mayor.
Lawrence is down as flat as a flounder,
On his belly stands the trumpet type founder,
The Aldermen in rotation playing at rounder,
   When they open the Viaduct and Bridge.

Next comes the Queen, so pretty indeed,
How nicely she sits on the velocipede,
With high heels and buckles she treads with 'ease,
   She's getting quite young is our Queen.
That Alderman Salomon out of the lane,
He holds up so stately poor Vickey's train,
Prince of Wales and Prince Tick will come if they can,
   Just to open the Viaduct and Bridge.

Horses and donkeys will caper like fleas,
No more sore shoulders and broken knees,
The animal Society may take their ease,
   Good-bye to the once Holborn Hill.

(Hindley 1871: 88, 111, 152)

60 HIPPOLYTE TAINE, FROM *NOTES ON ENGLAND* (1872), CHAPTERS 2 AND 3

Taine (1828–93), French philosopher, historian and critic, was a leading advocate of the idea that history and culture, including literature, are analysable and explicable by the methods of natural science. *Notes on England* – based on several visits during the previous decade and first published in serial form in the Paris *Temps* (and in translation in the *Daily News*) – accordingly contains an extensive taxonomy of English 'types' and numerous hypotheses regarding the relationship between behaviour and environment. Much more persuasive, however, is the unscientifically personal observation of passages such as these, sharpened and shaped by comparison with the writer's own country and others in Europe. In the first and third excerpts, unattractive aspects of London thus appear all the grimmer; in the second, however, Taine interestingly reverses the received contemporary view that the English capital was far behind the French in metropolitan grandeur and modernity.

Sunday in London in the rain: the shops are shut, the streets almost deserted; the aspect is that of an immense and a well-ordered cemetery. The few passers-by under their umbrellas, in the desert of squares and streets, have the look of uneasy spirits who have risen from their graves; it is appalling.

I had no conception of such a spectacle, which is said to be frequent in London. The rain is small, compact, pitiless; looking at it one can see no reason why it should not continue to the end of all things; one's feet churn water, there is water everywhere, filthy water impregnated with an odour of soot. A yellow, dense fog fills the air, sweeps down to the ground; at thirty paces a house, a steam-boat appear as spots upon blotting-paper. After an hour's walk in the Strand especially, and in the rest of the City, one has the spleen, one meditates suicide. The lofty lines of fronts are of sombre brick, the exudations being encrusted with fog and soot. Monotony and silence; yet the inscriptions on metal or marble speak and tell of the absent master, as in a large manufactory of bone-black closed on account of a death. . . .

When the Romans disembarked here they must have thought themselves in Homer's hell, in the land of the Cimmerians. . . . [I]n this pale smoke objects are but fading phantoms, Nature has the look of a bad drawing in charcoal which someone has rubbed with his sleeve. . . .

On returning to my hotel I read the following proclamation in Friday's *Gazette*: 'Victoria R. . . . [W]e do hereby strictly enjoin and prohibit all our loving subjects, of what degree or quality soever, from playing on the Lord's-day, at dice, cards, or any other game whatsoever, either in public or private house, or other place or places whatsoever; and we do hereby require and command them, and every [sic] of them decently and reverently to attend the worship of God on every Lord's-day.' . . . Other traces of Puritanical severity, among the rest, are the recommendations on the stairs which lead down to the Thames, and elsewhere; one is requested to be decent. At the railway-station there are large Bibles fastened to chains for the use of the passengers while waiting for the train. . . . Other tokens denote an aristocratic country. At the gate of St. James's Park is the following notice: 'The park-keepers have orders to prevent all beggars from entering the gardens, and all persons in ragged or dirty clothes, or who are not outwardly decent and well-behaved.' At every step one feels oneself further removed from France. . . .

Enormous, enormous – this is the word which always recurs. Moreover, all is rich and well ordered; consequently, they must think us neglected and poor. Paris is mediocre compared with these squares, these crescents, these circles and rows of monumental buildings of massive stone, with porticoes, with sculptured fronts, these spacious streets; there are sixty of them as vast as the Rue de la Paix; assuredly Napoleon III demolished and rebuilt Paris only because he had lived in London. In the Strand, in Piccadilly, in Regent Street, in the neighbourhood of London Bridge, in twenty places, there is a bustling crowd, a surging traffic, an amount of obstruction which our busiest and most frequented boulevard cannot parallel. Everything is on a large scale here; the clubs are palaces, the hotels are monuments; the river is an arm of the sea; the cabs go twice as fast; the boatmen and the omnibus-conductors condense a sentence into a word; words and gestures are economised; actions and time are turned to the utmost possible account; the human being produces and expends twice as much as among us.

From London Bridge to Hampton Court are eight miles, that is, nearly three leagues of buildings. After the streets and quarters erected together as one piece by wholesale, like a hive after a model, come the countless pleasure retreats, cottages surrounded with verdure and trees in all styles – Gothic, Grecian, Byzantine, Italian, of the Middle Age or the Revival, with every mixture and every shade of style, generally in lines or clusters of five, ten, twenty of the same sort, apparently the handiwork of the same builder, like so many specimens of the same vase or the same bronze. They deal in houses as we deal in Parisian articles. What a multitude of well-to-do, comfortable and rich existences! One divines accumulated gains, a wealthy and spending middle class quite different from ours, so pinched, so straitened. . . .

Shadwell, one of the poor neighbourhoods . . . by the vastness of its distress and by its extent . . . is in keeping with the hugeness and the wealth of London. I have seen the bad quarters of Marseilles, of Antwerp, of Paris, they do not come near to it. . . . Beggars, thieves, harlots, the latter especially, crowd Shadwell Street. One hears a grating music in the spirit cellars; sometimes it is a negro who handles the violin; through the open window one perceives unmade beds, women dancing. Thrice in ten minutes I saw crowds collected at the doors; fights were going on, chiefly fights between women; one of them, her face bleeding, tears in her eyes, drunk, shouted with a sharp and harsh voice, and wished to fling herself upon a man. The bystanders laughed; the noise caused the adjacent lanes to be emptied of their occupants; ragged, poor children, harlots – it was like a human sewer suddenly discharging its contents. . . .

I recall the alleys which run into Oxford Street, stifling lanes encrusted with human exhalations; troops of pale children nestling on the muddy stairs; the seats on London Bridge where families, huddled together with drooping heads, shiver through the night; particularly the Haymarket and the Strand in the evening. Every hundred steps one jostles twenty harlots; some of them ask for a glass of gin; others say, 'Sir, it is to pay my lodging.' This is not debauchery which flaunts itself but destitution – and such destitution! The deplorable procession in the shade of the monumental streets is sickening; it seems to me a march of the dead. That is a plague-spot – the real plague-spot of English society.

(Taine 1872: 9–11, 14–17, 33–6)

Plate 14 'Ludgate Hill – A Block in the Street', G. Doré, *London: A Pilgrimage*, 1872.

PART IV
'IN DARKEST ENGLAND AND SOME WAYS OUT'

The Late Nineteenth and Early Twentieth Centuries

61   OCTAVIA HILL, FROM 'SPACE FOR THE PEOPLE', *HOMES OF THE LONDON POOR* (1875)

Hill (1838–1912) came from radical campaigning stock: her grandfather was the sanitary reformist, Dr Thomas Southwood Smith, her mother a progressive educationalist, her father an Owenite socialist–communitarian. A protégée of Ruskin and F. D. Maurice, she taught at the Working Men's and Women's Colleges before embarking on her chief mission, the improvement of working-class housing conditions. As a leading figure in the Charity Organisation Society, Hill promoted self-help schemes in which regular visits by mostly female rent-collectors were intended to inculcate thrifty habits in their tenants. Although this moralistic market system largely failed to remedy London's growing housing crisis in the last quarter of the nineteenth century (see especially Stedman-Jones 1971: 193–6), Hill was more far-sighted, and somewhat tougher on property-owners, when campaigning for 'space for the people'. This essay was first published in *Macmillan's Magazine* (August 1875) as part of an appeal for funds to buy Swiss Cottage Fields above North London for common use. This particular battle was lost, but Hill's tireless efforts in the longer campaign prepared the way for the Garden City movement and culminated in her co-founding of the National Trust in 1895.

There is perhaps no need of the poor of London which more prominently forces itself on the notice of anyone working among them than that of space. .... I go sometimes on a hot summer evening into a narrow paved court, with houses on each side. The sun has heated them all day, till it has driven nearly every inmate out of doors. Those who are not at the public-house are standing or sitting on their door-steps, quarrelsome, hot, dirty; the children are crawling or sitting on the hard hot stones till every corner of the place looks alive, and it seems as if I must step on them, do what I would, if I am to walk up the court at all. Everyone looks in everyone else's way, the place echoes with words not of the gentlest. .... Sometimes on such a hot summer evening in such a court when I am trying to calm excited women shouting their execrable language at one another, I have looked up suddenly and seen one of those bright gleams of light the summer sun sends out just before he sets, catching the top of a red chimney-pot, and beautiful there, though too directly above their heads for the crowd below to notice it much. But to me it brings sad thought of the fair and quiet places far away, where it is falling softly on tree, and hill, and cloud, and I feel as if that quiet, that beauty, that space, would be more powerful to calm the wild excess about me than all my frantic striving with it. . . .

It is strange to think it must be a gift recovered for Londoners with such difficulty. . . . The house is an individual possession, and should be worked for, but the park or the common which a man shares with his neighbours, which descends as a common inheritance from generation to generation, surely this may be given without pauperising.

How can it best be given? And what is it precisely which should be given? I think we want four things. Places to sit in, places to play in, places to stroll in, and places to spend a day in. As to the last named . . . a visit to Wimbledon, Epping, or Windsor means for the workman not only the cost of the journey but the loss of a whole day's wages; we want, besides, places where the long summer evenings or the Saturday afternoon may be enjoyed without effort or expense.

First, then, as to places to sit in. These should be very near the homes of the poor, and might be really very small, so that they were pretty and bright, but they ought to be well-distributed and abundant. The most easily available places would be our disused churchyards. . . .

Secondly, the children want playgrounds. I am glad the Board Schools are providing these, and I wish they would arrange to have them rendered available after school hours, and on the Saturday holiday. So far as I know, this is not done. If it were, children would not be obliged to play in alleys and in the street, learning their lessons of evil, in great danger of accident, and without proper space or appliances for games. . . .

And thirdly, we come to the places to stroll in. We could not have a better instance than the Embankment. What a boon it has been to London! Of course the parks come under this head; and to what thousands of people they give pleasure! But beyond these thousands are many who never find their way to these open spaces. . . . Brought up in dirt, close quarters, and the excitement of the street tragedies; ashamed of their neglected clothes; shy of a neatly-dressed public, they burrow in courts and alleys out of sight. . . . They must be invited to come out in little companies for a walk, taken out again, and again, and again during the summer. . . .

There are a few fields just north of this parish of Marylebone which . . . have been our constant resort for years: they are within an easy walk for most of us, and a twopenny train takes the less vigorous within a few yards of the little white gate by which they are entered. . . . [T]here on a summer Sunday or Saturday evening you might see hundreds of working people, who have walked up there from the populous and very poor neighbourhood of Lisson Grove and Portland Town. . . . There the May still grows; there thousands of buttercups crown the slope with gold: there, best of all, as you ascend, the hill lifts you out of London, and will always lift you of it, even when houses are built all around; for far away the view stretches over blue distances to the ridge where Windsor stands. As you come home – yes, as your children's children come home – if you will save the fields from being built over now, will be seen from them the great sun going down, with all his clouds about him, or the fair space of cloudless summer sky, London lying hushed below you – even London hushed for you for a few minutes, so far it lies beneath – though you will be in it in a short ten minutes.

These fields may be bought now, or they may be built over: which is it to be? . . . I feel myself as if the question ought, in a measure, to be taken up by the large London landowners. . . . [T]he possession of the land is a very great responsibility, and if there be so *very* little land on their own estates which they can dedicate to the service of the poor, surely they might feel it incumbent on them to do the next best thing, that is, to secure and throw open such fields as lie nearest to London on any side. The same duty appears to me to lie before the Corporation and the City Companies, and the more because the poor, having been a good deal driven out, the funds left for their benefit from the City, which these bodies have inherited, might well be applied to such an object as this. . . .

We all need space; unless we have it we cannot reach that sense of quiet in which whispers of better things come to us gently. Our lives in London are over-crowded, over-excited, over-strained. This is true of all classes; we all want quiet; we all want beauty for the refreshment of our souls. . . .

(Hill 1875: 196–212)

62   [WILLIAM HALE WHITE], FROM *MARK RUTHERFORD'S DELIVERANCE* (1885), CHAPTERS 2, 5, 6

White (1831–1913) was born in Bedford, where his father, a politically radical bookseller, was also deacon at the Old (Bunyan) Meeting of Independents. White's own college training for the Independent Ministry ended abruptly in expulsion for questioning dogmatic Biblical teaching. He subsequently pursued a dual career as a civil servant in the Admiralty and as a literary and political journalist. After the semi-fictional 'spiritual' *Autobiography of Mark Rutherford* (1881), most of his writings, including four novels, were published under this pseudonym. In its tone and preoccupations Rutherford's is a representative later-nineteenth-century voice. The oppressively prisonous city and the apparently irremediable condition of its poor inhabitants cast a pall over the somewhat misleadingly titled second part of the autobiography: 'deliverance', such as it is, is gained by curbing speculation regarding life's impenetrable mysteries and by learning to make the most of whatever genuine though modest means to happiness and improvement lie to hand.

M'Kay had a passionate desire to reform the world. The spectacle of the misery of London, and of the distracted swaying hither and thither of the multitudes who inhabit it, tormented him incessantly. He always chafed at it, and he never seemed sure that he had a right to the enjoyment of the simplest pleasures so long as London was before him. What a farce, he would cry, is all this poetry, philosophy, art, and culture, when millions of wretched mortals are doomed to the eternal darkness and crime of the city! Here are the educated classes occupying themselves with exquisite emotions, with speculations upon the Infinite, with addresses to flowers, with the worship of waterfalls and flying clouds, and with the incessant portraiture of a thousand moods and variations of love, while their neighbours lie grovelling in the mire, and never know anything more of life or its duties than is afforded them by a police report in a bit of newspaper picked out of a kennel. We went one evening to hear a great violin-player, who played such music, and so exquisitely, that the limits of life were removed. But we had to walk up the Haymarket home, between eleven and twelve o'clock, and the violin-playing became the merest trifling. M'Kay had been brought up on the Bible. . . . He recurred to the apostles and Bunyan, and was convinced that it was possible even now to touch depraved men and women with an idea which should recast their lives.

M'Kay had found a room near Parker Street, Drury Lane, in which he proposed to begin. . . . The first Sunday I went with him. . . . As we walked over the Drury Lane gratings of the cellars a most foul stench came up, and one in particular I remember to this day. A man half dressed pushed open a broken window beneath us, just as we passed by, and there issued such a blast of corruption, made up of gases bred by filth, air breathed and rebreathed a hundred times, charged with odours of unnameable personal uncleanness and disease, that I staggered to the gutter with a qualm which I could scarcely conquer. At the doors of the houses stood grimy women with their arms folded and their hair disordered. Grimier boys and girls had tied a rope to broken railings, and were swinging on it. The common door to a score of lodgings stood ever open, and the children swarmed up and down the stairs carrying with them patches of mud every time they came in from the street. There was no break in the uniformity of squalor. . . . All self-respect, all effort to do anything more than to satisfy somehow the grossest wants, had departed. . . . The desire to decorate existence in some way or other with more or less care is nearly universal. . . . I have known selfish, gluttonous, drunken men spend their leisure moments in trimming a bed of scarlet geraniums, and the vulgarest and most commonplace of mortals considers it a necessity to put a picture in the room or an ornament on the mantelpiece. The instinct, even in its lowest forms, is divine. It is the commentary on the text that man shall not live by bread alone. It is evidence of an acknowledged compulsion – of which art is the highest manifestation – to *escape*. In the alleys behind Drury Lane this instinct, the very salt of life, was dead, crushed out utterly, a symptom which seemed to me ominous, and even awful to the last degree. The only house in which it survived was in that of the undertaker, who displayed the willows, the black horses, and the coffin. These may have been nothing more than an advertisement, but from the care with which the cross was elaborated, and the neatness with which it was made to resemble a natural piece of wood, I am inclined to believe that the man felt some pleasure in his work for its own sake, and that he was not utterly submerged. The cross in such dens, in such sewers! If it be anything, it is a symbol of victory, of power to triumph over resistance, and even death. Here was nothing but sullen subjugation, the most grovelling slavery, mitigated only by a tendency to mutiny. . . . The preaching of Jesus would have been powerless here; in fact, no known stimulus, nothing ever held up before men to stir the soul to activity, can do anything in the back streets of great cities so long as they are the cess-pools which they are now. . . .

It was an awful thought to me, ever present on those Sundays, and haunting me at other times, that men, women, and children were living in such brutish degradation, and that as they died others would take their place. Our civilisation seemed nothing but a thin film or crust lying over a volcanic pit, and I often wondered whether some day the pit would not break up through it and destroy us all. . . . The filthy gloom of the sky, the dirt of the street, the absence of fresh air, the herding of the poor into huge districts which cannot be opened up by those who would do good, are tremendous agencies of corruption which are active at such a rate that it is appalling to reflect what our future will be if the accumulation of population be not checked. To stand face to face with the insoluble is not pleasant. . . .

M'Kay's dreams therefore were not realised, and yet it would be a mistake to say that they ended in nothing. . . . He did not convert Drury Lane, but he saved two or three. . . . Our main object was to create in our hearers contentment with their lot, and even some joy in it. That was our religion. . . .

(Rutherford 1969: 166–71, 209, 227)

63 [W. T. STEAD], FROM 'THE MAIDEN TRIBUTE OF MODERN BABYLON', *PALL MALL GAZETTE* (6 JULY 1885)

This famous piece of exposé journalism maintains an urban tradition (going back at least as far as Defoe) which blends salacious sensationalism with moralistic realism. Under the colourful editorship of Stead (1849–1912) in the 1880s, the *Pall Mall Gazette* acquired a socially radical edge; it exploited the populist techniques of the New Journalism to the full in giving supportive publicity to Josephine Butler's campaigns against the Contagious Diseases Act (suspended 1883) and child prostitution. Through its revelations on the latter, the four-part 'Maiden Tribute' certainly hastened passage of the Criminal Law Amendment Act (1885), raising the age of consent to 16.

Ironically, though, the articles also led to Stead's imprisonment for abduction of a 13-year-old girl. In a probing reappraisal, Walkowitz (1992: 81–125) finds his critical radicalism compromised by sentimental melodrama and quasi-pornographic voyeurism. But as these excerpts show, the histrionics often give a memorable vigour to Stead's attack upon exploitation and double standards in the name of humanity, justice and democracy.

The Report of our Secret Commission, Part I

In ancient times, if we may believe the myths of Hellas, Athens, after a disastrous campaign, was compelled by her conqueror to send once every nine years a tribute to Crete of seven youths and seven maidens. The doomed fourteen, who were selected by lot amid the lamentations of the citizens, returned no more. The vessel that bore them to Crete unfurled black sails as the symbols of despair, and on arrival her passengers were flung into the famous Labyrinth of Daedalus, there to wander about blindly until such time as they were devoured by the Minotaur, a frightful monster, half man, half bull, the foul product of an unnatural lust. 'The labyrinth was as large as a town and had countless courts and galleries. Those who entered it could never find their way out again. . . .'

The fact that the Athenians should have taken so bitterly to heart the paltry maiden tribute that once in nine years they had to pay to the Minotaur seems incredible, almost inconceivable. This very night in London, and every night, year in and year out, not seven maidens only, but many times seven, selected almost as much by chance . . . will be offered up as the Maiden Tribute to Modern Babylon. Maidens they were when this morning dawned, but tonight their ruin will be accomplished, and tomorrow they will find themselves within the portals of the maze of London brotheldom. Within that labyrinth wander, like lost souls, the vast host of London prostitutes, whose number no man can compute, but who are probably not much below 50,000 strong. . . . The maw of the London Minotaur is insatiable, and none that go into the secret recesses of his lair return again. After some years' dolorous wandering in this palace of despair . . . most of those ensnared tonight will perish, some of them in horrible torture. Yet, so far from this great city being convulsed with woe, London cares for none of these things. . . .

Nevertheless, I have not yet lost faith in the heart and conscience of the English folk, the sturdy innate chivalry and right thinking of our common people. . . . [I]f we must cast maidens . . . nightly into the jaws of vice, let us at least see to it that they assent to their own immolation, and are not unwilling sacrifices procured by force and fraud. That is surely not too much to ask from the dissolute rich. Even considerations of self-interest might lead our rulers to assent to so modest a demand. For the hour of Democracy has struck, and there is no wrong which a man resents like this. . . . [U]nless the levying of the maiden tribute in London is shorn of its worst abuses . . . resentment . . . may hereafter be the virus of social revolution. It is the one explosive which is strong enough to wreck the Throne. . . .

For four weeks, aided by two or three coadjutors of whose devotion and self-sacrifice, combined with a rare instinct of investigation and a singular personal fearlessness, I cannot speak too highly, I have been exploring the London Inferno. It has been a strange and unexampled experience. . . . London beneath the gas glare of its innumerable lamps became . . . a resurrected and magnified City of the Plain, with all the vices of Gomorrah, daring the vengeance of long-suffering Heaven. It seemed a strange, inverted world, that in which I lived those terrible weeks – the world of the streets and of the brothel. It was the same, yet not the same, as the world of business and the world of politics. I heard of much the same people in the house of ill-fame as those of whom you hear in caucuses, in law courts, and on 'Change. But all were judged by a different standard. . . .

Here . . . is a statement made to me by a brothel-keeper who formerly kept a noted house in the Mile-end road: '. . . I have gone and courted girls in the country under all kinds of disguises, occasionally assuming the dress of a parson, and made them believe that I intended to marry them. . . . I bring her up [to London], take her here and there, giving her plenty to eat and drink – especially drink. . . . [T]hen I contrive it so that she loses her last train. . . . I offer her nice lodgings for the night: she goes to bed in my house, and then the affair is managed. My client gets his maid, I get my £10 or £20 commission, and in the morning the girl, who has lost her character, and dare not go home, in all probability will do as the others do, and become one of my "marks" – that is, she will make her living in the streets, to the advantage of my house. . . . Another very simple mode of supplying maids is by breeding them. . . . When they get to be 12 or 13 they become merchantable. For a very likely "mark" of this kind you may get as much as £20 or £40. I sent my own daughter out on the streets from my own brothel. . . . In the East-end, you can always pick up as many fresh girls as you want. In one street in Dalston you might buy a dozen. . . .'

Anxious to test the truth of his statement, I asked him, through a trusty agent, if he would undertake to supply me in three days with a couple of fresh girls, maids, whose virginity would be attested by a doctor's certificate. . . . In two days I received . . . an intimation that for £10 commission he would undertake to deliver to my chambers, or to any other spot which I might choose to select, two young girls, each with a doctor's certificate of the fact that she was a *virgo intacta*. . . .

(*PMG*, 6 July 1885: 1–6)

64 BEATRICE POTTER (WEBB), FROM 'DIARY' (8 NOVEMBER 1886; 1926)

My Apprenticeship, in which this and many other diary entries are quoted, recounts an earnest Victorian's search for a creed. But Potter (1858–1943), a generation younger than White (doc. 62), escaped spiritual anguish, as well as the trivial pursuits of a young lady 'coming out' into society, by becoming an East-End rent-collector: 'the time-spirit had seized me and compelled me to concentrate all my free energy in getting the training and the raw material for applied sociology . . . with a view to bettering the life and labour of the people' (Webb 1926: 130). Potter's important contributions to Booth's field-study of London poverty (see doc. 72) were the first significant fruits of this project, followed by an investigation of the Co-operative Movement. Her commitment thereafter to the advancement of 'scientific' socialism was sealed in marriage to Sidney Webb in 1892, the formidable 'partnership' of subsequent autobiographical volumes. However, Potter wrote this passage when feeling depressed and isolated as acting manager of Katherine Buildings, a bleak housing block in Whitechapel.

Plate 15 'Wentworth Street, Whitechapel', G. Doré, *London: A Pilgrimage*, 1872.

Where is the wish for better things in these myriads of beings hurrying along the streets night and day? Even their careless, sensual laugh, coarse jokes, and unloving words depress one as one presses through the crowd, and almost shudders to touch them. It is not so much the actual vice, it is the low level of monotonous and yet excited life; the regular recurrence to street sensations, quarrels and fights; the greedy street-bargaining, and the petty theft and gambling. The better natures keep apart from their degraded fellow citizens and fellow-workers, live lonely and perforce selfish lives, not desiring to lead their more ignorant and unself-controlled neighbours. Social intercourse brings out, and springs from, the worst qualities in East London; as a society it is an ever-increasing and ever-decomposing mass; the huge mass smothering the small centres containing within them the seeds of social life and growth. Even the faculty for manual labour becomes demoralised, and its capability is reduced.

These buildings, too, are to my mind an utter failure. In spite of Ella Pycroft's heroic efforts, they are not an influence for good. The free intercourse has here, as elsewhere in this dismal mass, a demoralising effect. The bad and indifferent, the drunken, mean and lowering elements overwhelm the effect of higher motive and noble example. The respectable tenants keep rigidly to themselves. To isolate yourself from your surroundings seems to be here the acme of social morality: in truth, it is the only creed one dare preach. 'Do not meddle with your neighbours' is perforce the burden of one's advice to the newcomer. The meeting-places, there is something grotesquely coarse in this, are the water-closets! Boys and girls crowd on these landings – they are the only lighted places in the buildings – to gamble and flirt. The lady collectors are an altogether superficial thing. Undoubtedly their gentleness and kindness brings light into many homes: but what are they in face of this collective brutality, heaped up together in infectious contact; adding to each other's dirt, physical and moral?

And how can one raise these beings to better things without the hope of a better world, the faith in the usefulness of effort? Why resist the drink demon? A short life and a merry one, why not? A woman diseased with drink came up to me screaming, in her hand the quart pot, her face directed to the Public [House]. What could I say? Why dissuade her? She is half-way to death – let her go – if death ends all. But with her go others; and these others may be only on the first step downwards. Alas! *there* is the pitifulness in this long chain of iniquity, children linked on to parents, friends to friends, and lovers to lovers, bearing down to that bottomless pit of decaying life.

The bright side of the East End life is the sociability and generous sharing of small means. This, of course, brings in its train quarrels and backbiting;

for it is easier to give than to bear ingratitude, or to be grateful. And as the 'Public' is the only meeting-place, the more social and generous nature is led away even by its good qualities; while the crabbed mind and sickly constitution isolates itself, and possibly thrives in isolation. The drink demon destroys the fittest and spares the meaner nature: undermines the constitution of one family, and then passes on to stronger stuff. There are times when one loses all faith in *laisser-faire* and would suppress this poison at all hazards, for it eats the life of the nation. For hardworking men are tied to drunken wives, and hardworking women to drunken husbands; so that the good are weighted down, and their striving after a better life made meaningless.

And yet there are glimpses into happy homes; sights of love between men and women, and towards little children, and, rarely enough, devotion to the aged and the sick. And, possibly, it is this occasional rest from dirt and disorder that makes the work more depressing; for one must hear unheeded the sickening cry of the sinking man or woman dragging the little ones down into poverty from which there is no rising.

(Webb 1926: 276–8)

65   GEORGE GISSING, FROM *THYRZA* (1887), CHAPTER 9

Though struggling grimly for professional status and financial security as a novelist throughout the 1880s, Gissing (1857–1903) was in tune with the times in setting five of the seven novels he published during that decade amid London working-class life. For *Thyrza*, the fourth of these, he undertook particularly careful research in the streets of Lambeth, 'doing my best to get at the meaning of that strange world, so remote from our civilisation' (Mattheisen *et al.* 1990–7: 111, 47). The chronic tension between attraction and alienation in Gissing's relationship to that world is evident in the cultural refinement bestowed upon the novel's working-class hero, Gilbert Grail (note the initials!), and heroine, Thyrza Trent, a beautiful singer. One of the functions of this moving passage, in which street music is taken as emblematic of 'the hunger of unshaped desire', is to make the central characters more representative in their unattainable aspirations. Yet it also 'goes deep to the contradictions in Gissing' (Poole 1975: 82) in that revulsion from the ineluctable taint of the 'semi-human' contends with sympathetic testimony to 'all that is purely human in those darkened multitudes'.

He turned towards Lambeth Walk. The market of Christmas Eve was flaring and clamorous; the odours of burning naphtha and fried fish were pungent on the wind. He walked a short distance among the crowd, then found the noise oppressive and turned into a by-way. As he did so, a street organ began to play in front of a public-house close by. Grail drew near; there were children forming a dance, and he stood to watch them.

Do you know that music of the obscure ways, to which children dance? Not if you have only heard it ground to your ears' affliction beneath your

174

windows in the square. To hear it aright you must stand in the darkness of such a by-street as this, and for the moment be at one with those who dwell around, in the blear-eyed houses, in the dim burrows of poverty, in the unmapped haunts of the semi-human. Then you will know the significance of that vulgar clanging of melody; a pathos of which you did not dream will touch you, and therein the secret of hidden London will be half revealed. The life of men who toil without hope, yet with the hunger of an unshaped desire; of women in whom the sweetness of their sex is perishing under labour and misery; the laugh, the song of the girl who strives to enjoy her year or two of youthful vigour, knowing the darkness of the years to come; the careless defiance of the youth who feels his blood and revolts against the lot which would tame it; all that is purely human in these darkened multitudes speaks to you as you listen. It is the half-conscious striving of a nature which

Plate 16 'The Organ in the Court', G. Doré, *London: A Pilgrimage*, 1872.

knows not what it would attain, which deforms a true thought by gross expression, which clutches at the beautiful and soils it with foul hands.

The children were dirty and ragged, several of them bare-footed, nearly all bare-headed, but they danced with noisy merriment. One there was, a little girl, on crutches; incapable of taking a partner, she stumped round and round, circling upon the pavement, till giddiness came upon her and she had to fall back and lean against the wall, laughing aloud at her weakness. Gilbert stepped up to her, and put a penny into her hand; then, before she had recovered from her surprise, passed onwards.

(Gissing 1927: 111–12)

66 [MARGARET HARKNESS], FROM *OUT OF WORK* (1888), CHAPTERS 1, 6, 10

Harkness (c. 1861–1921), a cousin of Beatrice Webb and associate of the socialist-feminists, Eleanor Marx and Olive Schreiner, wrote politically engaged fiction of contemporary East-End life under the pseudonym of John Law. Her work is probably best known for occasioning (in an 1888 letter regarding her first novel, *A City Girl*) Engels' most famous pronouncements on realism ('typical characters in typical circumstances'). While praising the author's courageous truthfulness, he complained that in this book 'the working class appears as a passive mass'; but then, contradictorily, he admitted 'that nowhere in the civilised world are the working people . . . more passively submitting to fate . . . than in the East End of London' (Craig 1975: 269–71). As though in response to Engels' comments, *Out of Work* opens by recording a dissentient spirit in the crowd at a recent historical event (14 May 1887) planned as part of the Golden Jubilee celebrations. This was the official opening by Victoria herself of Queen's Hall, the first stage of the projected People's Palace in Mile End Road; the narrator's reference to a collective mood 'which may a year or so hence prove dangerous' appears prophetic in the light of the Great Dock Strike of 1889. Yet the ensuing story is of a skilled carpenter from the countryside, forced to accept casual labour in the docks on the way down to chronic unemployment, personal betrayal and a wretched early death.

It was the day after the Queen's visit to the East End. Whitechapel was gay with flags. Mile End had coloured banners, and festoons of red, yellow, green, and blue paper flowers 'all along the line'. About seventeen hours earlier Her Majesty had been enthusiastically welcomed by crowds of West End visitors at the London Hospital and the great breweries. Cheers from the lungs of medical students still echoed in the air; scents from the pocket-handkerchiefs of brewers' wives and doctors' daughters rose upwards. Reporters were busy at work concocting stories of the royal progress through the East End for the Monday papers; artists were preparing for the illustrated weekly papers pictures of Whitechapel as it may possibly appear in the Millenium. No one would speak about the hisses which the denizens of the slums had mingled with faint applause as Her Majesty neared her destination; no one would hint that the crowd about the Palace of Delight had had a sullen, ugly look which may a year or so hence prove dangerous. . . .

He left the block, and walked towards Lockhart's shop, which is close to the Mint. As he went he saw men sitting on the stones by the post-office, rough fellows with hungry faces and famished eyes. It was nearly time for them to begin hanging about the docks, to commence looking out for a job, at the only place where a man can get work without having a character. . . . The company there is more mixed than anywhere else in London, so whoever sinks into it can never rise up again, is socially branded.

'Shall I come to *that*?' wondered Jos, as he swallowed his halfpenny cup of coffee, and ate a stale bun. 'Not if I can help it.' . . .

Half-past six o'clock . . . found Jos at Fenchurch Street station. Half-past six is an unpleasant hour in that part of the city. The streets look greasy. There are not enough people about to enliven the houses. Shops have shutters up; untidy girls are scrubbing doorsteps; no one is there, except men on their way to work, old women going to market, and that scum of the populace who sleep in any hole they can, and live in any way they may; bleating sheep and lowing cattle are being driven along by butchers; yawning policemen are talking over a suicide here, a murder there; lean dogs are acting as scavengers; ragged children are seeking breakfast in dust heaps and gutters. The damp morning air is adding to the unpleasant smells in the atmosphere.

Little wonder that public-houses entice customers! Before Jos reached Fenchurch Street station he had had 'a glass of something to raise his spirits', for the dock-labourer had lent him a shilling, and the gin had done him so much good the previous evening that he thought it wise to begin the day with the same remedy.

He found the train for Tidal Basin crowded with dock-labourers, all on their way to the Albert and Victoria Docks, where about one thousand men find employment.

It is reckoned that twenty thousand Londoners call themselves dock-labourers; of which number nearly the half is daily turned away to swell the number of the unemployed, to seek, by fair means or foul, a living. . . .

The carriage held about forty men, all untidy, unshaven, hungry people. A few had food tied up in pocket-handkerchiefs, one or two had bottles sticking out of their pockets. All had unbrushed hair, muddy boots, filthy hands, and dirty faces; some were sleeping, some were smoking, three or four were trying to laugh at the others. . . .

''Ave you 'eard what we unemployed's got to do Jubilee day?' . . .

'What then?'

177

'We've got to walk two and two down Cheapside afore the Queen; we've got to do penance in white sheets and candles; so I've read in the newspapers.'

Then the men began to sing: –

'Starving on the Queen's highway.'

The carriage was full of stale tobacco. All the windows were up. The men seemed to enjoy the stuffiness, to relish the smell and taste of it. But Jos, whose lungs still had some traces of country air in them, felt stifled. He sat upright, with his hands in his pockets, silent, looking steadily in front of him.
. . .

At each station fresh passengers jumped in; and as they could not sit down, room was made for them in the centre of the carriage, against the windows, or on the knees of other men. It was 'Ulloa, Tom!' and 'Well, Bill!' at every platform, a desire to share tobacco, to show kindness, and receive favours. These men exist by the generosity of their fellows; and the only good thing that comes of being unemployed is 'I help you, and you help me, because we've no place in society.' This is the *one*, the *only* good thing among the legions of evil which are the outcome of enforced idleness. For loss of self-respect, bitterness, the loosening of all social restraints, the lifting of that dam called Civilisation which keeps the passions of men from making beasts of them, are the results of telling a human being, 'there is no work for you to do, you are not wanted.'

At Tidal Basin all the men turned out of the train, and left the station. They went towards the docks, and some stopped at the public-house on the way, letting the others press on to the gates, where hundreds of men already stood waiting. Is any artist in need of a subject for his next Academy picture? If so, he had better visit the dock gates some early morning, and watch the men 'taken on'.

By the gates of the Albert and Victoria Docks stand policemen, who keep order while the men pass into a covered pen, pass through . . . to crave, as a favour, the boon of slaving all day, in order to carry home to wives and children a little money.

(Law 1888: 1–2, 88–9, 126–30)

67 HENRY JAMES, FROM 'LONDON', *CENTURY ILLUSTRATED MONTHLY MAGAZINE* (DECEMBER 1888)

Like most of James' earlier essays of European travel and topography, this one was first published in an American periodical. Unlike them, however, 'London' is not written from the perspective of a New-World traveller but from that of 'an adoptive son', James

(1843–1916) having settled in the English capital in 1876. Although the essay begins with a powerful recollection of being at first overwhelmed by 'the infernal town' – one of the classic accounts of dreadful initiation – he testifies to having since taken imaginative possession of the whole, pursuing the role of 'the accommodated haunter' for whom 'the impression of suffering is a part of the general vibration'. James here writes as the recent author of *The Princess Casamassima* (1886), a novel which endows London, in the words of his 1907 Preface, with 'some sinister anarchic underworld'. Written not long after the republication of 'London' in *English Hours*, this Preface strikingly echoes it in referring to 'the habitual observer, the preoccupied painter, the pedestrian prowler' with a commitment 'to haunt the great city and by this habit to penetrate it, imaginatively, in as many places as possible' (James 1934: 77). Walkowitz (1992: 15–17) makes effective use of this self-image in discussing late-nineteenth-century *flânerie* and 'the literary construct of the metropolis as a dark, powerful and seductive labyrinth'.

There is a certain evening that I count as virtually a first impression – the end of a wet, black Sunday, twenty years ago, about the first of March. There had been an earlier vision, but it had turned to grey, like faded ink, and the occasion I speak of was a fresh beginning. No doubt I had mystic prescience of how fond of the murky modern Babylon I was one day to become; certain it is that as I look back I find every small circumstance of those hours of approach and arrival still as vivid as if the solemnity of an opening era had breathed upon it. . . .

The impression . . . was, strictly, that of the drive from Euston, after dark, to Morley's Hotel in Trafalgar Square. It was not lovely – it was in fact rather horrible; but as I move again through dusky tortuous miles, in the greasy four-wheeler to which my luggage had compelled me to commit myself, I recognise the first step in an initiation of which the subsequent stages were to abound in pleasant things. It is a kind of humiliation in a great city not to know where you are going, and Morley's Hotel was then, to my imagination, only a vague ruddy spot in the general immensity. The immensity was the great fact, and that was a charm; the miles of housetops and viaducts, the complication of junctions and signals through which the train made its way to the station had already given me the scale. . . . [B]ut this momentous cab-drive was an introduction to the rigidities of custom. The low black houses were as inanimate as so many rows of coal-scuttles, save where at frequent corners, from a gin-shop, there was a flare of light more brutal still than the darkness. . . .

A day or two later, in the afternoon, I found myself staring at my fire, in a lodging of which I had taken possession on foreseeing that I should spend some weeks in London. . . . The uproar of Piccadilly hummed away at the end of the street, and the rattle of a heartless hansom passed close to my ears. A sudden horror of the whole place came over me, like a tiger-pounce of homesickness which had been watching its moment. London was hideous, vicious, cruel, and above all overwhelming; whether or no she was 'careful of the type',[1] she was as indifferent as Nature herself to the single life. ... It appeared to me that I would rather remain dinnerless, would rather even starve, than sally forth into the infernal town, where the natural fate of an obscure stranger would be to be trampled to death in Piccadilly and have his carcass thrown into the Thames. I did not starve, however, and I eventually attached myself by a hundred human links to the dreadful, delightful city. ...

It is, no doubt, not the taste of everyone, but for the real London-lover the mere immensity of the place is a large part of its savour. A small London would be an abomination, as it fortunately is an impossibility, for the idea and the name are beyond everything an expression of extent and number. Practically, of course, one lives in a quarter, in a plot; but in imagination and by a constant mental act of reference the accommodated haunter enjoys the whole – and it is only of him that I deem it worthwhile to speak. He fancies himself, as they say, for being a particle in so unequalled an aggregation; and its immeasurable circumference, even though unvisited and lost in smoke, gives him the sense of a social, an intellectual margin. ...

And yet I should not go so far as to say that it is a condition of such geniality to close one's eyes upon the immense misery; on the contrary, I think it is partly because we are irremediably conscious of that dark gulf that the most general appeal of the great city remains exactly what it is, the largest chapter of human accidents. ... Certain it is, at any rate, that the impression of suffering is a part of the general vibration; it is one of the things that mingle with all the others to make the sound that is supremely dear to the consistent London-lover – the rumble of the tremendous human mill. This is the note which, in all its modulations, haunts and fascinates and inspires him. ... We are far from liking London well enough till we like its defects: the dense darkness of much of its winter, the soot on the chimney-pots and everywhere else, the early lamplight, the brown blur of the houses, the splashing of hansoms in Oxford Street or the Strand on December afternoons.

(James 1905: 1–4, 7–9, 30–1)

Note

1 *careful ... type*: Tennyson, *In Memoriam* LV.

68 GEORGE GISSING, FROM *THE NETHER WORLD* (1889), CHAPTERS 2 AND 31

Just as he had done in Lambeth prior to writing *Thyrza* (doc. 65), Gissing conducted thorough field-research for this novel in frequent rambles through Clerkenwell, the centre of London's precious-metal industries and, on and around the 'Green', of its radical politics. Gissing had long since lost sympathy with the latter, but the shocking sight of his estranged, alcoholic wife's corpse in a squalid Lambeth slum just three weeks before he began *The Nether World* moved him to write in his diary (1 March 1888): 'Henceforth I never cease to bear testimony against the accursed social order' (Coustillas 1978: 23). The testimony in the first passage below endorses contemporary socialist critiques such as William Morris' 'Useful Work *vs* Useless Toil' (Morton 1973: 86–108), which Gissing certainly knew. But unlike Morris, Gissing had no faith in revolutionary change, nor even in reformist solutions. All schemes for social and personal improvement are nullified in the course of the novel; Clara Hewitt, the observing consciousness in the second passage, has had her bid to escape through a theatrical career cruelly aborted by facial disfigurement in an acid attack, and finds herself more trapped than ever in a new, prison-like tenement.

It was the hour of the unyoking of men. In the highways and byways of Clerkenwell there was a thronging of released toilers, of young and old, of male and female. Forth they streamed from factories and workrooms, anxious to make the most of the few hours during which they might live for themselves. Great numbers were still bent over their labour, and would be for hours to come, but the majority had leave to wend stablewards. Along the main thoroughfares the wheel-track was clangorous; every omnibus that clattered by was heavily laden with passengers; tarpaulins gleamed over the knees of those who sat outside. This way and that the lights were blurred into a misty radiance; overhead was mere blackness, whence descended the lashing rain. There was a ceaseless scattering of mud; there were blocks in the traffic, attended with rough jest or angry curse; there was jostling on the crowded pavement. Public-houses began to brighten up, to bestir themselves for the evening's business. Streets that had been hives of activity since early morning were being abandoned to silence and darkness and the sweeping wind.

At noon to-day there was sunlight on the Surrey hills; the fields and lanes were fragrant with the first breath of spring, and from the shelter of budding copses many a primrose looked tremblingly up to the vision of blue sky. But of these things Clerkenwell takes no count; here it had been a day like any other, consisting of so many hours, each representing a fraction of the weekly wage. Go where you may in Clerkenwell, on every hand are multiform evidences of toil, intolerable as a nightmare. It is not as in those parts of London where the main thoroughfares consist of shops and warehouses and workrooms, whilst the streets that are hidden away on either hand are devoted in the main to dwellings. Here every alley is thronged with small industries; all but every door and window exhibits the advertisement of a craft that is carried on within. Here you may see how men have multiplied toil for toil's sake, have wrought to devise work superfluous, have worn their lives away in imagining new forms of weariness. The energy, the ingenuity daily put forth in these grimy burrows task the brain's power of wondering. But that those who sit here through the livelong day, through every season, through all the years of the life that is granted them, who strain their eyesight, who overtax their muscles, who nurse disease in their frames, who put resolutely from them the thought of what existence *might* be – that these do it all without prospect or hope of reward save the permission to eat and sleep and bring into the world other creatures to strive with them for bread, surely that thought is yet more marvellous.

Workers in metal, workers in glass and in enamel, workers in wood, workers in every substance on earth, or from the waters under the earth, that can be made commerically valuable. In Clerkenwell the demand is not so much for rude strength as for the cunning fingers and the contriving brain. The inscriptions on the house-fronts would make you believe that you were in a region of gold and silver and precious stones. In the recesses of dim byways, where sunshine and free air are forgotten things, where families herd together in dear-rented garrets and cellars, craftsmen are for ever handling jewellery, shaping bright ornaments for the necks and arms of such as are born to the joy of life. Wealth inestimable is ever flowing through these workshops, and the hands that have been stained with gold-dust may, as likely as not, some day extend themselves in petition for a crust. In this house, as the announcement tells you, business is carried on by a trader in diamonds, and next door is a den full of children who wait for their day's one meal until their mother has come home with her chance earnings. A strange enough region wherein to wander and muse. Inextinguishable laughter were perchance the fittest result of such musing; yet somehow the heart grows heavy, somehow the blood is troubled in its course, and the pulses begin to throb hotly. . . .

Presently she was standing at her window, the blind partly raised. On a clear day the view from this room was of wide extent, embracing a great part of the City; seen under a low, blurred, dripping sky, through the ragged patches of smoke from chimneys innumerable, it had a gloomy impressiveness well in keeping with the mind of her who brooded over it. Directly in front, rising mist-detached from the lower masses of building, stood in black majesty the dome of St. Paul's; its vastness suffered no diminution from this high outlook, rather was exaggerated by the flying scraps of mirky vapour which softened its outline and at times gave it the appearance of floating on a vague troubled sea. Somewhat nearer, amid many spires and steeples, lay the surly bulk of Newgate, the lines of its construction shown plan-wise; its little windows multiplied for points of torment to the vision. Nearer again, the markets of Smithfield, Bartholomew's Hospital, the tract of modern deformity, cleft by a gulf of railway, which spreads between Clerkenwell Road and Charterhouse Street. Down in Farringdon Street the carts, waggons, vans, cabs, omnibuses, crossed and intermingled in a steaming splash-bath of mud; human beings, reduced to their due paltriness, seemed to toil in exasperation along the strips of pavement, bound on errands, which were a mockery, driven automaton-like by forces they neither understood nor could resist.

(Gissing 1974: 10–11, 280)

69   AMY LEVY, 'LONDON IN JULY' (1889)

Born into a middle-class Jewish family, Levy (1861–89) had a poem published at the age of 13; her poetry and fiction continued to appear in print throughout a tragically brief life. She also had an active interest in social issues, working as a secretary for the Beaumont Trust which raised funds for educational and cultural facilities in the East End, including the People's Palace project (see headnote to doc. 66). Among her friends were the socialist-feminists, Olive Schreiner and Eleanor Marx; the latter translated into German one of Levy's novels, *Reuben Sachs* (1888), a critical representation of the London Jewish community. In most of the short poems in her final collection, *The London Plane Tree*, the city functions as a correlative of shifting, contradictory moods, and it is often, as in this example, preferred to the conventionally more attractive countryside. In 'The Village Garden', this preference is explicitly related to personal psychology: 'For me, the roar and hurry of the town,/Wherein more lightly seems to press the burden/Of individual life that weighs me down' (Levy 1889: 30–1). Sadly, even in London the burden became insupportable: only a week after correcting proofs for this volume, Levy committed suicide.

What ails my senses thus to cheat?
　　What is it ails the place,
That all the people in the street
　　Should wear one woman's face?

The London trees are dusty-brown
　　Beneath the summer sky;
My love, she dwells in London town,
　　Nor leaves it in July.

O various and intricate maze,
　　Wide waste of square and street;
Where, missing through unnumbered days,
　　We twain at last may meet!

And who cries out on crowd and mart?
　　Who prates of stream and sea?
The summer in the city's heart –
　　That is enough for me.

(Levy 1889: 18)

70   ARTHUR MORRISON, FROM 'A STREET'(1891), *TALES FROM MEAN STREETS* (1894)

Morrison (1863–1945) was born and bred in the East End, the son of an engine fitter in the docks. 'A Street', first published in *Macmillan's* (October 1891), was noticed by W. E. Henley (see doc. 73), who recruited Morrison to write on East-End themes for his *National Observer*. A number of stories first published there were included in *Tales of Mean Streets*. 'A Street' (slightly revised) reappeared as the collection's Introduction. Morrison here sets out to demythologise the East End, widely perceived in the wake of the Ripper murders, strikes and unemployment marches as a theatre of dark melodrama and social unrest. The typical street is not – as Morrison's later books, *A Child of the Jago* (1896) and *The Hole in the Wall* (1902), might suggest – one that Booth (see doc. 72) would colour-code black or dark blue. 'A Street' nevertheless serves as an apt prelude to naturalistic tales with a strong element of economic and environmental determinism, and its corrective keynote of dreary monotony chimes with a prevailing pessimism regarding the inescapable ghettoisation of London's working class (compare, for example, docs 62 and 68).

This street is in the East End. There is no need to say in the East End of what. The East End is a vast city, as famous in its way as any the hand of man has made. But who knows the East End? It is down through Cornhill and out beyond Leadenhall Street and Aldgate Pump, one will say: a shocking place, where he once went with a curate; an evil plexus of slums that hide human creeping things; where filthy men and women live on penn'orths of gin, where collars and clean shirts are decencies unknown, where every citizen wears a black eye, and none ever combs his hair. The East End is a place, says another, which is given over to the Unemployed. And the Unemployed is a race whose token is a clay pipe, and whose enemy is soap: now and again it migrates bodily to Hyde Park with banners, and furnishes adjacent police courts with disorderly drunks. Still another knows the East End only as the place whence begging letters come; there are coal and blanket funds there, all perennially insolvent, and everybody always wants a day in the country. Many and misty are the people's notions of the East End; and each is commonly but the distorted shadow of a minor feature. Foul slums there are in the East End, of course, as there are in the West; want and misery there are, as wherever a host is gathered together to fight for food. But they are not often spectacular in kind.

Of this street there are about one hundred and fifty yards – on the same pattern all. It is not pretty to look at. A dingy little brick house twenty feet high, with three square holes to carry the windows, and an oblong hole to carry the door, is not a pleasing object; and each side of this street is formed by two or three score of such houses in a row, with one front wall in common. And the effect is as of stables. . . .

They are not a very noisy or obtrusive lot in this street. They do not go to Hyde Park with banners, and they seldom fight. It is just possible that one or two among them, at some point in a life of ups and downs, may have been indebted to a coal and blanket fund; but whosoever these may be, they would rather die than publish the disgrace, and it is probable that they very nearly did so ere submitting to it.

Some who inhabit this street are in the docks, some in the gasworks, some in one or other of the few shipbuilding yards that yet survive on the Thames. Two families in a house is the general rule, for there are six rooms behind each set of holes: this, unless 'young men lodgers' are taken in, or there are grown sons paying for bed and board. As for the grown daughters, they marry as soon as may be. Domestic service is a social descent, and little under millinery and dressmaking is compatible with self-respect. The general servant may be caught young among the turnings at the end where mangling is done; and the factory girls live still further off, in places skirting slums.

Every morning at half-past five there is a curious demonstration. The street resounds with thunderous knockings, repeated upon door after door, and acknowledged ever by a muffled shout from within. These signals are the work of the night-watchman or the early policeman, or both, and they summon the sleepers to go forth to the docks, the gasworks, and the ship-yards. . . .

The knocking and the shouting pass, and there comes the noise of opening and shutting of doors, and a clattering away to the docks, the gasworks and the ship-yards. Later more door-shutting is heard, and then the trotting of sorrow-laden little feet along the grim street to the grim Board School three grim streets off. Then silence, save for a subdued sound of scrubbing here and there, and the puny squall of croupy infants. After this, a new trotting of little feet to docks, gasworks, and ship-yards with father's dinner in a basin and a red handkerchief, and so to the Board School again. More muffled scrubbing and more squalling, and perhaps a feeble attempt or two at decorating the blankness of a square hole here and there by pouring water into a grimy flower-pot full of dirt. Then comes the trot of little feet toward the oblong holes, heralding the slower tread of sooty artisans; a smell of bloater up and down; nightfall; the fighting of boys in the street, perhaps of men at the corner near the beer-shop; sleep. And this is the record of a day in this street; and every day is hopelessly the same. . . .

Nobody laughs here – life is too serious a thing; nobody sings. There was once a woman who sang – a young wife from the country. But she bore children, and her voice cracked. Then her man died, and she sang no more. They took away her home, and with her children about her skirts she left this street for ever. The other women did not think much of her. She was 'helpless.' . . .

Where in the East End lies this street? Everywhere. The hundred-and-fifty yards is only a link in a long and a mightily tangled chain – is only a turn in a tortuous maze. This street of the square holes is hundreds of miles long. That it is planned in short lengths is true, but there is no other way in the world that can more properly be called a single street, because of its dismal lack of accent, its sorbid uniformity, its utter remoteness from delight.

(Morrison 1894: 7–14, 17–18, 25)

71 OSCAR WILDE, FROM *THE PICTURE OF DORIAN GRAY* (1891), CHAPTER 16

This, the only novel by Wilde (1854–1900), is one of the notable contributions to the literature of duality which enjoyed a florescence in the late nineteenth century (see Miller 1985: 209–44). In the set of binary oppositions characterising Dorian's double life, that of the upper and the lower world, surface and depths, is of central importance. In pursuit of knowledge and beauty, he tells his friend and mentor Lord Henry Wotton in Chapter 4, 'I went out and wandered eastward, soon losing my way in a labyrinth of grimy streets and black, grassless squares.' Dorian thus discovers 'the greatest romance of my life' (1891: 71–2), but this also initiates his secret corruption, which is far advanced by the time of the episode extracted below. In contrast to the initial quest, it is now oblivion and ugliness that he seeks in an East-End opium den. The urban underworld of *Dorian Gray* draws upon a melodramatic tradition going back at least to Reynolds (doc. 41), though it completely lacks Reynolds' geographical precision. But then Wilde's is in large part a symbolic landscape, suggestive of the protagonist's psychic and moral condition.

A cold rain began to fall, and the blurred street-lamps looked ghastly in the dripping mist. The public-houses were just closing, and dim men and women were clustering in broken groups round their doors. From some of the bars came the sound of horrible laughter. In others, drunkards brawled and screamed.

Lying back in the hansom, with his hat pulled over his forehead, Dorian Gray watched with listless eyes the sordid shame of the great city, and now and then he repeated to himself the words that Lord Henry had said to him on the first day they had met: 'To cure the soul by means of the senses, and the senses by means of the soul.' Yes, that was the secret. He had often tried it, and would try it again now. There were opium-dens, where one could buy oblivion, dens of horror where the memory of old sins could be destroyed by the madness of sins that were new.

The moon hung low in the sky like a yellow skull. From time to time a huge misshapen cloud stretched a long arm across and hid it. The gas-lamps grew fewer, and the streets more narrow and gloomy. Once the man lost his way, and had to drive back half a mile. A steam rose from the horse as it splashed up the puddles. The side-windows of the hansom were clogged with a grey-flannel mist. . . .

The way seemed interminable, and the streets like the black web of some sprawling spider. The monotony became unbearable, and, as the mist thickened, he felt afraid. . . .

After some time they left the clay road, and rattled again over rough-paven streets. Most of the windows were dark, but now and then fantastic shadows were silhouetted against some lamp-lit blind. He watched them curiously. They moved like monstrous marionettes, and made gestures like live things. He hated them. A dull rage was in his heart. As they turned a corner a woman yelled something at them from an open door, and two men ran after the hansom for about a hundred yards. The driver beat at them with his whip. . . .

Suddenly the man drew up with a jerk at the top of a dark lane. Over the low roofs and jagged chimney stacks of the houses rose the black masts of ships. Wreaths of white mist clung like ghostly sails to the yards.

'Somewhere about here, sir, ain't it?' he asked huskily through the trap.

Dorian started, and peered round. 'This will do,' he answered, and, having got out hastily, and given the driver the extra fare he had promised him, he walked quickly in the direction of the quay. Here and there a lantern gleamed at the stern of some huge merchantman. The light shook and splintered in the puddles. A red glare came from an outward-bound steamer that was coaling. The slimy pavement looked like a wet mackintosh.

He hurried on towards the left, glancing back now and then to see if he was being followed. In about seven or eight minutes he reached a small shabby house, that was wedged in between two gaunt factories. In one of the top windows stood a lamp. He stopped, and gave a peculiar knock.

After a little time he heard steps in the passage, and the chain being unhooked. The door opened quietly, and he went in without saying a word to the squat misshapen figure that flattened itself into the shadow as he passed. At the end of the hall hung a tattered green curtain that swayed and shook in the gusty wind which had followed him in from the street. He dragged it aside, and entered a long, low room which looked as if it had once been a third-rate dancing saloon. Shrill flaring gas-jets, dulled and distorted in the fly-blown mirrors that faced them, were ranged round the walls. Greasy reflectors of ribbed tin backed them, making quivering disks of light. The floor was covered with ochre-coloured sawdust, trampled here and there into mud, and stained with dark rings of spilt liquor. Some Malays were crouching by a little charcoal stove playing with bone counters, and showing their white teeth as they chattered. In one corner, with his head buried in his arms, a sailor sprawled over a table, and by the tawdrily painted bar that ran across one complete side stood two haggard women mocking an old man who was brushing the sleeves of his coat with an expression of disgust. 'He thinks he's got red ants on him,' laughed one of them, as Dorian passed by. The man looked at her in terror and began to whimper.

At the end of the room there was a little staircase, leading to a darkened chamber. As Dorian hurried up its three rickety steps, the heavy odour of opium met him. He heaved a deep breath, and his nostrils quivered with pleasure.

(Wilde 1891: 274–9)

72 CHARLES BOOTH, FROM *LABOUR AND LIFE OF THE PEOPLE*, VOL. 2 (1891)

Born into a wealthy family of Liberal-Unitarian shipowners, Booth (1840–1916) married the cousin of Beatrice Potter, who contributed to his monumental investigation of the condition of the London populace (see doc. 64 and, for her excellent account of this grand project, Webb 1926, Ch. 5). It was launched in the East End in 1886 and brought to completion (under a slightly modified title) with a seventeen-volume edition seventeen years later. The 'headline' finding of the metropolitan-wide survey was that 30.7 per cent of the population were in poverty. However, Booth's complex research methodology processes qualitative as well as quantitative data regarding standards of living and occupations; in the stratification of the populace and of the streets it occupies, moral as much as socio-economic criteria are invoked; and a good deal of the material is presented in an impressionistic and far from impersonal style. The (literally) most colourful feature is the famous set of maps of poverty, whereon the streets are colour-coded in accordance with 'the percentage of poverty found in each' and 'their prevailing social character' (Booth 1902–3: II (1902), 16). Black signifies 'lowest class. Vicious, semi-criminal'; dark blue, 'very poor, casual. Chronic want.' Each of the sample street descriptions such as those below is followed by detailed household profiles. However, with the exception of a group of already demolished 'black' streets off Drury Lane, including Shelton Street, the real names of neither streets nor their occupants are used.

Shelton Street was just wide enough for a vehicle to pass either way, with room between curb-stone and houses for one foot-passenger to walk; but vehicles would pass seldom, and foot-passengers would prefer the roadway to the risk of tearing their clothes against projecting nails. The houses, about forty in number, contained cellars, parlours, and first, second, and third floors, mostly two rooms on a floor, and few of the 200 families who lived here occupied more than one room. In little rooms no more than 8 ft square, would be found living father, mother, and several children. ... Most of the people described are Irish Roman Catholics getting a living as market porters, or by selling flowers, fruit, fowls or vegetables in the streets, but as to not a few it is a mystery how they live. Drunkenness and dirt and bad language prevailed, and violence was common, reaching at times even to murder. ... Not a room would be free from vermin, and in many life at night was unbearable.

Several occupants have said that in hot weather they don't go to bed, but sit in their clothes in the least infested part of the room. What good is it, they said, to go to bed when you can't get a wink of sleep for bugs and fleas? A visitor in these rooms was fortunate indeed if he carried nothing of the kind away with him. . . . Most of the doors stood open all night as well as all day, and the passage and stairs gave shelter to many who were altogether home-less. Here the mother could stand with her baby, or sit with it on the stairs, or companions could huddle together in cold weather. . . . The houses looked ready to fall, many of them being out of the perpendicular. Gambling was the amusement of the street. Sentries would be posted, and if the police made a rush the offenders would slip into the open houses and hide until danger was past. Sunday afternoon and evening was the hey-day time for this street. Every doorstep would be crowded by those who sat or stood with pipe and jug of beer, while lads lounged about, and the gutters would find amuse-ment for not a few children with bare feet, their faces and hands besmeared, while the mud oozed between their toes. Add to this a group of fifteen or twenty young men gambling in the middle of the street and you complete the general picture. . . .

Fount Street and Summer Gardens are both coloured dark blue. Baxter Street is black, the houses which are interspersed with the business premises having a bad character. The three together are part of one of the poorest districts in all London, a district where poverty is almost solid. Summer Gardens is a narrow street, all dwelling-houses. Fount Street is mostly dwellings, but has some places of business and a mission-house. . . . There was soup going at the mission-house . . . , a very large old house with wooden front, the boards overlapping like the sides of a boat. At each of its two doors a group was gathered; . . . I passed several times and still the same women, and I think the same children, stood waiting in the freezing air. . . . At the corner as I passed along two boys met. ''Ad dinner?' said one. 'Yes.' 'Was it good?' I put in, and the answer came promptly, 'No.' . . .

In Summer Gardens there live some costermongers, and in Fount Street also, empty barrows stood about and one or two baked potato vans, ready to turn out at night. Before one door stood two barrows well loaded with oranges ready for a start (12.30); the man may have returned to dinner, but more likely his hours begin and end late. Summer Place, the next street to Summer Gardens, is more completely in the occupation of costers. Here, and still more in the yet smaller courts round about, the roads are much littered with paper unwrapped from the fruit. Amongst the scraps of paper and garbage and frozen dirt there is as usual a great quantity of bread strewn about (surest sign of extreme poverty all over London). The streets are all covered and the gutters filled with frozen dirt. . . .

In one street is the body of a dead dog and near by two dead cats, which lie as though they had slain each other. All three have been crushed flat by the traffic which has gone over them. . . . The houses in Baxter Street and Fount Street are interspersed with little shops. Except the old clothes shops, every shop, whatever else it deals in, sells sweets, and with most of them the sweets seem the 'leading article'. . . .

(Booth 1902–3: II (1902), 46–8, 94–6)

73   W. E. HENLEY, FROM *LONDON VOLUNTARIES* (1892)

Although or because he was crippled by serious ill-health from childhood, Henley (1849–1903) promulgated and lived by a creed of strenuous activism (which in the sphere of political ideology came to mean a belligerent imperialism). In 1877 he settled in London to pursue a miscellaneous literary career, wherein his undoubtedly major achievements were as a journal editor, publishing new work by a distinguished array of established and younger writers, and championing notable innovators in the visual arts. His poetry, diverse and often experimental in form, is generally affirmative in spirit; *London Voluntaries* is thus personally characteristic, but also representative of the shift in the early 1890s to a decisively appreciative poetry of the city. *Voluntaries* has five musical movements evoking the atmosphere of different London localities in a seasonal sequence. After the summer of the first two, the golden autumn of this third movement is followed by winter in 'the poisonous East' (End) in the fourth. But the 'Wind-Fiend' of the latter is in turn countered by Pan as 'the gay genius' of Piccadilly in the spring of the final movement, a consummatory celebration of (London) life's wanton joys.

3. Scherzando[1]

Down through the ancient Strand
The spirit of October, mild and boon
And sauntering, takes his way
This golden end of afternoon,
As though the corn stood yellow in all the land,   5
And the ripe apples dropped to the harvest-moon.

Lo! the round sun, half-down the western slope –
Seen as along an unglazed telescope –
Lingers and lolls, loath to be done with day:
Gifting the long, lean, lanky street   10
And its abounding confluences of being
With aspects generous and bland;
Making a thousand harnesses to shine
As with new ore from some enchanted mine,
And every horse's coat so full of sheen   15
He looks new-tailored, and every 'bus feels clean,

190

And never a hansom but is worth the feeing;
And every jeweller within the pale
Offers a real Arabian Night for sale;
And even the roar   20
Of the strong streams of toil, that pause and pour
Eastward and westward, sounds suffused –
Seems as it were bemused
And blurred, and like the speech
Of lazy seas on a lotus-haunted beach –   25
With this enchanted lustrousness,
This mellow magic, that (as a man's caress
Brings back to some faded face, beloved before,
A heavenly shadow of the grace it wore
Ere the poor eyes were minded to beseech)   30
Old things transfigures, and you hail and bless
Their looks of long-lapsed loveliness once more;
Till Clement's, angular and cold and staid,
Gleams forth in glamour's very stuffs arrayed;
And Bride's, her aëry, unsubstantial charm   35
Through flight on flight of springing, soaring stone
Grown flushed and warm,
Laughs into life full-mooded and fresh-blown;
And the high majesty of Paul's
Uplifts a voice of living light, and calls –   40
Calls to his millions to behold and see
How goodly this his London Town can be!

For earth and sky and air
Are golden everywhere,
And golden with a gold so suave and fine   45
The looking on it lifts the heart like wine.
Trafalgar Square
(The fountains volleying golden glaze)
Shines like an angel-market. High aloft
Over his couchant Lions, in a haze   50
Shimmering and bland and soft,
A dust of chrysoprase,[2]
Our Sailor takes the golden gaze
Of the saluting sun, and flames superb,
As once he flamed it on his ocean round.   55
The dingy dreariness of the picture-place,

Turned very nearly bright,
Takes on a luminous transiency of grace,
And shows no more a scandal to the ground.
The very blind man pottering on the curb   60
Among the posies and the ostrich feathers
And the rude voices touched with all the weathers
Of the long, varying year,
Shares in the universal alms of light.
The windows, with their fleeting, flickering fires,   65
The height and spread of frontage shining sheer,
The quiring signs, the rejoicing roofs and spires –
'Tis El Dorado – El Dorado plain,
The Golden City! And when a girl goes by,
Look! as she turns her glancing head,   70
A call of gold is floated from her ear!
Golden, all golden! In a golden glory,
Long-lapsing down a golden coasted sky,
The day not dies, but seems
Dispersed in wafts and drifts of gold, and shed   75
Upon a past of golden song and story
And memories of gold and golden dreams.

(Henley 1893: 10–14)

Notes

1 *Scherzando*: in a light-hearted manner.
2 *chrysoprase*: apple-green quartz.

74   J. P. DE OLIVEIRA MARTINS, FROM
THE ENGLAND OF TODAY (1893), CHAPTERS 4 AND 22

Oliveira Martins (1845–94) has been described as 'the most brilliant and original of Portuguese historians, one of the most interesting literary figures of nineteenth-century Europe' (Oliveira Martins 1930: ix). Despite a deprived childhood in Lisbon, he rose to prominence in many spheres – as railway engineer and director, as distinguished writer in several disciplines, and, having started in politics as a revolutionary socialist, as Minister of Finance for a few months in 1891. In *A Inglaterra de Hoje*, based on a visit to London the following summer, personal observation is blended with sociological, economic and political commentary in a manner reminiscent of Taine (doc. 60), a figure whom Oliveira Martins indeed resembles. He is one of the first to note the domination of the face of London by advertisements in the late Victorian era. His later account of a guided tour of Whitechapel, which also takes in the Jewish quarter and a Chinese opium den, shows the image of the East End as dark foreign territory reinforced by the Ripper murders four years before, and thereby melodramatised for the tourist gaze.

The real monuments of the London of today are in my opinion seen in the buildings spontaneously born of the necessities of the dominant character of this Carthaginian civilisation. They are the Crystal Palaces of the popular Exhibitions; they are the massive and utilitarian bridges; the awe-inspiring railway stations, where the people huddle together in the vertigo of bustle, and the walls, inside and outside, the roofs, the ground, the seats, the glass-work, absolutely everything is bedaubed with advertisements in colossal letters of strident colours to force the attention of passers-by.

Advertisement – the bill-frenzy – was among the things that impressed me most. They persecute one everywhere. In the stations they are a delirium. They paint omnibuses with them. They line carriages with them. They put them above the roofs of houses in great letters of gold hanging up for the wind to shake. They are the English æolian harps.

Everything is advertised, absolutely everything: clothes, shoes, furniture, articles of luxury, poverty, the most extravagant medicines, the most curious utensils, with nauseating names, extracted from rare or dead languages, with certificates from the medical faculty and the learned generally. It is even a Carnival scene. I saw in a journey, I know not where, hung up from the roof more than a hundred bills successively announcing with an irritating obstinacy a certain substance which washed and yet was not soap.

And as these dodges pay, and as rivers of money are spent in advertisement, it is sad to think that the colossal metropolis of a great people bows down to such an extent before quackery, or that it is necessary to use quack measures to attract attention. English eccentricity shows itself in the stupid proportions of advertisement; though advertisement in general is an ailment of all great cities. . . .

The detective that accompanied us was a broad-shouldered giant. He infused into us a confidence we were very glad of in the middle of the quarter renowned for the exploits of Jack the Ripper. To one observation I made to him the detective answered me gravely: 'Certainly. It would be rash to come alone to these places even by day. By night, even inhabitants of London do not venture – much less strangers! This is no longer London. London ends with the *City*. This is the *East End*. The greater part of these people do not know of the existence of Hyde Park. They are born and they die here.' . . .

The detective . . . took us towards a street as dark as pitch. Along the sides there passed the shadows of queer-looking men talking to themselves. We went in file. The detective kept his policeman's whistle in his hand. We arrived at a square where the houses, miserable little cottages . . . formed a dismal recess. On the ground there were heaps of rotten mud. On one side lay the wreck of a cart with a broken axle. Absolute solitude. 'Here it was,' said the detective to us, stopping and pointing to the corner, 'here it was that Jack the Ripper operated upon his first victim.'

We followed behind, and ... the policeman ... knocked at the door of a dirty cottage. A hoarse voice grunted out an answer from within. The door opened and we entered, going down from the level of the street, for the tenement was partly underground. It was an enclosure that was at most double the size of the little iron bedstead placed on one side of it. A petroleum lamp, without screen, gave an uneasy light over the room, if such a place wherein we were could be called. On the bedstead, upon a straw mattress reeking with filthy moisture and covered with indescribable rags, lay a bald-headed man with a bottle of spirits. His breath, mingling with the smell of the petroleum and the ferment of the rottenness, formed an atmosphere impossible to breathe. A woman by his side said to the detective, 'He has had no work at the docks for a fortnight.'

I really do not know if the term woman could be applied to this creature, old before her time, her scanty hair plastered to her head, dragging over her bare shoulders a shawl yellow with grease, wearing a dirty petticoat, and trailing along on her feet a pair of loathsome slippers. She had the expression of an idiot.

'She drinks as well,' said the policeman to us seriously.

You might have cut the air of the room with a knife. There were also a broken chair, some remnants of clothes hung up on a line, and in a corner, in the dark shade, something that appeared to me to stir. I went near and stooped down; it was a child entirely naked. I wished to amuse the little creature but it bit me like an animal, with a savage air lighting up its eyes. The mother grunted, the father breathed with difficulty, and the detective, as we went out, said to us: 'It was on that bed that Jack the Ripper mutilated another woman. Did you not see on the wall at the side some dark splashes? It was the blood that gushed upon it, and it is there still.'

(Oliveira Martins 1896: 33–5, 252, 254–6)

75   CHARLOTTE MEW, FROM 'PASSED' (1894)

Mew (1869–1928), the daughter of a prosperous architect, was born and lived most of her rather unhappy life in the Bloomsbury district of London. Two of her siblings were permanently confined in mental asylums, and she herself committed suicide in a mentally disturbed condition. Although the publication of 'Passed' in the second issue of *The Yellow Book* gave her access to a literary-artistic milieu associated with that quintessentially 'Nineties' magazine, it was only after the appearance of her collection of verse, *The Farmer's Bride*, in 1916 that she achieved significant recognition, with Thomas Hardy (a personal friend) and Virginia Woolf among the admirers regarding her as the best woman poet of the age. In 'Passed', the opening of which is reproduced here, the narrator-agent wanders through the poorer streets of London alone as Mew herself apparently did at a time when this was still unusual for a middle-class woman. Yet this initial gesture of independence is misleading: in a sequence of passing encounters with female figures, especially that in which a destitute girl met in a church takes her home to a slum dwelling where the mother lies dead, there is an increasing loss of psychological and emotional control. That central scene is prefigured in the encounter near the end of this opening passage, with religious imagery embodying a romantic allure which is to be swiftly negated by unglamorous realities.

> 'Like souls that meeting pass,
> And passing never meet again.'

Let those who have missed a romantic view of London in its poorest quarters – and there will romance be found – wait for a sunset in early winter. They may turn North or South, towards Islington or Westminster, and encounter some fine pictures and more than one aspect of unique beauty. This hour of pink twilight has its monopoly of effects. Some of them may never be reached again.

On such an evening in mid-December, I put down my sewing and left tame glories of fire-light (discoverers of false charm) to welcome, as youth may, the contrast of keen air outdoors to the glow within.

My aim was the perfection of a latent appetite, for I had no mind to content myself with an apology for hunger, consequent on a warmly passive afternoon.

The splendid cold of fierce frost set my spirit dancing. The road rung hard underfoot, and through the lonely squares woke sharp echoes from behind. This stinging air assailed my cheeks with vigorous severity. It stirred my blood grandly, and brought thought back to me from the warm embers just forsaken, with an immeasurable sense of gain.

But after the first delirium of enchanting motion, destination became a question. The dim trees behind the dingy enclosures were beginning to be succeeded by rows of flaring gas jets, displaying shops of new aspect and evil smell. Then the heavy walls of a partially demolished prison reared themselves darkly against the pale sky.

By this landmark I recalled – alas that it should be possible – a church in the district, newly built by an infallible architect, which I had been directed to seek at leisure. I did so now. A row of cramped houses, with the unpardonable bow window, projecting squalor into prominence, came into view. Robbing these even of light, the portentous walls stood a silent curse before them. I think they were blasting the hopes of the sad dwellers beneath them – if hope they had – to despair. Through spattered panes faces of diseased and dirty children leered into the street. One room, as I passed, seemed full of them. The window was open; their wails and maddening requirements sent out the mother's cry. It was thrown back to her, mingled with her children's screams, from the pitiless prison walls.

These shelters struck my thought as travesties – perhaps they were not – of the grand place called home.

Leaving them I sought the essential of which they were bereft. What withheld from them, as poverty and sin could not, a title to the sacred name?

An answer came, but interpretation was delayed. Theirs was not the desolation of something lost, but of something that had never been. I thrust off speculation gladly here, and fronted Nature free.

Suddenly I emerged from the intolerable shadow of the brickwork, breathing easily once more. Before me lay a roomy space, nearly square, bounded by three-storey dwellings, and transformed, as if by quick mechanism, with colours of sunset. Red and golden spots wavered in the panes of the low scattered houses round the bewildering expanse. Overhead a faint crimson sky was hung with violet clouds, obscured by the smoke and nearing dusk.

In the centre, but towards the left, stood an old stone pump, and some few feet above it irregular lamps looked down. They were planted on a square of paving railed in by broken iron fences, whose paint, now discoloured, had once been white. Narrow streets cut in five directions from the open roadway. Their lines of light sank dimly into distance, mocking the stars' entrance into the fading sky. Everything was transfigured in the illuminated twilight. As I stood, the dying sun caught the rough edges of a girl's uncovered hair, and hung a faint nimbus round her poor desecrated face. The soft circle, as she glanced toward me, lent it the semblance of one of those mystically pictured faces of some medieval saint.

A stillness stole on, and about the square dim figures hurried along, leaving me stationary in existence (I was thinking fancifully), when my medieval saint demanded 'who I was a-shoving of?' and dismissed me, not unkindly, on my way. Hawkers in a neighbouring alley were calling, and the monotonous ting-ting of the muffin-bell made an audible background to the picture. I left it, and then the glamour was already passing. In a little while darkness possessing it, the place would reassume its aspect of sordid gloom.

(Mew 1894: 121–3)

76 JOHN DAVIDSON, FROM 'A WOMAN AND HER SON' (1897)

Davidson (1857–1909) spent most of his early life in Greenock on Clydeside, where his father was a minister of the Evangelical Union and where he first worked as a laboratory assistant and school teacher. He moved to London in 1889 to pursue a full-time literary career, but, despite some initial popular and critical success as poet and dramatist, he was soon struggling against the financial difficulties and deteriorating health which ultimately drove him to suicide. The city is a major presence in

Davidson's work, ambivalently regarded both as a concentration of the ruthlessly energetic forces he came to admire, and as a drearily confining environment for the exploited masses (especially in the new, soulless suburbs) with whom he never ceased to sympathise. Contradiction often finds expression in the dramatic form in which many of his poems are cast. Most of the 250-line 'A Woman and Her Son' is a dialogue between a dying (and then temporarily resurrected) widow of an evangelical preacher, hoping 'to soften you . . . before I die' (l. 37) and her son, who is determined to harden her into recognising force and strength as the only values in a godless universe; characteristically, the resolution involves some convergence of polarities. The extract below shows Davidson as a forerunner of T. S. Eliot (a legacy the latter acknowledged) in his use of blank verse to render the rhythms and cadences of informal speech, and more particularly in the vision of a 'raw waste land where doleful suburbs thrive'.

'Has he come yet?' the dying woman asked.
'No,' said the nurse. 'Be quiet.'
                  'When he comes
Bring him to me: I may not live an hour.'
'Not if you talk. Be quiet.'
                  'When he comes
Bring him to me.'
         'Hush, will you!'

                        Night came down.
The cries of children playing in the street
Suddenly rose more voluble and shrill;
Ceased, and broke out again; and ceased and broke
In eager prate; then dwindled and expired.

'Across the dreary common once I saw   10
The moon rise out of London like a ghost.
Has the moon risen? Is he come?'
                        'Not yet.
Be still, or you will die before he comes.'

The working-men with heavy iron tread,
The thin-shod clerks, the shopmen neat and plump
Home from the city came. On muddy beer
The melancholy mean suburban street
Grew maudlin for an hour; pianos waked
In dissonance from dreams of rusty peace,
And unpitched voices quavered tedious songs   20
Of sentiment infirm or nerveless mirth.

'Has he come yet?'
                'Be still or you will die!'

And when the hour of gaiety had passed,
And the poor revellers were gone to bed,
The moon among the chimneys wandering long
Escaped at last, and sadly overlooked
The waste raw land where doleful suburbs thrive.
Then came a firm quick step – measured but quick;
And then a triple knock that shook the house
And brought the plaster down.

                  'My son!' she cried.   30
'Bring him to me!'
          He came; the nurse went out . . .

He set his teeth, and saw his mother die.
Outside a city-reveller's tipsy tread
Severed the silence with a jagged rent;
The tall lamps flickered through the sombre street,   160
With yellow light hiding the stainless stars:
In the next house a child awoke and cried;
Far off a clank and clash of shunting trains
Broke out and ceased, as if the fettered world
Started and shook its irons in the night;
Across the dreary common citywards,
The moon, among the chimneys sunk again,
Cast on the clouds a shade of smoky pearl.

                  (Davidson 1897: 22–5, 33–5)

77 ARNOLD BENNETT, FROM *A MAN FROM THE NORTH* (1898), CHAPTER 3

A Man from the North is a semi-autobiographical first novel, in which Bennett (1867–1931) was perhaps expiating the fear of failure in the metropolitan literary world. The protagonist, Richard Larch, arrives in London from the Potteries with ambitions to write and, as this early scene shows, with a thirst for the glamorous excitement and freedom of the great city. In the sphere of late nineteenth-century popular culture, these properties were supremely represented by 'Theatres of Varieties' – glorified music-halls – of which the Empire (Bennett's 'Ottoman') in Leicester Square was the most famous (or infamous in respect of the prostitutes frequenting its promenade). However, in keeping with the tone and style of Bennett's French realist models, Richard's story is predominantly downbeat; by the end he has given up trying to write a novel and has settled for the placidities of married life in a 'suburban doll's house' (p. 177).

He walked slowly up Park Side and through Piccadilly, picking out as he passed them the French Embassy, Hyde Park Corner, Apsley House, Park

198

Lane, and Devonshire House. As he drank in the mingled glare and glamour of Piccadilly by night – the remote stars, the high sombre trees, the vast, dazzling interiors of clubs, the sinuous, flickering lines of traffic, the radiant faces of women framed in hansoms – he laughed the laugh of luxurious contemplation, acutely happy. At last, at last, he had come into his inheritance. London accepted him. He was hers; she his; and nothing should part them. Starvation in London would itself be bliss. But he had no intention of starving! Filled with great purposes, he straightened his back, and just then a morsel of mud thrown up from a bus-wheel splashed warm and gritty on his cheek. He wiped it off caressingly, with a smile. . . .

At Piccadilly Circus he loitered, and then crossed over and went along Coventry Street to Leicester Square. The immense façade of the Ottoman Theatre of Varieties, with its rows of illuminated windows and crescent moons set against the sky, rose before him, and the glory of it was intoxicating. It is not too much to say that the Ottoman held a stronger fascination for Richard than any other place in London. The British Museum, Fleet Street, and the Lyceum were magic names, but more magical than either was the name of the Ottoman. The Ottoman, on the rare occasions when it happened to be mentioned in Bursley, was a synonym for all the glittering vices of the metropolis. It stank in the nostrils of the London delegates who came down to speak at the annual meetings of the local Society for the Suppression of Vice. But how often had Richard, somnolent in chapel, mitigated the rigours of a long sermon by dreaming of an Ottoman ballet – one of those voluptuous spectacles, all legs and white arms, which from time to time were described so ornately in the London daily papers.

The brass-barred swinging doors of the Grand Circle entrance were simultaneously opened for him by two human automata dressed exactly alike in long semi-military coats, a very tall man and a stunted boy. He advanced with what air of custom he could command, and after taking a ticket and traversing a heavily decorated corridor, encountered another pair of swinging doors; they opened, and a girl passed out, followed by a man who was talking to her vehemently in French. At the same moment a gust of distant music struck Richard's ear. As he climbed a broad, thickpiled flight of steps the music became louder, and a clapping of hands could be heard. At the top of the steps hung a curtain of blue velvet; he pushed aside its stiff, heavy folds with difficulty, and entered the auditorium.

The smoke of a thousand cigarettes enveloped the furthest parts of the great interior in a thin bluish haze, which was dissipated as it reached the domed ceiling in the rays of a crystal chandelier. Far in front and a little below the level of the circle lay a line of footlights broken by the silhouette of the conductor's head. A diminutive, solitary figure in red and yellow

stood in the centre of the huge stand; it was kissing its hands to the audience with a mincing, operatic gesture; presently it tripped off backwards,
stopping at every third step to bow; the applause ceased, and the curtain fell
slowly.

The broad, semicircular promenade which flanked the seats of the grand
circle was filled with a well-dressed, well-fed crowd. The men talked and
laughed, for the most part, in little knots, while in and out, steering their way
easily and rapidly among these groups, moved the women: some with rouged
cheeks, greasy vermilion lips, and enormous liquid eyes; others whose faces
were innocent of cosmetics and showed pale under the electric light; but all
with a peculiar, exaggerated swing of the body from the hips, and all surreptitiously regarding themselves in the mirrors which abounded on every glowing wall. . . .

The band suddenly began to play, and after a few crashing bars the curtain
went up for the ballet. The rich *coup d'œil* which presented itself provoked a
burst of clapping from the floor of the house and the upper tiers, but to
Richard's surprise no one in his proximity seemed to exhibit any interest in
the entertainment. . . .

Richard never took his dazed eyes from the stage. The moving pageant
unrolled itself before him like a vision, rousing new sensations, tremors of
strange desires. He was under a spell, and when at last the curtain descended
to the monstrous roll of drums, he awoke to the fact that several people were
watching him curiously. Blushing slightly, he went to a far corner of the
promenade. At one of the little tables a woman sat alone. She held her head
at an angle, and her laughing, lustrous eyes gleamed invitingly at Richard.
Without quite intending to do so he hesitated in front of her, and she twit-
tered a phrase ending in *chéri*.

He abruptly turned away. He would have been very glad to remain and
say something clever, but his tongue refused its office, and his legs moved
themselves.

At midnight he found himself in Piccadilly Circus, unwilling to go home.
He strolled leisurely back to Leicester Square. The front of the Ottoman was
in darkness, and the square almost deserted.

(Bennett 1973: 5–9)

78   CLARENCE ROOK, FROM *THE HOOLIGAN NIGHTS* (1899), CHAPTER 1

Rook (1862–1915) was a London journalist about whom little else is known. In *The Hooligan Nights* he presents a non-judgemental narrative portrait of a young criminal and gang-leader in Lambeth, claiming indeed to do so 'as far as possible in his own words' (1899: xxi); the book thus displays some characteristic features of late nineteenth-century urban naturalism. However, Rook's introductory over-insistence that it 'is neither a novel, nor in any sense a work of the imagination' (p. xxi) also recalls Defoe's rhetorical strategy in, for example, *Moll Flanders* (doc. 10), placing the work in a long tradition of rogue literature.

''Ere we are,' said young Alf ... as we turned suddenly from the glaring, shouting, seething Walk,[1] redolent of gas, naphtha, second-hand shoe-leather, and fried fish, into a dark entrance. Dimly I could see that the entrance broadened a few yards down into a court of about a dozen feet in width. No light shone from any of the windows, no gas-lamp relieved the gloom. The court ran from the glare of the street into darkness and mystery. . . .

'Where them women's standing is where Pat Hooligan lived, 'fore he was pinched.'

It stood no higher than the houses that elbowed it, and had nothing to distinguish it from its less notable neighbours. But if a Hooligan boy prayed at all, he would pray with his face toward that house half-way down Irish Court.

'And next door – this side,' continued young Alf, 'that's where me and my muvver kipped when I was a nipper.'

The tone of pride was unmistakable, for the dwelling-place of Patrick Hooligan enshrines the ideal towards which the Ishmaelites of Lambeth are working; and as I afterwards learned, young Alf's supremacy over his comrades was sealed by his association with the memory of the Prophet. . . .

I inquired of his plans for the night, and he explained that there was a bit of a street-fight in prospect. The Drury Lane boys were coming across the bridge, and had engaged to meet the boys from Lambeth Walk at a coffee-stall on the other side. Then one of the Lambeth boys would make to one of the Drury Lane boys a remark which cannot be printed, but never fails to send the monkey of a Drury Lane boy a considerable way up the pole. Whereafter the Drury Lane boys would fall upon the Lambeth boys, and the Lambeth boys would give them what for.

As we came under the gas-lamps of Upper Kennington Lane, young Alf opened his coat. He was prepared for conflict. Round his throat he wore the blue neckerchief, spotted with white, with which my memory will always associate him; beneath that a light jersey. His trousers were supported by a strong leathern belt with a savage-looking buckle.

Diving into his breast pocket, and glancing cautiously round, he drew out a handy-looking chopper which he poised for a moment, as though assuring himself of its balance.

'That's awright, eh?' he said, putting the chopper in my hand.

'Are you going to fight with that?' I asked, handing it back to him.

He passed his hand carefully across the blade.

'That oughter mean forty winks for one or two of 'em. Don't you fink so?' he said.

His eyes glittered in the light of the gas-lamp as he thrust the chopper back into his pocket and buttoned up his coat, having first carefully smoothed down the ends of his spotted neckerchief.

'Then you'll have a late night, I suppose?' I said as we passed along up the lane.

''Bout two o'clock I shall be back at my kip,' he replied.

We parted for the night at Vauxhall Cross, where a small crowd of people waited for their trams. We did not shake hands. The ceremony always seems unfamiliar and embarrassing to him. With a curt nod he turned and slid through the crowd, a lithe, well-knit figure, shoulders slightly hunched, turning his head neither to this side nor to that, hands close to his trouser pockets, sneaking his way like a fish through the scattered peril of rocks.

(Rook 1899: 8, 10, 17–19)

Note

1   *Walk*: Lambeth Walk was the site of a well-known working-class market; compare the opening of doc. 65.

79   EDGAR BATEMAN (AND EUSTACE BAYNES), TWO MUSIC-HALL SONGS (1901)

These pieces provide a refreshing antidote to the sombre, if not despairing, views of London working-class life generally purveyed in middle-class writing up to and around the turn of the century. But like other Bateman songs, several of them performed by the coster comedian, Gus Elen, they also show, as Featherstone (1996) effectively argues, that late-Victorian music-hall had not become as socially and politically anaemic as some other modern accounts have suggested. Bateman (1860–1946) was 'a Cockney bred and born' (Abbott 1952: 14) who worked as a compositor on the *Sunday Referee* before joining the pioneer popular-music publishers, Francis, Day & Hunter. His aptitude as a songwriter for giving a piquant twist to lexical and thematic clichés is apparent in these two treatments of the city workers' holiday outing. In the first piece (music by George Le Brunn, sung by Bella Lloyd), the Bryants and May match girls (historically famed for their successful company strike of 1888) crash through the class barriers at the Henley Regatta with brazen belligerence, a comic confirmation in reverse perspective of the disorderly eruptions from 'the abyss' apprehensively recorded by Masterman (doc. 80) at just this time. In Baynes and Bateman's 'A Nice Quiet Day' (performed by Elen), the ironies of the title derive not only from the day's chain of calamities, but also from the fact that although (or rather because) 'I works like a nigger', the postman's excursion is a thoroughgoing busman's holiday, including a compulsive trek round the most far-flung postal districts of London.

The Girls from Bryants and May

Now me and all the other gals from Bryants and May,
We thought we'd 'ave a day to lark about and play –
We'd got the sick of 'Ampstead and the places up our way,
So off we went to 'Enley up the river all so gay!
We got there as 'appy as could be,
All the sights to see – cake and shrimps for tea.
'Let's go boating,' Bill 'e sez to me,
And 'e knows all about it 'cos 'e once fell in the Lea.[1]

CHORUS

And never will they forget the day,
The day we 'ad the beano:
   We all 'ad 'ticklers' in our 'and,
   With us the concertina band,
All the swells 'ad come from town upon Regatta day,
And all us bloomin' aristocrats that work for Bryants and May!

We all went on the towing path to try and get a boat,
Some masher[2] in a boat – 'ouse-flannel round his coat –
Said, 'What a beastly bally noise – they cannot play a note!'
So Bill 'e rammed 'is concertina down the Johnny's throat!
Toffs and stuck-up gals began to flock,
But they 'ad a shock – soon they took the knock!
I 'eard one marm sneezing at my frock
So then she got a shove which sent 'er flying in the lock.

CHORUS

And never will they forget the day,
The day we 'ad the beano:
   Just two 'undred jolly girls,
   'Aving a game with all the swells.
We made a target of their 'ats with whacking lumps of clay,
And got the bullseye every time, the girls from Bryants and May!

I 'eard a fat old geezer say 'O fetch a policeman, Bert!'
And 'e put on a spurt – though 'e was on a 'cert.'
We got three-quarters of 'is coat and 'alf his 'Dicky-dirt'![3]
And we found such lovely lots of loot.
Bill 'e looked a bute in someone's summer suit,

Made some toff change – then we shouted 'scoot!'
And sent him home in corduroys, assisted by a boot!

CHORUS

And never will they forget the day,
The day we 'ad the beano:
   'Arriet, Sall, and Ann Maria,
   Setting the blooming Thames afire!
And ev'ry time they strike a match the folks up 'Enley way,
They always think of brimstone and the girls from Bryants and May.

(Bateman 1901)

A Nice Quiet Day; or The Postman's Holiday

I works just like a nigger, and I isn't over strong,
   And I'm mostly on my trotters all the time;
So I'm glad when Easter Monday or a Whitsun comes along,
   'Cause a day of puffick rest is really prime.
So I lately took it easy 'cause I 'ad a day to spare,
   Wiv the wife and kiddies in their Sunday clothes;
'Twas a treat to make my mind up for a little country air,
   And the pleasures of a quiet day's repose.

CHORUS

There was me and the Missus, and the 'arf-a-dozen kids,
   Starting in the morning for the Zoo.
'Twas a precious way, you know, but we made our minds to go,
   And we took the lot to Eppin' Forest too.
Highgate, Barnet, 'Ampstead, Peckham Rye,
   At the Crystal Palace made a stay;
We got weary on our pins, and we lost the blooming twins,
   But I'm glad we 'ad a nice quiet day.

The night before none of us thought o' getting into bed,
   'Cause we'd got all day tomorrow for the rest;
And 'arf the night was taken up in cutting meat and bread,
   And in getting all the youngsters ready dressed.
I felt a bit lop-sided 'cause I carried all the grub,
   It's surprising wot a lot the kids can peck;
And I got a gallon bottle full of porter from the pub,
   'Cause it balanced all the grub around my neck.

CHORUS

There was me and the Missus, and the 'arf-a-dozen kids,
    Climbing up the Monument so 'igh;
Then we played at Jack and Jill when we sampled Greenwich Hill,
    And we 'ad a run to Chiswick bye-and-bye.
Acton, 'Endon, Kilburn, Kensal Green,
    Loaded wiv the lilac and the may;
There was blisters on my heel, from an 'arf an inch o' steel,
    But I'm glad we 'ad a nice quiet day.

'Twas grand to see the London smoke from the Monument,
    When I dragged the pram-ber-looter to the top;
As soon as I got up there to the bottom I was sent,
    'Cause the Missus let a beef-steak pudden drop.
And when we reached the Ser-pin-tine, the nipper tumbles in,
    We 'eld 'im upside down a bit to drain;
And soon as we 'ad scraped the mud from off his nose and chin,
    Well, blow me, if he don't fall in again.

CHORUS

There was me and the Missus, and the 'arf-a-dozen kids,
    Wiv nuffink in the bottle but the bung;
But I gave the kids a treat when we got to Newgate Street,
    'Cause I showed 'em where their uncle 'e was 'ung.
West Ham, Wanstead, Woolwich, Walthamstow,
    Reached a spot they called St Mary's Cray;[4]
And then I sez to Ma, 'Now we mustn't go too far,
    'Cause I finks we've had a nice quiet day.' . . .

(Baynes and Bateman 1901)

Notes

1 *Lea*: London river which then ran into the Thames at Poplar.
2 *masher*: dandy, fop.
3 *Dicky-dirt*: shirt (rhyming slang).
4 *St Mary's Cray*: Kentish village then on the extreme south-east edge of London.

80 C. F. G. MASTERMAN, FROM *FROM THE ABYSS* (1902)

Born into an upper-middle-class evangelical family, Masterman (1873–1927) gained high academic distinction and became an accomplished, committed writer and orator on social questions. Elected Liberal MP for West Ham (North) in 1906, he held office in several government departments over the next eight years, though his political career never quite reached the expected heights. Having become interested in the East-End settlement movement while at Cambridge, Masterman went with two friends to live in a tenement flat in Camberwell, South London, in 1900. Out of this experience emerged *From the Abyss*, anonymously published but subtitled 'Of the Inhabitants by One of Them'. However, the rhetorical strategy of speaking as a denizen of the lower depths is not pursued in the arresting opening section, an index of the alarm felt even by this young progressive in the face of what seems like an invasion of 'kindly, familiar London' by 'dense black masses' of subterranean aliens. These are described, as Keating (1976: 21–2) has pointed out, in terms strongly reminiscent of Wells' *The Time Machine* (1895). Masterman's final scene offers another view from above, but with a quite different tonality: in this panoramic vision of 'the interminable city' transfigured by evening sunlight, with the towers of Westminster gleaming in the distance, the figure of the abyss, so shockingly expressive of brutal social divisions, and its associated imagery of wild beasts and deep-sea monsters give way to the idea of a human collectivity, albeit confused, *in specie aeternitatis*.

At intervals during the late war events have demonstrated the necessity for a readjustment of our outlook to an altered environment. . . . Without warning or observation, a movement and a sound have arisen in those unknown regions surrounding the kindly, familiar London that we know. . . . Our streets have suddenly become congested with a weird and uncanny people. They have poured in as dense black masses from the eastern railways; they have streamed across the bridges from the marshes and desolate places beyond the river; they have been hurried up in incredible number through tubes sunk in the bowels of the earth, emerging like rats from a drain, blinking in the sunshine. They have surged through our streets, turbulent, cheerful, indifferent to our assumed proprietorship; their sound has been in all ways, their going and their coming in all men's ears. Three times at least during these months the richest city in the world was in the hollow of their hands. They brushed the police away like an elephant dispersing flies. They could have looted and destroyed, plundered and razed it to the ground. We gazed at them in startled amazement. Whence did they all come, these creatures with strange antics and manners, these denizens of another universe of being? They themselves seemed half afraid of their power, awed by unaccustomed daylight and squares and open spaces. They drifted through the streets hoarsely cheering, breaking into fatuous, irritating laughter, singing quaint militant melodies. . . . As the darkness drew on they relapsed more and more into bizarre and barbaric revelry. . . . They blew trumpets; they hit each other with bladders; they tickled passers-by with feathers; they embraced ladies in the streets, laughing genially and boisterously. Later the drink got into them, and they reeled and struck and swore, walking and leaping and blaspheming God. At night we left them, a packed and sodden multitude, howling under the quiet stars. We woke in the morning, and lo! they had gone – vanished, 'as a dream when one awaketh.' . . .

Further investigation discovers the perpetual presence of an existence which only rises to menacing gaiety upon occasions of national rejoicing. One may, for example, descend a great while before civilization awakens to any of the bridges that stretch towards the chaotic region beyond the river. The immediate impression is as of some gigantic upheaval and catastrophe in the unknown land; as if the inhabitants, like the fugitives from the cities of the plain, without time to gather up their household goods, were hurrying from a coming destruction and forbidden to look backward. A turbid river of humanity, pent up on the narrow bridge, is pouring into London; aged men in beards and bowlers shambling hastily forward; work girls, mechanics, active boys, neat little clerks in neat little high hats shining out conspicuous in the rushing stream. The pace is even lest one should fall; the general aspect is of a harassed but good-tempered energy, as of those driven along ways not clearly comprehended towards no definite goal. The Abyss is disgorging its denizens for the labour of the day. . . .

So as if propelled by the systole and diastole of some mighty unseen heart, the wave of humanity from north, east, and south rolls daily in and out of London. It floods into every crevice, depositing its burden at every door. No street or pathway is untouched by its influence. During the working hours the hum of industry arises in workshop and counting-house and factory; a vast enterprise is perpetually fermenting; threads are being woven towards every corner of the world. At night the gigantic machine stands idle and empty. In the unknown lands beyond, in the marshes of the South and on the hills of the North, four million people are sleeping under the stars. They have a life apart; their own existences are sharply severed asunder. The life they have made for themselves, when liberated from the forced service of others, is a life whose characteristics we are only just commencing dimly to discern.

We had thought that a city of four million people was merely a collection of one hundred cities of forty thousand. We find it differing not only in degree, but in kind, producing a mammoth of gigantic and unknown possibility. Hitherto it has failed to realize its power. It has counted for nothing; it has been hedged within isolated districts, each separate, apart, ignorant of the other. It has been wheedled into amiability and smoothed with honeyed words. Through the action of a benevolent autocratic Government it has now been invited to contemplate its strength. It has crept out into the daylight. At first it has moved painfully in the unaccustomed glare, as a cave bear emerging from his dark den. Now it is straightening itself and learning to gambol with heavy and grotesque antics in the sunshine. It finds the exercise pleasant; it uproots a small tree, displaces a rock, laughing with pleased good-humour. How long before, in a fit of ill-temper, it suddenly realizes its tremendous unconquerable might?

One last impression remains. We are gazing down from the high roof of our dwellings upon the great city, in the late afternoon of a November day – one of those occasional hours of magical clearness before sun-setting which are given by the little summer before the season of fog and rain and cold. The vast acreage of human dwellings, picturesque now in their very dishevelment and irregularity, stands out golden-tipped and clear; in the west the saffron melts to rose and the rose to a deep glare of crimson; church beyond church, spire beyond spire reflect the evening light, with far on the horizon in the heart of the glow the distant towers of Westminster. Great masses of smoke from chimneys drift across the sunset and hang heavy in the still air; the west deepens to purple, then to grey shadow; a million fairy lights enkindle in the mazes of the lamp-lit streets; above, the sky darkens into a deep blue curtain studded with innumerable stars. The confused noises of the multitude, of a bewildered and restless people, rise here but as the presence of an atmosphere charged with human emotion; and the 'sound of many-voiced life' has become 'not a maddening discord, but a melting one; with inarticulate cries and sobbings as of a dumb creature which in the ear of heaven are prayers.' It is London's one incalculable hour. Still the vastness, the aimlessness, the inevitable, unanswered inquiry of the meaning of it all. But to those who have been engaged all day in the hot and dusty struggle below, here is the Infinite banished from the eager traffic of men cooped up in narrow ways. And I have never watched the glow changing to darkness, and the lights creep out over the interminable city without a sudden and passionate conviction that the divine pity must transcend the human suffering, and the sorrows of man find solace in the heart of God.

([Masterman] 1902: 1–8, 94–6)

81   SIGURD FROSTERUS, FROM 'LONDON RHAPSODY' (1903)

Frosterus (1876–1956) was an important Swedish-Finnish modernist critic and architect. At the beginning of the century his creed was 'iron and brain style'; he was a rationalistic and Futurist-minded Machine Romantic, believing in the dominion of man and machine over nature. Unusually among educated Finns of his generation, Frosterus was powerfully attracted to Anglo-Saxon culture: from childhood onwards he visited Britain on many occasions; in 1906 he published a popular book on H. G. Wells. Earlier in the same decade he wrote travel essays on three cities, Siena, London and Berlin, all of which appeared in the cultural criticism magazine, *Euterpe*. The influence of Siena's Palazzo Pubblico, which he deeply admired, is evident in his major architectural work, the Stockmann department store in Helsinki. In the London and Berlin 'Rhapsodies', Frosterus appraised old and new means of transport in accordance with the principles of technical aesthetics. For him the Hansom cab was a magnificent poem to the past, the underground train its futuristic match.[1]

At Victoria Station . . . under the smoky spider's web of soot-blackened glass and iron . . . into a waiting cab . . . a 'Hansom', this too . . . a perfected poem; one's thoughts are spontaneously led to the beautiful gondolas of Venice. . . . An exquisite contrivance, an ingenious cultural product; the vertical design determined by the vast crowd. A means of conveyance so firmly rooted in London that it is not amenable to acclimatisation on foreign ground.

Past Buckingham Palace, that modest royal residence, which soon fades into the mist along the grand avenue of trees in The Mall. But the impression is gloomy, depressing. No broad perspectives, no unobstructed views. The haze, even when the sun is shining, forms an impenetrable circle – wider or more constricted depending on the time of day or the wind – that closes tightly around one. . . .

But, on Trafalgar Square, blackened and lop-sided – the metropolis' most splendid square with the high chimney of Nelson's Column in front of the elongated bulk of the National Gallery – surrounded by the most heterogeneous of building complexes, the tableau changes.

The Strand and St Martin's Lane open out like rivers of fire, the fog billows and glows like a solar flare, illuminated and pricked by innumerable points of light. Stretching in unbroken chains, along all the pavements are theatres, restaurants and Music Halls, a fantastic, electric architecture that does not recognise even the simplest laws of statics. All the means of technology are encountered so as to provide variations in colour and value: murky, smoking flames from the lampions, with an undertone of the Middle Ages and Honthorst-esque[2] nocturnal scenes, to the soft green tones of the Auer lamps, from the white teardrops of the incandescent lamps to the vast suns of the arc-lights, in limpid shades of blue-violet and blazing red, with finally, high in the air, a unifying frame: the barbaric, shameless advertisements of the transparencies. . . .

The new underground electric railway, like a parabola of energy – admittedly only visible on the map – with its apex at the Bank of England, runs through London's most central parts, and is likewise a work of art; monumental in its practical simplicity, splendid in its solid elegance. . . .

A slow rumbling, an indeterminate reddish gleam adds colour to the dark rat-hole, which gapes blackly in the back wall of the station. And the next moment there stops at the platform a strange, coiled steel monster with staring insect's eyes, behind which, like the brain, the train-driver hides; this is a creature almost of flesh and blood, a manifestation of the most modern art, worthy of being treated with the same reverence with which we honour tools or utensils perfected in vanished centuries: they too in their day no more than base necessities. Then one is sucked in unawares through the automatically opening double iron doors into the bogie-carriages of the accordion-like train, and before one has had time to settle into the wide, comfortable arm-chair, one is already out in the darkness, far beneath the streets of London or the muddy bed of the Thames. Round about – serene, immobile faces, news-paper held up to their eyes, pipes in mouths – representatives of various social classes sit in fraternal harmony, as carefree as though they were in their own homes, until the conductors loudly announce the name of the station, just before the train comes to a stop. A sudden jolt, a metallic clicking, the doors burst open; and along the wide centre-aisle the contents of the train flow out, as quickly as if someone had opened a lock gate.

Then up with the lift again, out into the crowd and the fog, out onto the swarming surface of the ant-heap, out into the heart of the city, out onto the crowded square in front of the Bank of England.

Like an impregnable fortress, vainly surrounded by high siege-towers, without a single window in its façades, the bank complex, which is only one storey high, lies at the focal point of the City. But here the architecture becomes a side-issue; put the Parthenon on this site and nobody would have time or occasion to see it. The movement, irresistible and mighty like the sea, absorbs all the visitor's interest. For, what do the rows of houses, palaces and churches signify here other than the walls between which the swirling torrent of humanity is pressed; who cares about the polished stones that lie along the banks of this river when one's gaze is fixed upon the thing itself?

The sun rarely shines over London's City. A lemon-yellow blotch with no clear outline, radiating only the most diffuse of lights in the turbid, absinthe-coloured air, peeps out for a few hours over the looming bulk of the build-ings. But it is unable to dispel and cleanse the dense, viscous air, which, immobile like standing water, fills the level, high-banked street canals, which lack adequate slope or outlet. And immersed in this unpleasant medium, where sound is muffled and dies in the absence of resonance, where vision and smell become indolent, the massed traffic drags past like a ghost, uni-formly, sullenly and incessantly, calculated and regulated, mathematically pre-cise like clockwork. Without interruption, like the tide, hour after hour, day after day, the stream of vehicles glides forward with neither beginning or end. The murmur of voices, the neighing of the horses, the sound of the omnibus bells, the delicate, off-key peel of church bells; everything is immersed and swallowed up by the low, indescribable undertone, which, in its constancy – generated by the rolling of innumerable carriage wheels along the damp, wooden paving of the carriageway – soon fades from one's consciousness. Ultimately everything seems silent as in a dream. No newspaper boy's call, no living, picturesque moment. Silently but commandingly, a rubber truncheon is raised aloft; a moment's stagnation at a given point. Silently the policeman lowers it again, silently the file moves on at the same calm but doggedly energetic pace as before.

A colourless and toneless spectacle, a magnificent picture in relief, a living, British, modern-day Parthenon frieze, the ancient myth of the giant's cauldron become reality.

(Frosterus 1994: 8–11)

Notes

1 I am wholly indebted to Kimmo Sarje for this headnote.
2 *Honthorst-esque*: the candlelight effects in the early pictures of the Dutch painter, Gerrit van Honthorst (1590–1656), earned him the nickname 'Gherardo delle Notti' (Gerard of the Night Scenes).

82 ARTHUR W. SYMONS, FROM *LONDON: A BOOK OF ASPECTS* (1903), CHAPTERS 1, 2 AND 6

Brought up in a pious Methodist household in the West Country, Symons (1865–1945) made an apostatic move to London as a young man. In verse and prose he carried the banner of Decadence and related creeds; a follower of Pater, he also imitated and championed the French Symbolists. Symons' severe mental breakdown in 1908, after which he never fully recovered his intellectual and creative powers, partly accounts for his having been too narrowly typecast as a man of the Nineties. However, these extracts from an early twentieth-century work do tend to reinforce that period identity, and this is not only true of the extravagant aesthetic impressionism of the first passage. The third, in which the writer wonders why the poor on the Edgware Road 'take the trouble to go on existing' given their conspicuous lack of beauty, charm or the philosophic wisdom of their South European counterparts, reveals the unacceptable face of aestheticism. The second passage offers an interesting comparison with Frosterus' machine aesthetics of the same year (doc. 81). Symons' recoil from modernity is most pronounced in his elegiac invocation of the London of Lamb (see doc. 24), who was himself inclined to look back to the *eighteenth* century in a similarly nostalgic way. Yet Symons feels an equally strong affinity with a great mid-nineteenth-century celebrant of the modern city, Charles Baudelaire, allusion to whom appropriately launches a powerful valedictory to the distinctively urban freedoms and pleasures of *flânerie* (see Introduction, pp. 6–7).

It is not only on the river that London can make absolute beauty out of the material which lies so casually about in its streets. A London sunset, seen through vistas of narrow streets, has a colour of smoky rose which can be seen in no other city, and it weaves strange splendours, often enough, on its edges and gulfs of sky, not less marvellous than Venice can lift over the Giudecca, or Siena see stretched beyond its walls. At such a point as the Marble Arch you may see conflagrations of jewels, a sky of burning lavender, tossed abroad like a crumpled cloak, with broad bands of dull purple and smoky pink, slashed with bright gold and decked with grey streamers; you see it through a veil of moving mist, which darkens downwards to a solid block, coloured like lead, where the lighted road turns, meeting the sky. . . .

London was once habitable, in spite of itself. The machines have killed it. The old, habitable London exists no longer. Charles Lamb could not live in this mechanical city, out of which everything old and human has been driven by wheels and hammers and the fluids of noise and speed. When will his affectionate phrase, 'the sweet security of streets,' ever be used again of London? No one will take a walk down Fleet Street any more, no one will shed tears of joy in the 'motley Strand,' no one will be leisurable any more, or turn over old books at a stall, or talk with friends at the street corner. Noise and evil smells have filled the streets like tunnels in daylight; it is a pain to walk in the midst of all these hurrying and clattering machines; the multitude of humanity, that 'bath' into which Baudelaire loved to plunge, is scarcely discernible, it is secondary to the machines; it is only in a machine that you can escape the machines. London that was vast and smoky and loud, now stinks and reverberates; to live in it is to live in the hollow of a clanging bell, to breathe its air is to breathe the foulness of modern progress.

London as it is now is the wreck and moral of civilization. . . .

It is the machines, more than anything else, that have done it. Men and women, as they passed each other in the street or on the road, saw and took cognizance of each other, human being of human being. The creatures that we see now in the machines are hardly to be called human beings, so are they disfigured out of all recognition, in order that they may go fast enough not to see anything themselves. Does anyone any longer walk? If I walk I meet no one walking, and I cannot wonder at it, for what I meet is an uproar, and a whizz, and a leap past me, and a blinding cloud of dust, and a machine on which scarecrows perch is disappearing at the end of the road. The verbs to loll, to lounge, to dawdle, to loiter, the verbs precious to Walt Whitman, precious to every lover of men and of himself, are losing their currency; they will be marked 'o' for obsolete in the dictionaries of the future. All that poetry which Walt Whitman found in things merely because they were alive will fade out of existence like the Red Indian. It will live on for some time yet in the country where the railway has not yet smeared its poisonous trail over the soil; but in London there will soon be no need of men, there will be nothing but machines.

As I walk to and fro in Edgware Road, I cannot help sometimes wondering why these people exist, why they take the trouble to go on existing. Watch their faces, and you will see in them a listlessness, a hard unconcern, a failure to be interested, which speaks equally in the roving eyes of the man who stands smoking at the curbstone with his hands in his pockets, and in the puckered cheeks of the woman doing her shopping, and in the noisy laugh of the youth leaning against the wall, and in the gray, narrow face of the child whose thin legs are too tired to dance when the barrel-organ plays jigs. Whenever anything happens in the streets there is a crowd at once, and this crowd is made up of people who have no pleasures and no interests of their own to attend to, and to whom any variety is welcome in the tedium of their lives. In all these faces you will see no beauty, and you will see no beauty in the clothes they wear, or in their attitudes in rest or movement, or in their voices when they speak. They are human beings to whom nature has given no grace or charm, whom life has made vulgar, and for whom circumstances have left no escape from themselves. In the climate of England, in the atmosphere of London, on these pavements of Edgware Road, there is no way of getting any simple happiness out of natural things, and they have lost the capacity for accepting natural pleasures graciously, if such came to them. Crawling between heaven and earth thus miserably, they have never known what makes existence a practicable art or a tolerable spectacle, and they have infinitely less sense of the mere abstract human significance of life than the fachino[1] who lies, a long blue streak in the sun, on the Zattere[2] at Venice, or the girl who carries water from the well in an earthen pitcher, balancing it on her head, in any Spanish street.

(Symons 1909: 5–6, 14–17, 71–3)

Notes

1 *facchino*: porter, rough fellow.
2 *Zattere*: quayside looking across the lagoon to the island of Giudecca.

83   FORD HERMANN HUEFFER, FROM *THE SOUL OF LONDON* (1905), CHAPTER 1

Hueffer (1873–1939), better known as Ford Madox Ford, the name he adopted in 1919, was born in London. His German father was a journalist and music critic, his maternal grandfather the painter Ford Madox Brown. The Pre-Raphaelite and Aesthete circles in which he grew up exerted a lasting though not exclusive influence. As editor of the *English Review* (1908–9) and, in Paris, of the *Transatlantic Review* (1924), he published many of the greatest names of the modernist age; as critic and as novelist, for a time in collaboration with Conrad, he strongly promoted a modern aesthetics of fiction. In this sequence of essays, including the representative passage below, he champions Impressionism not only as a prose style but, in its relativist philosophy, as the only authentic way of seeing the modern city in all its multitudinous immensity.

A brilliant, wind-swept, sunny day, with the fountains like hay-cocks of prismatic glitter in the shadow of Nelson's column, with the paving stones almost opalescent, with colour everywhere, the green of the orange trees in tubs along the façade of the National Gallery, the vivid blue of the paper used by flower-sellers to wrap poet's narcissi, the glint of straws blown from horses' feeds, the shimmer of wheel-marks on the wood pavement, the shine of bits of harness, the blaze of gold lettering along the house fronts, the slight quiver of the nerves after a momentarily dangerous crossing accentuating the perception – is that 'London'? Does that rise up in your Londoner's mind's eye, when, in the Boulevard Haussman, or on the Pyramids, he thinks of his own places?

Or is it the chaotic crowd, like that of baggage wagons huddled together after a great defeat, blocked in the narrow ways of the City, an apparently indissoluble muddle of gray wheel traffic, of hooded carts, of 'buses drawing out of line, of sticky mud, with a pallid church wavering into invisibility towards the steeple in the weeping sky, of grimy upper windows through which appear white faces seen from one's level on a 'bus-top, of half the street up, of the monstrous figure of a horse 'down' – and surely there is no more monstrous apparition than that of a horse down in the sticky streets with its frantic struggles, the glancing off of its hoofs, the roll of eyes, the sudden apparition of great teeth, and then its lying still – is this, with its black knot of faces leaning a little over the kerbstone, with its suggestion of the seashore in the unconcerned, tarpaulin-shrouded figure of the traffic policeman – is this again 'London', the London we see from a distance?

Or do we see it in the glare of kerosene lamps, the diffused blaze of shop fronts, the slowly moving faces revealed for a moment, then as it were, washed out, of the serried, marketing crowds. They will be carrying string bags, carrying paper parcels, carrying unwrapped green stuff, treading on layers of handbills, treading on the white scrolls of orange peels, on small heaps of muddy sawdust, standing in shawled groups round the glare of red joints in butchers' shops, standing in black groups round the carts of nostrum sellers, round the carts of dutch auctioneers; with ears deafened by the cries of vendors of all things meet for a Saturday night, by the incessant whistle of trams looming at a snail's pace through the massed humanity; by the incessant, as if vindictively anvil-like, peals of notes of barrel organs. In a patch of shadow left in a vacant space, you will hardly make out the figure of a forlorn man standing still. With a pendent placard on his chest, announcing one of the ills of the flesh, he offers for sale things that you would think nobody could stop to buy, or indistinguishable quavers of melody that nobody could stay to hear. Is this again the London that comes to one at a distance?

For, almost assuredly, it will be some minute detail of the whole, we seeing things with the eye of a bird that is close to the ground. And with the eye of a bird seeking for minute fragments of seed, minute insects, tiny parasites, we also look for things that to us are the constituents of our mental or visual pabula. The tendency of 'carriage folk' must be to think of the Saturday night market as nothing but the swinging doors of public-houses and of pawnshops, as nothing but the architectural arrangements of translucent gin bottles in pale shop windows. The marketer has his tendency to regard those he sees in carriages as insolent servants conducting people who 'are no better than they should be'. The essential Bohemian must think of those whose sign visual is the aligned brass knockers of suburban streets, as sluggish-minded and intolerable. Thus, humanity not caring to think about what it does not like, the villa resident away from London will see a vision of 'Parks' and 'Gardens', surrounded by uninteresting or repulsive districts of small houses; the working man thinks of High Streets, of small streets, of tenement blocks, set down on the fringes of villadom.

(Hueffer 1905: 16–19)

84 OLIVE CHRISTIAN MALVERY, FROM *THE SOUL MARKET* (1906), CHAPTER 13

See Introduction, pp. 19–21, and Winter (1993: 103–7). Malvery (1884?–1914) came to London from her native India in 1900 to receive training as a vocalist at the Royal College of Music. However, much of the remainder of her tragically brief life was devoted to investigating and publicising the lot of some of the city's most exploited and destitute groups of inhabitants, especially working women and children, and to implementing, in the best traditions of Christian and Conservative paternalism, practical welfare schemes on their behalf. *The Soul Market* was the first and most popular of her numerous books, going through at least eleven editions in six years. Following its appearance Malvery was also in great demand as a public speaker, another of the several roles in which her performative talents were effectively displayed. The chapter from which these extracts are taken is entitled: 'The Simple Life, with Variations – How I Lived on Sixpence a Day, and Earned it.'

To begin with, I had of course to dress for the part. I had to leave a respectable neighbourhood and go forth looking as much like the people amongst whom I was going to live as possible. After rummaging in my 'property box', we secured a really dreadful assortment. . . .

Our way lay through mean streets in the Westminster borough. In these foetid alleys there seems no idea of bed-time for the babies: there were scores of them playing in the gutters. Untidy women and filthy men herded at lowering doors. Here and there a public-house flung broad beams of light on to the squalid pavement. Strange that these places should be the only spots in poverty-haunted streets that do not bear an impress of poverty. It is always a mystery to me why these miserable victims of drink and over-crowding do not rise in desperation and tear down the places that batten on their shrunken fortunes.

When, after some wandering, we got out of Westminster slums, we found ourselves by the Houses of Parliament. The streets were alight and pulsating with life.

We passed on to the Embankment, which might well be called the Waiting-Room of Travellers in Poverty Station. I was already tired – for we had covered about four miles, passing in and out of those horrid streets – so we sat down on one of the benches.

Presently a woman came and dropped down on the other end of the bench; her clothes were fairly good, but her shoes were battered and she limped slightly. We watched her quietly for a while, then my companion began talking to her. Conversation progressed very slowly. I have since learnt that these children of suffering speak but little. . . .

We gathered from stray remarks that she had come from the country with a tiny capital to seek work in London. She never found it. The money was spent, her clothes wore out, and she found herself one of the many for whom the world had no place. She noticed that I was crying, and thinking it was my own misfortune that troubled me, she pressed a halfpenny into my hand.

'You can't buy anything for a ha'penny till morning,' she said. 'The coffee is a penny a cup at night, but at five o'clock you can get a cup for a ha'penny; it is dreadful to be hungry till you're used to it.' I walked swiftly away, and she said to Mr C.: 'Don't be hard on her, she's such a little thing.'

Can you imagine the heavenly charity of the poor creature; she had eaten nothing that livelong day, but she gave me her last halfpenny.

I never understood charity till I lived with the poor. The grand dames of London might do worse than study this grace with those who go hungry that some worse fated creature may be fed.

We heard the Westminster clock chime two, and set our faces towards the Bridge. Mr C. asked me if I would mind waiting there for a few minutes while he went to look for a coffee-stall. . . .

I was terribly tired when my companion returned, and it was with very lagging feet that we wandered on towards Blackfriars. We walked up Thames Street towards Billingsgate Market. Who would know these long, soundless streets, with dark, gaping alleys here and there, for those same busy highways we are accustomed to in London? When we reached Billingsgate we felt we were in a city of the dead – here and there a predatory cat or a skulking dog slipped past, or a sleepy policeman yawned loudly as he strolled by. It was too early for the market, so we went on to Smithfield. Sleepy butchers were dragging out sacks and carcases from high-piled carts; here and there a fat cat rubbed herself against the benches.

It was not a very enlivening scene, so we sought a coffee-stall, and finding none, went into Lockhart's; the butchers' boys and carters were drinking coffee at little tables, but they refused to serve us. 'No females in here,' said the man, looking suspiciously at me. I was ready to cry with disappointment, I wanted some coffee so much. However, presently we found a place where the despised sex might slip in unostentatiously, swallow some food, and depart. We were served with two hot cups of coffee and an enormous hunk of cake each for fourpence. . . .

From here we dragged our weary limbs to Covent Garden. By this time we had both fallen into the unmistakable slouch of the drag-footed stray. My feet were so badly blistered that I could hardly move. Our friend on the Embankment had told us that we could probably get a job at shelling peas at Covent Garden, or bottling fruit at one of the factories. I 'went for' the peas. . . .

Early as we were at the pea-shed, some hundred wretched creatures were already busy shelling peas with incredible speed. Only women are employed at this work. They sit on upturned baskets or stools in rows down the length of the shed. A man at one end gave each woman an apron or skirt full of peas. These she shelled into a flat tin pan and brought back to be measured. The 'boss' poured the peas into a tin quart measure and gave the women a metal disc for each quart done. These were exchanged later for threepence each. I was so worn out and exhausted that I only managed to earn twopence. Then Mr C. came and took me away. I had endured all that was possible for that one night.

(Malvery 1906: 224–31)

85 BECKLES WILLSON, GEORGE R. SIMS, FROM 'WHICH IS THE MOST INTERESTING LONDON STREET?' *STRAND MAGAZINE* (1907)

The *Strand* put the question to 'a group of representative men' (p. 314) – a dubious phrase, we might now think, yet the answers were suitably diverse, with a range of West-End, City and East-End streets receiving nominations. A number of respondents (obligingly) cited the Strand for its historic atmosphere and associations with pageantry, but it took a colonial, Beckles Willson (1869–1942), more English than the English, to invoke these with a veritable effusion of patriotic nostalgia. Sims (1847–1922) was a prolific writer of popular fiction, melodrama (most famously *The Lights o' London* (1881)) and ballads (for example 'In the Workhouse: Christmas Eve' (1876)), as well as a highly respected journalistic explorer of London's dark places (for example in *How the Poor Live* (1883)). While the Strand appeals to Willson as the least cosmopolitan of London's streets, an avenue to and of the nation's past, Mile End Road fascinates Sims as the precise opposite, its rival pageantry an emblem of London's multicultural future. Compare the more mundane photographic views, plates 18 and 19.

'If Fleet Street,' writes the Canadian historian, Mr Beckles Willson, 'be the brain and Piccadilly Circus the heart, then surely the Strand is the face of London. No street seems to me less cosmopolitan, more characteristic. I see in my mind's eye the long line of feudal palaces which gilded this historic link between the two great cities of London and Westminster; I think of the truly English pageants, cavalcades, and processions it has witnessed – at a time, too, when Piccadilly, Whitehall, and St James's Street were but green fields; I linger amidst the landmarks of Angevins, Tudors and Stuarts, and murmur with honest Evelyn when he saw King Charles go by: "I stood in the Strand and beheld it and blessed God!" It is the homely Strand that so often first greets the English home-comer after his exile, and the look and the smell and the gentle roar of it brings the lump to his throat.'

No one can speak with a more intimate knowledge of our great Metropolis than Mr George R. Sims, who writes: 'The most interesting street in London to me is the Mile End Road. From morning till night it is packed with pages from the Book of Life written in many European tongues.

'Here Asia jostles Europe and the dominant Oriental note carries you back to the Picture Bible of your childhood. Here are Abraham and Isaac, Jacob and Esau, Aaron and Miriam, the bearded Patriarchs, and the children of Israel, who have come through the wilderness to a Canaan that, if it does not flow with milk and honey for them just when they enter it, has promise of a golden harvest to be reaped in the fat years to come.

Plate 17 The Strand, Looking West, c. 1890, *The Queen's London.*

'The human panorama that unfolds itself night and day in the Mile End Road interests me so absorbingly that I have never yet looked up to see where the Mile End Road ends or begins. I pass into it from Aldgate and Whitechapel, and I wander it wonderingly till I come within sound of the bells of Bow that are not Bow Bells.

'Both the Ghettoes – the old Ghetto and the new Ghetto – pour strange streams of humanity into the Mile End Road. The English-speaking Jews are in the minority. Everywhere the world jargon of the Ashkenazim, which is "Yiddish", salutes your ear, and salutes it somewhat harshly if you have no familiarity with the German tongue.

'Most wonderful of all is the Mile End Road on a Saturday night when the Jewish Sabbath is over, and a brightly-dressed crowd of young Jewesses promenades with Oriental colours in their raiment, and Parisian *coiffures* under hats that to Parisians "are unknowe".

'You rarely see a sign of poverty or slatternliness among these young women, many of whom are only working girls.

'But it is not all festivity among the shows and stalls that line the roadway on Saturday night and make it a flaring fair. A large number of the business places open, the tailors and the shoemakers of the so-called "sweating dens"

Plate 18 The Mile End Road, c. 1890, *The Queen's London.*

219

renew their toil, and in the old-English houses that stand in long gardens at the Bow end you may see every floor aflare with gas, for these houses are now let out in floors to the fugitives from the Russian Pale and the Russian Pogroms, the Jews from Poland and the Jews from Roumania, and on every floor a different trade is often carried on.

'Mile End Road is quieter in the week-day, but it is always wonderful – always a picture of many lands and an object-lesson in the pushing back of one race by another. The Jewish note which dominates all along the Mile End Road ends almost suddenly when you come to Bow.

'There the land of your fathers begins again or rather still remains, for the unchanging East with its Bible pictures has vanished, and the English of "Stratford atte Bowe" has a cockney twang in it that after the eternal Yiddish is not ungrateful in our ears.'

(Strand 1907: 321, 316–17)

86   JOSEPH CONRAD, FROM *THE SECRET AGENT* (1907), CHAPTER 7

In a prefatory 'Author's Note', Conrad (1857–1924) recalled the importance of the London setting in the imaginative germination of this novel: 'the vision of an enormous town presented itself, of a monstrous town more populous than some continents and in its man-made might as if indifferent to heaven's frowns and smiles; a cruel devourer of the world's light' (1923: xii). As is illustrated by the extract below, the power of this vision partly lies in its alienness, in defamiliarising properties which imbue the benighted city with an almost surrealistic atmosphere of murkiness and confusion. There is nothing new about aquatic-piscatorial imagery in literary explorations of London's lower depths (see Greenwood 1876!). But Conrad's explorer in this scene, the Assistant Commissioner of Police whose 'adventurous disposition' has been curbed since he returned from colonial service under a bright tropical sun and became 'chained to a desk in the thick of four millions of men' (1923: 113), finds or rather loses himself in deep waters as soon as he plunges (in disguise) into the streets in the city centre; moreover, the 'sense of loneliness, of evil freedom . . . was rather pleasant'. Conrad's paradoxical, ironic wit functions as a tonal counterweight to the blacker implications of the novel's anarchic world, the epicentre of which is the goal of the Assistant Commissioner's diving expedition, the secret agent's shady property in Brett Street.

His descent into the street was like the descent into a slimy aquarium from which the water had been run off. A murky, gloomy dampness enveloped him. The walls of the houses were wet, the mud of the roadway glistened with an effect of phosphorescence, and when he emerged into the Strand out of a narrow street by the side of Charing Cross Station the genius of the locality assimilated him. He might have been but one more of the queer foreign fish that can be seen of an evening about there flitting round the dark corners.

He came to a stand on the very edge of the pavement, and waited. His exercised eyes had made out in the confused movements of lights and shadows thronging the roadway the crawling approach of a hansom. He gave no sign; but when the low step gliding along the curbstone came to his feet he dodged in skilfully in front of the big turning wheel, and spoke up through the little trap door almost before the man gazing supinely ahead from his perch was aware of having been boarded by a fare.

It was not a long drive. It ended by signal abruptly, nowhere in particular, between two lamp-posts before a large drapery establishment – a long range of shops already lapped up in sheets of corrugated iron for the night. Tendering a coin through the trap door the fare slipped out and away, leaving an effect of uncanny, eccentric ghostliness upon the driver's mind. But the size of the coin was satisfactory to his touch, and his education not being literary, he remained untroubled by the fear of finding it presently turned to a dead leaf in his pocket. Raised above the world of fares by the nature of his calling, he contemplated their action with a limited interest. The sharp pulling of his horse right round expressed his philosophy.

Meantime, the Assistant Commissioner was already giving his order to a waiter in a little Italian restaurant round the corner – one of those traps for the hungry, long and narrow, baited with a perspective of mirrors and white napery; without air, but with an atmosphere of their own – an atmosphere of fraudulent cookery mocking an abject mankind in the most pressing of its miserable necessities. In this immoral atmosphere the Assistant Commissioner, reflecting upon his enterprise, seemed to lose some more of his identity. He had a sense of loneliness, of evil freedom. It was rather pleasant. When, after paying for his short meal, he stood up and waited for his change, he saw himself in the sheet of glass, and was struck by his foreign appearance. He contemplated his own image with a melancholy and inquisitive gaze, then by sudden inspiration raised the collar of his jacket. This arrangement appeared to him commendable, and he completed it by giving an upward twist to the ends of his black moustache. He was satisfied by the subtle modification of his personal aspect caused by these small changes. 'That'll do very well,' he thought. 'I'll get a little wet, a little splashed – '. . . .

A pleasurable feeling of independence possessed him when he heard the glass doors swing to behind his back with a sort of imperfect baffled thud. He advanced at once into an immensity of greasy slime and damp plaster interspersed with lamps, and enveloped, oppressed, penetrated, choked, and suffocated by the blackness of a wet London night, which is composed of soot and drops of water.

Brett Street was not very far away. It branched off, narrow, from the side of an open triangular space surrounded by dark and mysterious houses, temples of petty commerce emptied of traders for the night. Only a fruiterer's stall at the corner made a violent blaze of light and colour. Beyond all was black, and the few people passing in that direction vanished at one stride beyond the glowing heaps of oranges and lemons. No footsteps echoed. They would never be heard of again. The adventurous head of the Special Crimes Department watched these disappearances from a distance with an interested eye. He felt light-hearted, as though he had been ambushed all alone in a jungle many thousands of miles away from departmental desks and official inkstands. This joyousness and dispersion of thought before a task of some importance seems to prove that this world of ours is not such a very serious affair after all. For the Assistant Commissioner was not constitutionally inclined to levity.

The policeman on the beat projected his sombre and moving form against the luminous glory of oranges and lemons, and entered Brett Street without haste. The Assistant Commissioner, as though he were a member of the criminal classes, lingered out of sight, awaiting his return. But this constable seemed to be lost for ever to the force. He never returned: must have gone out at the other end of Brett Street.

The Assistant Commissioner, reaching this conclusion, entered the street in his turn, and came upon a large van arrested in front of the dimly lit window-panes of a carter's eating-house. The man was refreshing himself inside, and the horses, their big heads lowered to the ground, fed out of nose-bags steadily. Farther on, on the opposite side of the street, another suspect patch of dim light issued from Mr. Verloc's shop front, hung with papers, heaving with vague piles of cardboard boxes and the shapes of books. The Assistant Commissioner stood observing it across the roadway. There could be no mistake. By the side of the front window, encumbered by the shadows of nondescript things, the door, standing ajar, let escape on the pavement a narrow, clear streak of gaslight within.

Behind the Assistant Commissioner the van and horses, merged into one mass, seemed something alive – a square-backed black monster blocking half the street, with sudden iron-shod stampings, fierce jingles, and heavy, blowing sighs. The harshly festive, ill-omened glare of a large and prosperous public-house faced the other end of Brett Street across a wide road. This barrier of blazing lights, opposing the shadows gathered about the humble abode of Mr. Verloc's domestic happiness, seemed to drive the obscurity of the street back upon itself, make it more sullen, brooding, and sinister.

(Conrad 1923: 147–51)

87   H. G. WELLS, FROM *TONO-BUNGAY* (1909), II, 1, 1 AND III, 2, 6

Like his fictional autobiographer, George Ponderevo, in this, 'perhaps my most ambitious novel' (1934: 53), Wells (1866–1946) came to London in the 1880s to study science. This move followed impressionable early years 'below stairs' at Uppark ('Bladesover'), the great house in West Sussex where his mother was housekeeper, and (among numerous 'starts in life') at nearby Midhurst ('Wimblehurst'), where Wells taught at the grammar school after a briefer spell than George's as a pharmacist's assistant. The fictional pharmacist, George's uncle, enjoys a meteoric rise to temporary opulence and power by zestful promotion of a quack medicine, 'Tono-Bungay', with George clinging half-reluctantly to his coat-tails. The ambitiousness of the novel partly lies in treating this story as a parable of the times within an expansive socio-historical context. This is one of the functions of the first passage below, which in its discursive method fulfils the narrator's declared intention to 'comment and theorize' on a 'comprehensive' scale. Yet the same passage also illustrates countervailing effects making for coherence of design; these include the novel's sustained 'architectural rhetoric' and its 'strain of disease and decay imagery' (Lodge 1984: 222, 219). In relation to the second passage, see Introduction, p. 23, on elevated views of the lower classes.

London!

At first, no doubt, it was a chaos of streets and people and buildings and reasonless going to and fro. I do not remember that I ever struggled very steadily to understand it, or explored it with any but a personal and adventurous intention. Yet in time there has grown up in me a kind of theory of London; I do think I see lines of an ordered structure out of which it has grown, detected a process that is something more than a confusion of casual accidents, though indeed it may be no more than a process of disease.

I said at the outset of my first book that I find in Bladesover the clue to all England. Well, I certainly imagine it is the clue to the structure of London. There have been no revolutions, no deliberate restatements or abandonments of opinion in England since the days of the fine gentry, since 1688 or thereabouts, the days when Bladesover was built; there have been changes, dissolving forces, replacing forces, if you will; but then it was that the broad lines of the English system set firmly. And as I have gone to and fro in London, in certain regions constantly the thought has recurred, this is Bladesover House, this answers to Bladesover House. The fine gentry may have gone; they have indeed largely gone, I think; rich merchants may have replaced them, financial adventurers or what not. That does not matter; the shape is still Bladesover.

I am most reminded of Bladesover and Eastry[1] by all those regions round about the West End parks, for example, estate parks, each more or less in relation to a palace or group of great houses. The roads and back ways of Mayfair and all about St James's again, albeit perhaps of a later growth in point of time, were of the very spirit and architectural texture of the Bladesover passages and yards; they had the same smells, the space, the large cleanness, and always going to and fro there one met unmistakable Olympians, and even more unmistakable valets, butlers, footmen in mufti. There were moments when I seemed to glimpse down areas the white panelling, the very chintz of my mother's room again. . . .

And the more I have paralleled these things with my Bladesover-Eastry model, the more evident it has become to me that the balance is not the same, and the more evident is the presence of great new forces, blind forces of invasion, of growth. The railway termini on the north side of London have been kept as remote as Eastry had kept the railway station from Wimblehurst, they stop on the very outskirts of the estates, but from the south, the South Eastern railway had butted its great stupid rusty iron head of Charing Cross station – that great head that came smashing down in 1905[2] – clean across the river, between Somerset House and Whitehall. The south side had no protecting estates. Factory chimneys smoke right over against Westminster with an air of carelessly not having permission, and the whole effect of industrial London and of all London east of Temple Bar and of the huge dingy immensity of London port, is to me of something disproportionately large, something morbidly expanded, without plan or intention, dark and sinister toward the clean clear social assurance of the West End. And south of this central London, south-east, south-west, far west, north-west, all round the northern hills, are similar disproportionate growths, endless streets of undistinguished houses, undistinguished industries, shabby families, second-rate shops, inexplicable people who in a once fashionable phrase do not 'exist'. All these aspects have suggested to my mind at times, do suggest to this day, the unorganized, abundant substance of some tumourous growth-process, a process which indeed bursts all the outlines of the affected carcass and protrudes such masses as ignoble comfortable Croydon, as tragic impoverished West Ham. To this day I ask myself will those masses ever become structural, will they indeed shape into anything new whatever, or is that cancerous image their true and ultimate diagnosis? . . .

Moreover, together with this hypertrophy there is an immigration of elements that have never understood and never will understand the great tradition, wedges of foreign settlement embedded in the heart of this yeasty English expansion. One day I remember wandering eastward out of pure curiosity – it must have been in my early student days – and discovering a shabbily bright foreign quarter, shops displaying Hebrew placards and weird unfamiliar commodities, and a concourse of bright-eyed, eagle-nosed people talking some incomprehensible gibberish between the shops and the barrows. And soon I became quite familiar with the devious, vicious, dirtily-pleasant exoticism of Soho. I found those crowded streets a vast relief from the dull grey interior of Brompton where I lodged and lived my daily life. In Soho, indeed, I got my first inkling of the factor of replacement that is so important in both the English and the American process.

Even in the West End, in Mayfair and the squares about Pall Mall, Ewart was presently to remind me, the face of the old aristocratic dignity was fairer than its substance, here were actors and actresses, here moneylenders and Jews, here bold financial adventurers, and I thought of my uncle's frayed cuff as he pointed out this house in Park Lane and that. That was so and so's who made a corner in borax, and that palace belonged to that hero among modern adventurers, Barmentrude, who used to be an I.D.B., – an illicit diamond buyer that is to say. A city of Bladesovers, the capital of a kingdom of Bladesovers, all much shaken and many altogether in decay, parasitically occupied, insidiously replaced by alien, unsympathetic and irresponsible elements; – and withal ruling an adventitious and miscellaneous empire of a quarter of this daedal earth. . . .

There comes back too, among these Hardingham memories an impression of a drizzling November day, and how we looked out of the windows upon a procession of the London unemployed.

It was like looking down a well into some momentarily revealed nether world. Some thousands of needy ineffectual men had been raked together to trail their spiritless misery through the West End with an appeal that was also in its way a weak and unsubstantial threat: 'It is Work we need, not Charity.'

There they were, half-phantom through the fog, a silent, foot-dragging, interminable, grey procession. They carried wet, dirty banners, they rattled boxes for pence; these men who had not said 'snap' in the right place, the men who had 'snapped' too eagerly, the men who had never said 'snap', the men who had never had a chance of saying 'snap'. A shambling, shameful stream they made, oozing along the street, the gutter waste of competitive civilization. And we stood high out of it all, as high as if we looked godlike from another world, standing in a room beautifully lit and furnished, skilfully warmed, filled with costly things.

'There,' thought I, 'but for the grace of God, go George and Edward Ponderevo.'

But my uncle's thoughts ran in a different channel, and he made that vision the text of a spirited but inconclusive harangue upon Tariff Reform.

(Wells 1909: 118–19, 121–3, 287–8)

Notes

1 *Eastry*: the great house at Wimblehurst: 'Eastry was far greater than Bladesover. . . . It ruled not two villages but a borough' (I, 3, 1).

2 *that ... 1905*: structures collapsing (5 December 1905) during maintenance work
on the arched roof of John Hawkshaw's enormous station shed (built 1860–4)
killed six people; it was rebuilt in a modified form.

88   H. G. WELLS, FROM *ANN VERONICA* (1909), V, 4

The frank treatment of sex and marriage was one of Wells's aims in several earlier
books, including *Ann Veronica*'s immediate predecessor, *Tono-Bungay* (see doc. 87). In
Ann Veronica these topics are not only given centrality but, more boldly and controversially, presented mainly from the point of view of a young heroine determined to
gain independence and then to take the initiative in securing the mate she wants (who
happens to be already married). There is much in later parts of the book to disappoint
feminists as well as to offend traditionalists of the day. However, the episode partly
reproduced below constitutes a remarkably convincing representation – in a realistic
London setting – of a fledgling flâneuse's short-lived pleasure in that role, and of its
being undermined by a sequence of disturbing encounters, culminating in a stalker's
harassment, which remind her that 'a girl does not go alone in the world unchallenged'. The 21-year-old Ann Veronica has just left her father's suburban home; having
booked into a hotel near the Embankment, she sets off to look for a cheaper room
and, more speculatively, a job.

She walked along the Strand and across Trafalgar Square, and by the Haymarket to Piccadilly, and so through dignified squares and palatial alleys to
Oxford Street; and her mind was divided between a speculative treatment of
employment on the one hand, and breezes – zephyr breezes – of the keen-
est appreciation for London, on the other. The jolly part of it was that for
the first time in her life so far as London was concerned, she was not going
anywhere in particular; for the first time in her life it seemed to her she was
taking London in. . . .

Her thoughts were deflected . . . by the peculiar behaviour of a middle-
aged gentleman in Piccadilly. He appeared suddenly from the infinite in the
neighbourhood of the Burlington Arcade, crossing the pavement towards
her and with his eyes upon her. He seemed to her indistinguishably about her
father's age. . . .

'Whither away?' he said very distinctly in a curiously wheedling voice. Ann
Veronica stared at his foolish, propitiatory smile, his hungry gaze, through
one moment of amazement, then stepped aside and went on her way with a
quickened step. But her mind was ruffled, and its mirror-like surface of satisfaction was not easily restored. . . .

That delightful sense of free, unembarrassed movement was gone.

As she neared the bottom of the dip in Piccadilly she saw a woman
approaching her from the opposite direction. . . . Behind this woman and a
little to the side of her, walked a man smartly dressed, with desire and
appraisal in his eyes. Something insisted that those two were mysteriously
linked – that the woman knew the man was there.

It was a second reminder that against her claim to go free and untram-melled there was a case to be made, that after all it was true that a girl does not go alone in the world unchallenged, nor ever has gone freely alone in the world, that evil walks abroad and dangers, and petty insults more irritating than dangers, lurk.

It was in the quiet streets and squares towards Oxford Stret that it first came into her head disagreeably that she herself was being followed. She observed a man walking on the opposite side of the way and looking towards her. . . .

[Ann Veronica seeks refuge and refreshment in a tea-shop, but the man fol-lows her in . . . and out.]

She became angry with herself. She would not be driven in by this persis-tent, sneaking aggression. She would ignore him. Surely she could ignore him. She stopped abruptly, and looked in a flower-shop window. He passed, and came loitering back and stood beside her, silently looking into her face.

The afternoon had passed now into twilight. The shops were lighting up into gigantic lanterns of colour, the street lamps were glowing into existence, and she had lost her way. She had lost her sense of direction, and was among unfamiliar streets. She went on from street to street, and all the glory of London had departed. Against the sinister, the threatening, monstrous inhu-manity of the limitless city, there was nothing now but this supreme, ugly fact of a pursuit – the pursuit of the undesired, persistent male.

For a second time Ann Veronica wanted to swear at the universe.

There were moments when she thought of turning upon this man and talking to him. But there was something in his face at once stupid and invin-cible that told her he would go on forcing himself upon her, that he would esteem speech with her a great point gained. In the twilight he had ceased to be a person one could tackle and shame; he had become something more general, a something that crawled and sneaked towards her and would not let her alone. . . .

Then, when the tension was getting unendurable, and she was on the verge of speaking to some casual passer-by and demanding help, her follower van-ished. For a time she could scarcely believe he was gone. He had. The night had swallowed him up, but his work on her was done. She had lost her nerve, and there was no more freedom in London for her that night. She was glad to join in the stream of hurrying homeward workers that was now welling out of a thousand places of employment, and to imitate their driven, preoc-cupied haste. She followed a bobbing white hat and grey jacket until she reached the Euston Road corner of Tottenham Court Road, and there, by the name on a bus and the cries of a conductor, she made a guess of her way. And she did not merely affect to be driven – she felt driven. She was afraid people would follow her, she was afraid of the dark, open doorways she passed, and afraid of the blazes of light; she was afraid to be alone, and she knew not what it was she feared.

It was past seven when she got back to her hotel. She thought then that she had shaken off the man of the bulging blue eyes for ever, but that night she found he followed her into her dreams. He stalked her, he stared at her, he craved her, he sidled slinking and propitiatory and yet relentlessly towards her, until at last she awoke from the suffocating nightmare nearness of his approach, and lay awake in fear and horror listening to the unaccustomed sounds of the hotel. . . .

(Wells 1943: 79–84)

89 YOSHIO MARKINO, FROM *A JAPANESE ARTIST IN LONDON* (1910), CHAPTERS 1 AND 17

Markino (1874–?) was born into an old Samurai family in the rural village of Koromo in Mikawa. He arrived in London in 1897 after spending four years in San Francisco, where he had received a smattering of art training, financed with difficulty by a variety of menial jobs, and where, according to this book, he had been continously subjected to anti-Japanese prejudice. Markino's first ten years in England were just as impoverished but, as the passages below indicate, he became an immediate anglophile, mainly on social grounds. The appeal of 'civilised' crowds, together with the atmospheric stimulus of London's weather, turned him into a painter specialising in urban scenes (see plate 20). The favourable reception of *The Colour of London* (1906), in which his watercolours were accompanied by textual commentaries, including a short essay in his own idiosyncratic English, led to successors in the same format on Paris and Rome. The Edwardians evidently found his 'artfully artless' prose (as one review described it) at least as charming as his pictures, and Markino was able to realise his earliest ambitions to become an 'English' writer in a rapid series of books of reminiscences and impressions, of which this is the first.

I started my first sightseeing from Hyde Park and the Green Park and St. James's Park. I could not understand all those iron railings. I thought they were to divide private grounds from the public ones. But I saw many people on both sides. I so timidly walked inside the rail. Nobody shouted me. Then I went near the crowds of people with still more fear. Being quite ignorant of the English civilisation I anticipated some pebble-showers every minute. I waited and waited with beating heart, but nothing happend to me at all. I walked into the crowds who were feeding birds in the lake of St. James's Park. Nobody spat on me! I ventured myself into the thickest crowds, and I was squeezed between the peoples. Nobody took any notice of me. 'Hallo, hallo, what's matter?' I said in my heart. 'Perhaps they don't know I am a Japanese.' I took off my hat on purpose to show my black hair. Finally one man pushed me quite accidentally, and he touched his hand to his hat and apologised me very politely. I realised at last that I was in the country where I could enjoy my liberty quite freely. Fancy polite apology instead of swearing and spitting! I felt as if I had come to a paradise in this world, and I was quite melted with comfort. . . .

At this time I went to a little newspaper shop to buy a box of cigarettes. The shopkeeper treated me quite same way with his countrymen. I asked him if he has seen Japanese before. He said 'No.' Then I asked him again if he was not curious of me? He said, 'No, sir. You see, sir, we 'ave our colonies all *hover* the world, sir – white men, yellow men, brown men and black men are forming parts of the British nation, so I am not curious of a Japanese gentle-man at all.'

What a broad mind he had! He was only a little shopkeeper, but he was worthy of being called one of the most civilised of the nations. I made a friendship with him at once, and I told him how I was treated in California. He said, 'Thut ain't fair, sir! Indeed, thut ain't fair!' How sweet this word was to me! I carried this sweet 'thut ain't fair' in my head, and slept with it all night so comfortably. . . .

It was just five days after I came back from Rome that I was invited to a dinner at the Parliament by one of my M.P. friends. When I arrived at Westminster station I was about a few minutes too soon to go in, so I had a little walk on the Embankment. It was still daylight. I saw St. Thomas's Hospital across the Thames. My head was still full of those old ruins in Rome, and those delicate

Plate 19 'Hyde Park Corner', Y. Markino, *A Japanese Artist in London*, 1910.

colours of Parisian buildings, and I said to myself, 'How ugly colours are those London buildings!'

The dinner was finished at 9.30, and we all went out to the Terrace to have a walk. London was in her most beautiful evening dress. I repented that I said St. Thomas's was ugly just a few hours ago. The rows of those Hospital Buildings were silhouetted up and down against the soft, misty sky; Westminster Bridge, just like many rainbows high up, connected that distance with the foreground. All of them were in bluish (perhaps a little greenish) grey. Pale electric lights, and the warm umber lights of 'buses on the Bridge, were reflected on the full tide. A few tugs were guided by small steamboats. These were all in one tone of greyish mist. In the foreground, the pavement of the Terrace, many semicircles were marked under many a lamp. Ladies in white, and gentlemen's white chests, broke the darkness here and there. They were walking together as light as butterflies. Where else could such romantic view be seen? Neither in Paris nor Rome, I am sure!

Perhaps the real colours of some buildings in London might be rather crude. But this crude colour is so fascinating in the mists. For instance, that house in front of my window is painted in black and yellow. When I came here last summer I laughed at its ugly colour. But now the winter fogs cover it, and the harmony of its colour is most wonderful, and I am sure I need a great deal of study to paint this beautiful colour. When I was in Rome I often exclaimed, 'Only if Rome had London fogs!' . . .

Then about the life of London, I have found out it is larger than any other town. London is on the extremely larger scale altogether. She is just like a vast ocean where sardines as well as whales are living together.

Perhaps I love humans more than even the mists. Let them be either good or bad, I cannot live without them. I hear that artists or writers generally seclude themselves in a lonely place to find out some idea to work out. I am quite reverse. Whenever I want to get idea for painting or writing, I always throw myself amongst the thickest crowds such as Earl's Court, Shepherd's Bush, or the music stands in the Parks. Let the crowds push me to and fro – I call it a human bath. In this human bath I always work out my ideas. And if I am left quite alone, I feel too miserable to do anything.

(Markino 1910: 7–9, 188–90, 192)

90 FROM 'MISS DAVISON'S FUNERAL: THE MARCH THROUGH LONDON', *MANCHESTER GUARDIAN* (16 JUNE 1913)

See Introduction, pp. 11 and 26–7, and plate 21. The funeral procession for Emily Davison, the militant suffragist, took place on 14 June, ten days after she had suffered mortal injuries running into the horses' path during the Epsom Derby. This ceremonial farewell to a martyr to the cause, though necessarily staged without long-term planning, came at the end of a sequence of impressively organised demonstrations in the streets of London over the previous six years. In these events, according to the most authoritative study of visual aspects of the campaign, 'the suffragists developed a new kind of political spectacle', distinctively feminine yet drawing upon traditional features of state ritual and exploiting the 'Edwardian fascination with pageantry' (Tickner 1987: 56). The Davison procession, as described in the detailed and respectful report below, answers fully to this characterisation, while its patriotic and quasi-military signifiers less consciously offer intimations of the greater conflict beginning only one year thence. Although Emily Davison's actual funeral was to take place near the family's Northumbrian home, this metropolitan ceremony was fitting on personal as well as political grounds: Gertrude Colmore's *Life* (1913) quotes a sonnet by Davison – 'Oh London! How I feel thy magic spell' – responding to the city's magnetic pull as strongly as any of its devotees quoted earlier in this book:

> The centre of the universe is here!
> This is the hub, the very fount of life.

(Stanley and Morley 1988: 19)

London, Saturday

The body . . . was carried through the streets this afternoon from Victoria Station to King's Cross on the way to the final journey to Morpeth. There was a halt of half an hour in the march while a memorial service was held in St George's Church, Bloomsbury. The passage of the body was made the occasion of an imposing demonstration, arranged with all the skill and practised organisation of the Women's Social and Political Union. Nearly five thousand members from all parts of the country marched in undisturbed quiet and orderliness behind the coffin. Any fears of interference from the crowd were soon seen to be quite baseless. The crowd – the huge multitude of a fine Saturday afternoon in the season – paid to the procession the reverence due to the dead, and the only difficulty came from the enormous numbers pressing almost irresistibly into the track of the marchers at every crossroads in the route, so that the police had a harassing time before they could master the affair sufficiently to prevent utter disorganisation of the traffic. . . . [S]hortly before the procession set out from Victoria the rumour spread by the mysterious wireless telegraphy of the street that the route had been altered and thousands of people deserted their stations in Piccadilly and rushed towards Shaftesbury Avenue (under the impression that the marchers had been diverted along Oxford Street). This caused a tremendous crush in the little open space where Oxford Street meets Hart Street, and where stands St George's Church, with its statue of George III perched grotesquely on the steeple. Here the police had to struggle hard to keep the way clear, riding their horses repeatedly into a wonderfully patient and long-suffering mass of people. . . .

Plate 20 Emily Davison's Funeral Procession through Piccadilly, 1913, Museum of London.

The pack of people between the station and Hyde Park Corner was especially great, and it is only rarely that you see a really big crowd in the discreet region of Grosvenor Gardens. The lordly porches of the grey mansions formed stands for sightseers; women sitting on the doorsteps had been waiting for hours. Hawkers bawled 'memory cards' and 'memorial handkerchiefs' along the pavements. The official 'programme' had upon it the words 'She died for women' and the text 'Greater love hath no man than this, that he lay down his life for his friends.' Perhaps what most impressed the London mind in it all was the note of colour. Among the women who walked there were hundreds dressed in black, but at the head was a young girl[1] in yellow silk carrying a gilt cross, and there were large companies all in white, and the bands scattered at intervals were dressed in scarlet or sky-blue coats. The crowd seized on this aspect of the demonstration, and the word most heard as the women marched slowly along was the word 'beautiful'. Seen from a window, as white succeeded purple and scarlet black, the procession resembled the long unfurling of the militant banner. It had, in a more sober key, something of the deliberate brilliance of a military funeral.

I saw the procession as it poured into the narrow space of roadway which was all the police could win for it from the multitude that crushed from half a dozen streets towards the church. The crowd, which had been hilarious a moment before, was astonishingly quiet when it saw the gleaming cross and the group of young girls in white – one a mere child – that followed, carrying huge laurel wreaths. . . . A purple banner appeared, inscribed 'Fight on! God will give the victory.' . . . Another banner, 'Thought have gone forth whose power can sleep no more. Victory, victory,' came along, preceding the hunger strikers, and then a row of carriages and motors filled with wreaths, one in the shape of a prison gate.[2] The coffin lay on a carriage drawn by four black horses. It was covered with a purple pall, on which white arrows were worked at the sides. Three girls in white holding up great lilies walked alongside. The relatives and personal friends followed close behind. Then came a group of women doctors and graduates wearing academic dress – a beautiful effect of colour. . . . Clergymen walked in their vestments, and a fairly large body of men followed the banner 'Dulce et decorum est pro patria mori.' . . . The chief mourners . . . followed the coffin up the steps of St George's. The other women stood quietly in Russell Square until the service was ended and it was time to form up again for the last walk to King's Cross. Here the biggest crowd of the day, a crowd of poor folk, was eagerly waiting for the heralding sound of muffled drums.

(*Manchester Guardian* 16 June 1913: 9–10)

Notes

1 *a young girl*: Charlotte Marsh. Like Davison herself, often referred to as a 'freelance' militant, she had acted as WSPU colour-bearer in previous processions.
2 *hunger strikers, prison gate*: Davison herself had been imprisoned on eight occasions, and had hunger-struck seven times.

BIBLIOGRAPHY

Full bibliographical information for articles in daily newspapers has been given in the text. In the case of pieces anthologised in this book, the document numbers are identified in bold type after the references. Although early editions have generally been cited, texts currently or recently in print in modern editions are asterisked. The place of publication is London unless otherwise stated.

Abbott, J. (1952) *The Story of Francis, Day & Hunter*, Francis, Day & Hunter.

Acton, W. (1857) *Prostitution, Considered in its Moral, Social and Sanitary Aspects, in London and Other Large Cities*, J. Churchill.

Altick, R. (1978) *The Shows of London*, Cambridge, MA: Harvard University Press.

Arnold, M. (1890) *Poetical Works*, Macmillan (**58***).

Bagehot, W. (1911) *Literary Studies*, 2 vols, Dent.

—— (1993) *The English Constitution*, Fontana.

Bateman, E. (1901) 'The Girls from Bryants and May', Francis, Day & Hunter (**79**).

Baudelaire, C. (1972) *Selected Writings on Art and Literature*, tr. P. E. Charvet, Harmondsworth: Penguin.

Baynes, E. and Bateman, E. (1901) 'A Nice Quiet Day; or The Postman's Holiday', Francis, Day & Hunter (**79**).

Bedarida, F. and Sutcliffe, A. (1980) 'The Street in the Structure and Life of the City: Reflections on Nineteenth-Century London and Paris', *Journal of Urban History* 6, 4: 379–96.

Belchem, J. (1985) *'Orator' Hunt: Henry Hunt and English Working-Class Radicalism*, Oxford: Clarendon Press.

Bell, C. [Brontë, C.] (1855) *Villette*, Smith, Elder (**47***).

Benjamin, W. (1983) *Charles Baudelaire: A Lyric Poet in the Era of High Capitalism*, tr. H. Zohn, Verso.

Bennett, A. (1973) *A Man from the North*, Hamish Hamilton (**77**).

Blake, W. (1868) *Songs of Innocence and of Experience*, ed. R. H. Shepherd, B. M. Pickering (**23***).

Booth, C. *et al.* (1902–3) *Life and Labour of the People in London*, 17 vols, Macmillan (**72**).

Booth, W. (1890) *In Darkest London and The Way Out*, International H.Q. of Salvation Army.

Boswell, J. (1950) *London Journal 1762–3*, ed. F. A. Pottle, Heinemann (**17**).

Brown, T. (1927) *Amusements Serious and Comical, and Other Works*, ed. A. L. Hayward, Routledge (**1**).

Browning, W. E. (ed.) (1910) *The Poems of Jonathan Swift*, 2 vols, Bell (**4***).

Buchanan, R. (1866) *London Poems*, London and New York: A. Strahan (**57**).

Buck-Morss, S. (1986) 'The Flaneur, The Sandwichman, and the Whore: The Politics of Loitering', *New German Critique* 39: 99–140.

Cannadine, D. (1983) 'The Context, Performance and Meaning of Ritual: The British Monarchy and the "Invention of Tradition", c. 1820–1977', in E. Hobsbawm and T. Ranger (eds), *The Invention of Tradition*, Cambridge: Cambridge University Press.

Chesney, K. (1970) *The Victorian Underworld*, Temple Smith.

Collins, P. (ed.) (1971) *Dickens: The Critical Heritage*, Routledge & Kegan Paul.

—— (1973) 'Dickens and London', in H. J. Dyos and M. Wolff (eds), *The Victorian City: Images and Realities*, 2 vols, Routledge & Kegan Paul, II: 537–57.

Conrad, J. (1923) *The Secret Agent*, Dent (**86***).

Corfield, P. J. (1990) 'Walking the City Streets: The Urban Odyssey in Eighteenth-Century England', *Journal of Urban History* 16, 1: 132–74.

Coustillas, P. (ed.) (1978) *London and the Life of Literature in Late Victorian England: The Diary of George Gissing, Novelist*, Harvester Press.

Craig, D. (ed.) (1975) *Marxists on Literature*, Harmondsworth: Penguin.

Cunningham, P. (ed.) (1857–9) *The Collected Letters of Horace Walpole*, 9 vols, Bentley (**12*, 19***).

Darley, G. (1990) *Octavia Hill: A Life*, Constable.

Davidson, J. (1897) *New Ballads*, London and New York: J. Lane, The Bodley Head (**76**).

De Quincey, T. (1896–7) *Collected Writings*, ed. D. Masson, 14 vols, A. & C. Black (**29*, 33**).

Defoe, D. (1923) *The Fortunes and Misfortunes of Moll Flanders*, Constable (**10***).

Dickens, C. (1873) *Bleak House*, Household Edn, Chapman & Hall (**48***).

—— (1874a) *Barnaby Rudge*, Household Edn, Chapman & Hall.*

—— (1874b) *The Pickwick Papers*, Household Edn, Chapman & Hall.*

—— (1876) *The Life and Adventures of Nicholas Nickleby*, Household Edn, Chapman & Hall (**35***).

—— (1877a) *Dombey and Son*, Household Edn, Chapman & Hall (**42***).

—— (1877b) *Sketches by Boz*, Household Edn, Chapman & Hall.*

—— (1892) *The Old Curiosity Shop and Master Humphrey's Clock*, rpt. of 1st (1841) edn, Macmillan (**38***).

—— (1914) *Miscellaneous Papers*, intro. B. W. Matz, Chapman & Hall (**50**).

Doré, G. and Jerrold, B. (1872) *London: A Pilgrimage*, Grant & Co.*

Dostoyevsky, F. (1955) *Summer Impressions*, tr. K. Fitzlyon, Calder (**55***).

Dyos, H. J. and Wolff, M. (eds) (1973) *The Victorian City: Images and Realities*, 2 vols, Routledge & Kegan Paul.

Egan, P. (1822) *Life in London: the Day and Night Scenes . . .* , Sherwood, Neely & Jones (**28**).

Eliot, T. S. (1963) *Collected Poems, 1909–1962*, Faber & Faber.

Ellis, S. M. (ed.) (1923) *A Mid-Victorian Pepys: The Letters and Memoirs of Sir William Hardman*, C. Palmer.

Featherstone, S. (1996) '"E Dunno Where 'E Are: Coster Comedy and the Politics of Music Hall', *Nineteenth-Century Theatre*, 24, 1: 7–33.

Forster, J. (1969) *The Life of Charles Dickens*, rev. Everyman edn, 2 vols, Dent.

Fox, C. (1987) *Londoners*, Thames & Hudson.

—— (ed.) (1992) *London – World City: 1800–1840*, Yale University Press.

Frosterus, S. (1994) 'London Rhapsody', tr. M. Garner, in L. Kelly (ed.) *The City as Art*, Belfast: I.A.C.A. (**81**).

Gattrell, V. A. C. (1994) *The Hanging Tree: Execution and the English People, 1770–1868*, Oxford: Oxford University Press.

Gay, J. (1720) *Poems on Several Occasions*, 2 vols in 1, Tonson & Lintot (**9**).

George, M. D. (1966) *London Life in the Eighteenth Century* (1st edn 1925), Harmondsworth: Penguin.

Gissing, G. (1927) *Thyrza*, Eveleigh Nash & Grayson (**65**).

—— (1974) *The Nether World*, rpt of 1st 1-vol. (1890) edn, Harvester Press (**68***).

Glen, H. (1976) 'The Poet in Society: Blake and Wordsworth on London', *Literature and History* 3 (March): 2–28.

Greenwood, J. (1876) *Low Life Deeps, and an Account of the Strange Fish to be Found There*, Chatto & Windus.

Grosley, P. J. (1772) *A Tour of London*, tr. T. Nugent, 2 vols, Lockyer Davis (**18**).

Harrison, R. (1965) *Before the Socialists: Studies in Labour and Politics, 1861–1881*, Routledge & Kegan Paul.

Hawthorne, N. (1941) *The English Notebooks*, ed. R. Stewart, New York: Modern Language Association of America and London: Oxford University Press (**52***).

Hayford, H., Parker, H. and Tanselle, G. T. (eds) (1982) *Israel Potter: His Fifty Years of Exile*, vol. 8 of *The Writings of Herman Melville*, Evanston, IL: Northwestern University Press and Chicago: The Newberry Library (**49***).

—— (eds) (1989) *Journals*, vol. 15 of *The Writings of Herman Melville*, Evanston, IL: Northwestern University Press and Chicago: The Newberry Library.

Haywood, E. (1751) *The History of Miss Betsy Thoughtless*, 4 vols, Gardner (**14***).

Heine, H. (1879) *Pictures of Travel*, tr. C. G. Leland, 8th edn, Philadelphia, PA: Schaefer & Koradi (**32**).

—— (1910) *Memoirs*, ed. G. Karpeles, tr. G. Cannan, 2 vols, Heinemann (**32**).

Henley, W. E. (1893) *London Voluntaries*, 2nd edn, D. Nutt (**73**).

Herzen, A. (1968) *Ends and Beginnings*, rev. tr. H. Higgens, ed. A. Kelly, Chatto & Windus.

Hill, O. (1875) *Homes of the London Poor*, Macmillan (**61**).

Himmelfarb, G. (1984) *The Idea of Poverty: England in the Early Industrial Age*, New York: A. A. Knopf and London: Faber.

[Hindley, C.] (ed.) (1871) *Curiosities of Street Literature*, Reeves & Turner (**59**).

Holmes, R. (1993) *Dr Johnson & Mr Savage*, Hodder & Stoughton.

Howe, P. P. (ed.) (1931–4) *The Works of William Hazlitt*, 21 vols, Dent (**30**).

Hudson, D. (1972) *Munby, Man of Two Worlds: The Life and Diaries of Arthur J. Munby, 1828–1910*, J. Murray.

Hueffer, F. H. (1905) *The Soul of London*, A. Rivers (**83**).

Humpherys, A. (1977) *Travels into the Poor Man's Country: The Work of Henry Mayhew*, Athens, GA: University of Georgia Press.

—— (1983) 'The Geometry of the Modern City: G. W. M. Reynolds and *The Mysteries of London*', *Browning Institute Studies* 11: 69–80.

—— (1991) 'Generic Strands and Urban Twists: The Victorian Mysteries Novel', *Victorian Studies* 34, 4: 463–72.

Hyde, R. (1988) *Panoramania! The Art and Entertainment of the 'All-Embracing' View*, Trefoil.

Irving, W. H. (1928) *John Gay's London*, Cambridge, MA: Harvard University Press.

Jackson, A. A. (1969) *London's Termini*, Newton Abbott: David & Charles.

James, H. (1905) *English Hours*, Heinemann (**67***).

—— (1934) *The Art of the Novel: Critical Prefaces*, New York and London: Charles Scribner's Sons.

Johnson, S. (1905) 'Savage' in *Lives of the English Poets*, ed. G. B. Hill, 3 vols, Oxford: Oxford University Press, II: 321–434 (**13***).

Keating, P. J. (1971) *The Working Classes in Victorian Fiction*, Routledge & Kegan Paul.

—— (ed.) (1976) *Into Unknown England, 1866–1913: Selections from the Social Explorers*, Fontana.

—— (1989) *The Haunted Study: A Social History of the English Novel, 1875–1914*, Secker & Warburg.

Lamb, C. (1929) *Essays*, 2 vols, Dent (**24***).

Langford, P. (1989) *A Polite and Commercial People: England 1727–1783*, Oxford: Oxford University Press.

Law, J. [Harkness, M.] (1888) *Out of Work*, Swan Sonnenschein (**66**).

Le Bon, G. (1896) *The Crowd: A Study of the Popular Mind*, Fisher Unwin.

Levy, A. (1889) *The London Plane Tree and Other Verse*, Fisher Unwin (**69**).

Lillywhite, B. (1972) *London Signs*, Allen & Unwin.

Lindop, G. (1981) *The Opium-Eater: A Life of Thomas De Quincey*, Dent.

Lodge, D. (1984) '*Tono-Bungay* and the Condition of England', *Language of Fiction*, 2nd edn, Routledge & Kegan Paul: 214–42.

Low Life: or One Half the World Knows Not How the Other Half Lives (1764), 3rd edn, Lever (**15**).

Maclean, C. M. (1955) *Mark Rutherford: A Biography of William Hale White*, Macdonald.

McWilliam, R. (1996) 'The Mysteries of G. W. M. Reynolds: Radicalism and Melodrama in Victorian Britain', in M. Chase and I. Dyck (eds), *Living and Learning: Essays in Honour of J. F. C. Harrison*, Aldershot: Scolar Press.

Malvery, O. C. (1906) *The Soul Market*, Hutchinson (**84**).

—— (1908) *Thirteen Nights*, Hodder & Stoughton.

—— (1912) *A Year and a Day*, Hutchinson.

Markino, Y. (1910) *A Japanese Artist in London*, Chatto & Windus (**89**).

—— (1912) *When I Was a Child*, Constable.

Marrs, E. W. (ed.) (1975) *The Letters of Charles and Mary Ann Lamb*, 3 vols, Ithaca, NY and London: Cornell University Press.

Masson, D. (1908) *Memories of London in the 'Forties*, Edinburgh and London: Blackwood.

[Masterman, C. F. G.] (1902) *From the Abyss*, Brimley Johnson (**80**).

—— (1960) *The Condition of England*, ed. J. T. Boulton, Methuen.

—— (ed.) (1973) *The Heart of the Empire: Discussions of Problems of Modern City Life*, ed. B. B. Gilbert, rpt. of 1st (1901) edn, Brighton: Harvester Press.

Mattheisen, P. F., Young, A. C. and Coustillas, P. (eds) (1990–7) *The Collected Letters of George Gissing*, 9 vols, Athens, OH: Ohio University Press.

Matthews, W. (ed.) (1939) *The Diary of Dudley Ryder, 1715–16*, Methuen (**8**).

Mayhew, H. (1967) *London Labour and the London Poor*, 4 vols, rpt. of 1861–2 edn, F. Cass (**45**).

—— and Binny, J. (1968) *The Criminal Prisons of London*, rpt. of 1st (1862) edn, F. Cass (**44**).

Metcalf, P. (1972) *Victorian London*, Cassell.

Mew, C. M. (1894) 'Passed', *The Yellow Book*, II (July), London: E. Mathews & J. Lane and Boston, MA: Copeland & Day (**75***).

Miles, D. (1988) *Francis Place: The Life of a Remarkable Radical*, Brighton: Harvester Press.

Miller, K. (1985) *Doubles: Studies in Literary History*, Oxford and New York: Oxford University Press.

Mingay, G. E. (1975) *Georgian London*, Batsford.

Morris, C. (ed.) (1947) *The Journeys of Celia Fiennes*, Cresset Press.

Morrison, A. (1894) *Tales of Mean Streets*, Methuen (**70***).

Morton, A. L. (ed.) (1973) *Political Writings of William Morris*, Lawrence & Wishart.

Mudie, R. (1825) *Babylon the Great*, C. Knight (**31**).

Munby, A. J. (1993) 'Diaries', 65 vols, in *Working Women in Victorian Britain, 1850–1910: The Diaries and Letters of Arthur J. Munby and Hannah Cullwick*, Microfilm, 24 reels, A. Matthew (**56**).

Murray, J. F. (1843) *The World of London*, 2 vols, Edinburgh and London: W. Blackwood (**39**).

Nadel, I. B. and Schwarzbach, F. S. (eds) (1980) *Victorian Artists and the City: A Collection of Critical Essays*, New York, Oxford: Pergamon Press.

Neuburg, V. E. (1977) *Popular Literature: A History and Guide*, Harmondsworth: Penguin.

Newlyn, L. (1981) '"In City Pent": Echo and Allusion in Wordsworth, Coleridge, and Lamb, 1797–1801', *Review of English Studies* 32 (November): 408–28.

Nord, D. E. (1995) *Walking the Victorian Streets: Women, Representation, and the City*, Ithaca, NY: Cornell University Press.

Oliveira Martins, J. P. de (1896) *The England of Today*, tr. C. J. Willdey, G. Allen (**74**).

—— (1930) *A History of Iberian Civilization*, tr. and intro. A. F. G. Bell, Oxford: Oxford University Press.

Place, F. (1972) *Autobiography*, ed. M. Thale, Cambridge: Cambridge University Press (**34**).

Poe, E. A. (1884) *Tales and Poems*, 4 vols, Nimmo (**40***).

Pollock, G. (1988) 'Vicarious Excitements: *London: A Pilgrimage* by Gustave Doré and Blanchard Jerrold, 1872', *New Formations* 4: 25–48.

Poole, A. (1975) *Gissing in Context*, Macmillan.

Porter, R. (1994) *London: A Social History*, Hamish Hamilton.

Rabinow, P. (ed.) (1986) *The Foucault Reader*, Harmondsworth: Peregrine.

Reynolds, G. W. M. (n.d.) *The Mysteries of London*, 1st series, 2 vols, J. Dicks (**41**).

Roche, S. V. la (1933) *Sophie in London: Diary of 1786*, tr. C. Williams, J. Cape (**22**).

Rogers, P. (1974) *The Augustan Vision*, Weidenfeld & Nicolson.

Rook, C. (1899) *The Hooligan Nights*, Grant Richards (**78**).

Rosenfeld, S. (1960) *The Theatres of the London Fairs in the Eighteenth Century*, Cambridge: Cambridge University Press.

Rudé, G. (1962) *Wilkes and Liberty*, Oxford: Oxford University Press.

—— (1964) *The Crowd in History: A Study of Popular Disturbances in France and England, 1730–1848*, John Wiley.

—— (1971) *Hanoverian London, 1714–1808*, Secker & Warburg.

Rutherford, M. (1969) *Autobiography and Deliverance*, rpt. of 1888 edn, intro. B. Willey, Leicester: Leicester University Press (**62**).

Sala, G. A. (1895) *The Life and Adventures of George Augustus Sala, Written by Himself*, Cassell.

—— (1971) *Twice Round the Clock, or the Hours of the Day and Night in London*, rpt. of 1859 edn, intro. P. Collins, Leicester: Leicester University Press (**54**).

Sales, R. (1983) *English Literature in History, 1780–1830: Pastoral and Politics*, Hutchinson.

Sammons, J. L. (1979) *Heinrich Heine: A Modern Biography*, Princeton, NJ: Princeton University Press.

Saussure, C. de (1902) *A View of England in the Reigns of George I and George II*, tr. & ed. Mme van Muyden, Murray (**11**).

Sennett, R. (1977) *The Fall of Public Man*, Cambridge: Cambridge University Press.

Sharpe, W. and Wallock, L. (eds) (1983) *Visions of the Modern City: Essays in History, Art and Literature*, New York: Columbia University Press.

Shelley, P. B. (1943) *Complete Poetical Works*, ed. T. Hutchinson (1905), Oxford University Press.*

Shesgreen, S. (ed.) *Engravings by Hogarth: 101 Prints*, New York: Dover.

Smith, A. (ed.) (1849) *Gavarni in London: Sketches of Life and Character*, D. Bogue (**43**).

Smith, C. M. (1853) *The Working Man's Way in the World*, Cash.

—— (1857) *The Little World of London*, Hall, Virtue & Co. (**51**).

Smith, D. N. and McAdam, E. L. (eds) (1941) *The Poems of Samuel Johnson*, Oxford: Clarendon Press.

Smith, G. G. (ed.) (1897–8) *The Spectator*, 8 vols, Dent (**6*, 7***).

Smollett, T. (1831) *The Expedition of Humphry Clinker*, Cochrane & Pickersgill (**20***).

Southey, R. (1951) *Letters from England*, Cresset Press (**26**).

Stange, R. (1973) 'The Frightened Poets', in H. J. Dyos and M. Wolff (eds) *The Victorian City: Images and Realities*, 2 vols, Routledge & Kegan Paul, II: 475–94.

Stanley, L. and Morley, A. (1988) *The Life and Death of Emily Wilding Davison*, Women's Press.

Stedman-Jones, G. (1971) *Outcast London*, Oxford: Oxford University Press.

—— (1989) 'The "Cockney" and the Nation, 1780–1988', in D. Feldman and G. Stedman-Jones (eds), *Metropolis, London: Histories and Representations Since 1800*, Routledge.

Steedman, C. (1992) *Past Tenses: Essays on Writing, Autobiography and History*, Rivers Drury Press.

Summerson, J. (1969) *Georgian London*, rev. edn, Harmondsworth: Penguin.

Symons, A. W. (1909) *London: A Book of Aspects*, privately printed (**82**).

Taine, H. (1872) *Notes on England*, tr. W. F. Rae, Strahan (**60**).

Tennyson, A. (1905) *In Memoriam*, Macmillan (**46***).

Tester, K. (ed.) (1994) *The Flâneur*, Routledge.

Thackeray, W. M. (1903) *Travels and Sketches*, ed. W. Jerrold, Dent (**37**).

The Life and Poetical Works of George Crabbe by His Son (1901), John Murray (**21**).

The Queen's London (1897), Cassell.

Thesing, W. B. (1982) *The London Muse: Victorian Poetic Responses to the City*, Athens, GA: University of Georgia Press.

Thomas, T. (1996) 'Introduction' to G. W. M. Reynolds, *The Mysteries of London*, Keele: Keele University Press.

Thompson, E. P. (1971) 'Mayhew and the *Morning Chronicle*', in E. P. Thompson and E. Yeo (eds), *The Unknown Mayhew*, Merlin.

—— (1993) *Witness Against the Beast: William Blake and the Moral Law*, Cambridge: Cambridge University Press.

Thomson, J. ('B. V.') (1880) *The City of Dreadful Night and Other Poems*, Reeves & Turner.

Thornbury, W. and Walford, E. (1873–8) *Old and New London: Its History, Its People, and Its Places*, 6 vols, Cassell Petter & Galpin.

Tickner, L. (1987) *The Spectacle of Women: Imagery of the Suffrage Campaign, 1907–14*, Chatto & Windus.

Tristan, F. (1980) *London Journal*, tr. D. Palmer and G. Pincetl, G. Prior (**36**).

Trudgill, E. (1973) 'Prostitution and Paterfamilias', in H. J. Dyos and M. Wolff (eds), *The Victorian City: Images and Realities*, 2 vols, Routledge & Kegan Paul, II: 693–705.

Uffenbach, Z. C. von (1934) *London in 1710*, tr. and ed. W. H. Quarrell and M. Mare, Faber (**5**).

Urry, J. (1990) *The Tourist Gaze: Leisure and Travel in Contemporary Societies*, Sage.

Vidler, A. (1978) 'The Scenes of the Street: Transformations in Ideal and Reality', in S. Anderson (ed.) *On Streets*, Cambridge, MA: MIT Press, 29–111.

Walkowitz, J. J. (1982) *Prostitution and Victorian Society: Women, Class and the State*, Cambridge: Cambridge University Press.

—— (1992) *City of Dreadful Delight: Narratives of Sexual Danger in Late-Victorian London*, Virago.

Ward, A. W. (ed.) (1870) *The Poetical Works of Alexander Pope*, Macmillan (**3***).

Ward, E. (1924) *The London Spy*, Casanova Society (**2**).

Webb, B. (1926) *My Apprenticeship*, Longmans Green (**61***).

Weiner, D. E. B. (1989) 'The People's Palace: An Image for East London in the 1880s', in D. Feldman and G. Stedman-Jones (eds), *Metropolis, London: Histories and Representations Since 1800*, Routledge.

Wells, H. G. (1909) *Tono-Bungay*, Macmillan (**87***).

—— (1934) *Experiment in Autobiography*, 2 vols, Gollancz & Cresset Press.

—— (1943) *Ann Veronica*, Dent (**88***).

'Which is the Most Interesting London Street? A Collection of Opinions' (1907) *Strand Magazine* 34, 201 (September): 314–22 (**85**).

Whitehead, W. (1754) *Poems on Several Occasions*, Dodsley (**16**).

Wilde, O. (1891) *The Picture of Dorian Gray*, Ward Lock (**71***).

Williams, R. (1973) *The Country and the City*, Chatto & Windus.

Wilson, E. (1992) 'The Invisible Flâneur', *New Left Review* 191: 90–110.

Winter, J. (1993) *London's Teeming Streets, 1830–1914*, Routledge.

Wolff, J. (1990) 'The Invisible Flâneuse: Women and the Literature of Modernity', *Feminine Sentences: Essays on Women and Culture*, Cambridge: Polity Press: 34–50.

Wordsworth, W. (1926) *The Prelude: or Growth of a Poet's Mind*, ed. E. de Selincourt, Oxford: Clarendon Press (**25***).

—— (1950) *Poetical Works*, ed. T. Hutchinson, rev. E. de Selincourt (1936), Oxford University Press.*

INDEX